AIBE

(ALL INDIA BAR EXAMINATION)

SUBJECT-WISE SOLVED PAPERS

(2012-2024)

DEVENDRA KUMAR SINGH

LL.B. (Faculty of Law, University of Delhi)

ISBN: 9781639741571

DEDICATION

This book is dedicated to all those unsung heroes who have strived hard to bring transparency and accountability in the working of judicial system of our country.

TABLE OF CONTENTS

PREFACE

The Bar Council of India (BCI), at its meeting held on 30th April 2010, passed a resolution that it shall conduct All India Bar Examination (AIBE), the passing of which would entitle the advocate to a Certificate of Practice which would permit him/her to practice the profession of law under the Advocates Act 1961. In view of the above resolution, Rules 9 to 11 were framed and inserted in Part VI, Chapter III of the Bar Council of India rules – Conditions for Right to Practice – under Section 49(1) (ah) of the Advocates Act 1961.

Rule 9 provided as following-
"***No advocate enrolled under Section 24 of the Advocates Act 1961 shall be entitled to practice under Chapter IV of the Advocates Act 1961 unless such advocate successfully passes the All-India Bar Examination conducted by the Bar Council of India. It is clarified that the Bar Examination shall be mandatory for all law students graduating from academic year 2009-10 and onwards and enrolled as advocates under Section 24 of the Advocates Act 1961.***"

Rule 10(1)(a) provided as following-
"***The Bar Examination shall be held at least twice each year in such month and such places that the Bar Council of India may determine from time to time.***"

The All-India Bar Examination has been held twice in years 2011, 2012, 2014, 2017, 2018 and 2021 and only once in years 2013, 2015, 2016, 2019 and 2023. In year 2021, the Bar Council of India decided that AIBE-XVI onwards, no books, notes, or study material will be allowed in the Examination Hall. However, the Candidates would be allowed to carry Bare Acts without notes.

In view of the above, it is required that the applicants acquaint themselves beforehand with the questions that have been asked in the previous Bar Examinations.

This book is an attempt in that direction.

Devendra Kumar Singh
12th November 2025

ABOUT THIS BOOK

In this book, efforts have been made to compile at one place, subject-wise as per the latest AIBE syllabus, all those questions which have been asked in the previous Bar Examinations to help the AIBE applicants acquaint themselves beforehand with the type of questions that have been repeatedly asked in the previous examinations.

To maintain the genuineness of the questions and their answers in this book, the author has thoroughly referred to the original Question Papers and the authentic Answer Keys released by the Bar Council of India from time to time. The answers to the Multiple-Choice Questions (MCQs) in this book have been provided in the questions itself by highlighting the correct option in **bold** fronts. Answers to only those questions, which were either deleted at the evaluation stage for some error, or for which grace marks were awarded to everybody, have not been highlighted.

While writing this book, the author has tried to correct some of those mistakes which could be corrected reasonably. Every effort has been made to avoid errors or omissions. Despite this, typing errors may creep in. Any mistake, error or discrepancy noted may be brought to the notice of the author by sending an email to **rtidevendra@gmail.com** which shall be taken care of.

It is notified that the author will not be responsible for any damage or loss of action to any one, of any kind, in any manner, there from. It is suggested that to avoid any doubt, the reader should cross-check the contents of this book with the material available on web and made available through original BCI/AIBE publications or notifications.

ABOUT ALL INDIA BAR EXAMINATION (AIBE)

All India Bar Examination (AIBE) is of three hours' duration and the question paper contains 100 multiple-choice questions, of one mark each, from the following topics/subjects: -

S. No.	Topic/Subject	No. of Questions
1.	Constitutional Law	10
2.	Code of Civil Procedure	10
3.	Criminal Procedure Code	10
4.	Indian Penal Code	8
5.	Evidence Act	8
6.	Family Law	8
7.	Law of Contract, Specific Relief, Property Laws, Negotiable Instruments Act	8
8.	Law of Tort, including Motor Vehicle Act and Consumer Protection Law	5
9.	Labour & Industrial Laws	4
10.	Law related to Taxation	4
11.	Professional Ethics & Cases of Professional Misconduct under BCI rules	4
12.	Public Interest Litigation	4
13.	Alternative Dispute Redressal including Arbitration Act	4
14.	Administrative Law	3
15.	Company Law	2
16.	Environmental Law	2
17.	Cyber Law	2
18.	Intellectual Property Laws	2
19.	Land Acquisition Act	2

There is no negative marking for the wrong answers.

TOPIC 1: CONSTITUTIONAL LAW

(10 questions are, generally, asked from this subject)

Q.1 In which case was a registered society held to be an "authority" for the purpose of Article 12 ?
(A) Som Prakash vs. Union of India
(B) Ajay Hasia vs. Khalid Mujib
(C) Sukhdev vs. Bhagatram
(D) R. D. Shetty vs. International Airport Authority [AIBE-XIX]

Q.2 In which case did the Supreme Court of India held that fundamental rights cannot be waived ?
(A) Gopala vs. State of Madras
(B) Kameshwar Singh vs. State of Bihar
(C) Golaknath vs. State of Punjab
(D) Basheshar Nath vs. I.T. Commissioner [AIBE-XIX]

Q.3 By which Constitutional Amendment was clause (4B) inserted into Article 16 ?
(A) 81
(B) 91
(C) 77
(D) 85 [AIBE-XIX]

Q.4 Which of the following statement is correct about 106th Constitutional Amendment Act ?
(i) It introduces Article 239A by which seats are reserved for women in legislative assembly of the national capital territory of Delhi.
(ii) It introduces Article 338 providing for the reservation of seats for women in the house of people.
(iii) It also adds Article 334A Which states in that the said amendment will commence after the first census have been taken after the commencement of the said Act.
(iv) The above stated shall cease to have effect on the expiration of a period of 15 years from such commencement.
(A) (i), (ii) & (iii)
(B) (i), (iii) & (iv)
(C) (ii), (iii) & (iv)
(D) All of these [AIBE-XIX]

Q.5 The Parliament enacts the "Fair Housing Act, 2024", which includes the following provisions:
(1) Section 3: Prohibits discrimination in renting or selling houses based on religion, caste, or gender.
(2) Section 6: Imposes a penalty of ₹10,000 for discrimination.
(3) Section 10: Makes it mandatory for landlords to disclose the religious background of all tenants in the previous 10 years.
A citizen challenges Section 10, arguing that it violates the right to

privacy under Article 21 of the Indian Constitution. The Supreme Court declares Section 10 unconstitutional but upholds the other provisions of the law.
What principle did the court apply in this decision ?
(A) Doctrine of Eclipse
(B) Doctrine of Severability
(C) Doctrine of Basic Structure
(D) Doctrine of Colourable Legislation [AIBE-XIX]

Q.6 The reports of the Comptroller and Auditor General of India relating to the accounts of a State shall be submitted to the
(A) Governor
(B) Committee on Public Undertakings
(C) Estimates Committee
(D) Public Accounts Committee [AIBE-XIX]

Q.7 Which of the following Article of the Constitution of India declares that the Supreme Court shall be a court of record ?
(A) Article 119
(B) Article 111
(C) Article 129
(D) Article 135 [AIBE-XIX]

Q.8 Which article deals with the powers, privileges, and immunities of Parliament and its members ?
(A) 107
(B) 105
(C) 108
(D) 102 [AIBE-XIX]

Q.9 Which Constitutional Amendment Act inserted provisions related to GST ?
(A) 99
(B) 100
(C) 101
(D) 102 [AIBE-XIX]

Q.10 Who can initiate impeachment proceedings against the President of India ?
(A) Either House of Parliament
(B) Supreme Court
(C) Only Lok Sabha
(D) Rajya Sabha [AIBE-XIX]

Q.11 The concept of freedom of trade and commerce mentioned in the Indian Constitution is motivated from the experience of the following country:
a) America
b) Australia
c) Ireland
d) United Kingdom [AIBE-XVIII]

Q.12 Which of the following writ is issued to enforce the performance of public duties by the authority?
a) Mandamus
b) Quo warranto
c) Certiorari
d) Prohibition [AIBE-XVIII]

Q.13 Which of the following Constitutional Amendment Act had made the provision for publishing Hindi translation of the Constitution?
a) 52nd amendment
b) 54th amendment
c) 56th amendment
d) 58th amendment
[AIBE-XVIII]

Q.14 Which of the following is the landmark judgment on the Colorable legislation?
a) State of Bihar v Kameshwar Singh
b) M. Karunanidhi v Union of India
c) State of Karnataka v Union of India
d) Keshavan Madhav Menon v State of Bombay [AIBE-XVIII]

Q.15 Which of the following Constitutional Amendment Act was passed in light of the advisory opinion received in *Re: Berubari* case?
a) The Constitution (Fourth Amendment) Act, 1955
b) The Constitution (Seventh Amendment) Act, 1956
c) The Constitution (Ninth Amendment) Act, 1960
d) The Constitution (Eleventh Amendment) Act, 1961
[AIBE-XVIII]

Q.16 Which of the following provisions of the Constitution of India is relevant for solving questions of repugnancy between a central law and a state law?
a) Article 248
b) Article 252
c) Article 254
d) Article 256 [AIBE-XVIII]

Q.17 What transition period was provided in the Constitution of India for changing official language of the Union from English to Hindi?
a) 5 years
b) 10 years
c) 15 years
d) 25 years [AIBE-XVIII]

Q.18 In which of the following cases was it held that there could be no reservation on a single post in the cadre?
a) Chakradhar Paswan v State of Bihar
b) K.C Vasanth Kumar v State of Karnataka
c) A.B.S.K. Sangh (Rly) v Union of India
d) State of Kerala v N.M. Thomas
[AIBE-XVIII]

Q.19 Sexual harassment of a working women at her place of work may also be considered as the violation of which of the following provisions of the Constitution of India?

a) Article 19(1)(b)
b) Article 19(1)(d)
c) Article 19(1)(e)
d) Article 19(1)(g)

[AIBE-XVIII]

Q.20 Which of the following doctrines has been applied to resolve the conflict between Article 25(2)(b) and Article 26(b) of the Constitution of India?

a) Doctrine of Harmonious Construction
b) Doctrine of Casus Omissus
c) Doctrine of Liberal Interpretation
d) Doctrine of Pith and Substance

[AIBE-XVIII]

Q.21 The title of the Constitution of India is laid down in _____.

a) Article 1
b) Article 5
c) Article 390
d) **Article 393** [AIBE-XVII]

Q.22 Constitutional provisions of fundamental rights are given under which part of the Constitution of India?

a) Part I
b) Part II
c) **Part III**
d) Part IV [AIBE-XVII]

Q.23 By which of the following Amendment Act of 1985, Anti Defection Law was added in the Constitution of India?

a) 51st Constitutional amendment
b) **52nd Constitutional amendment**
c) 53rd Constitutional amendment
d) 54th Constitutional amendment

[AIBE-XVII]

Q.24 In which one of the following cases, the Supreme Court decided that a constitutional amendment is a 'law' within the meaning of Article 13(2), and therefore if it violates any of the fundamental rights, it may be declared void:

a) Sajjan Singh Vs State of Rajasthan
b) Keshavananda Bharati Vs State of Kerala
c) Indra Sawhney Vs Union of India
d) **Golak Nath Vs State of Punjab**

[AIBE-XVII]

Q.25 Uniform Civil Code in India is _____:

a) Fundamental Rights
b) **Directive Principles of State Policy**
c) Government Policy
d) Constitutional Right

[AIBE-XVII]

Q.26 As per Article 16, no citizen shall, on grounds only of _____ or any of them, be ineligible for, or discriminated against in respect of, any employment or office under the State.

a) **religion, race, caste, sex, descent, place of birth, residence**
b) religion, age, caste, sex, descent, place of birth, residence
c) religion, race, age, sex, descent, place of birth, residence
d) religion, race, caste, sex, descent, place of birth, age [AIBE-XVII]

Q.27 The minimum number of Judges who are to sit for the purpose of deciding any case involving a substantial question of law as to the interpretation of this Constitution, or for the purpose of hearing any reference under Article 143, shall be __.

a) 2
b) 3
c) 4
d) **5** [AIBE-XVII]

Q.28 According to Article 300A of the Constitution of India, no _____ shall be deprived of his property save by authority of law.

a) **person**
b) citizen
c) foreigner
d) Indian [AIBE-XVII]

Q.29 Which of the following is not 'Law' according to Article 13 of Indian Constitution?

a) Rule
b) By-laws
c) Custom or usage
d) **None of these** [AIBE-XVII]

Q.30 Which of the following Schedule deals with Union List, State List and Concurrent List in the Constitution of India?

a) **Schedule 7**
b) Schedule 10
c) Schedule 11
d) Schedule 12 [AIBE-XVII]

Q.31 What is the leading decision in the case of Menaka Gandhi Vs Union of India?

a) **Right of hearing**
b) Separation of powers
c) Delegated legislation
d) Rule of evidence [AIBE-XVI]

Q.32 Freedom of residence under Article 19 of the Indian Constitution is available in which of the following clauses?

a) **Clause (1)(E)**
b) Clause (1)(D)
c) Clause (1)(B)
d) Clause (1)(C) [AIBE-XVI]

Q.33 Every person who is a member of a defence service or holds any civil post under the Union holds office during the pleasure of the _____.

a) Prime Minister
b) **President**
c) Council of Ministers
d) Both (a) and (b) [AIBE-XVI]

Q.34 According to the provisions of Article 315 of the Indian Constitution:
I. There shall be a Public Service Commission for the Union and a Public Service Commission for each state.
II. The Public Service Commission for the Union, if requested to do by the governor of a state may, with the approval of the president, agree to serve all or any of the needs of the state.
Which of the above statements is/are correct?
a) Only I
b) Only II
c) **I and II**
d) None of them [AIBE-XVI]

Q.35 The test of reasonableness is not wholly _____ test and its contours are fairly indicated by constitution.
a) **Subjective**
b) Objective
c) Descriptive
d) Summative [AIBE-XVI]

Q.36 The power to enact a law relating to the citizenship of India is left to _____ under the provisions of article 11 of the Indian Constitution.
a) President
b) Council of Ministers
c) House of people
d) **Parliament** [AIBE-XVI]

Q.37 A discrimination against a man or a woman, only on the grounds of ____ would be violative of Article 15(1).
a) **Sex**
b) Remuneration
c) Place of birth
d) Religion [AIBE-XVI]

Q.38 The "Objective Resolution" adopted by the Constituent Assembly on January 22, 1947 was drafted by:
a) **Jawaharlal Nehru**
b) Dr. B.R. Ambedkar
c) Dr. Rajendra Prashad
d) B.N. Rao [AIBE-XVI]

Q.39 Right to the property was eliminated from the list of Fundamental Rights during the tenure of:
a) Indira Gandhi
b) Charan Singh
c) Rajiv Gandhi
d) **Morarji Desai** [AIBE-XVI]

Q.40 Protection against arrest and detention in certain cases is mentioned in which of the

following Articles of Indian Constitution?
a) Article 21
b) Article 21A
c) **Article 22**
d) Article 22A [AIBE-XVI]

Q.41 Article 300A of Indian Constitution i.e. Right to Property has been inserted in the Constitution by:
a) **44th Amendment Act**
b) 42nd Amendment Act
c) 40th Amendment Act
d) 51st Amendment Act [AIBE-XVI]

Q.42 The Supreme Court invoked the principle of 'Transformative Constitutionalism' in the case of:
a) Navtej Singh Johar Vs. Union of India (2018)
b) Suresh Kumar Koushal Vs. Naz Foundation (2010)
c) Naz Foundation Vs. Government of NCT of Delhi (2009)
d) Aruna Roy Vs. Union of India (2002) [AIBE-XV]

Q.43 Section 66A of the Information Technology Act was struck down under Art.19(1)(a) read with Art.19(2) in the case of:
a) Justice K S Puttaswamy Vs. Union of India
b) Kharak Singh Vs. State of U. P.
c) Govinda Vs. State of M. P.
d) Shreya Singhal Vs. Union of India [AIBE-XV]

Q.44 Article 145(3) of the Indian Constitution states that the minimum number of judges who are to sit for the purpose of deciding any case involving a substantial question of law as to the interpretation of this Constitution or for the purpose of hearing any reference under Article 143 shall be:
a) Two
b) Three
c) Five
d) Nine [AIBE-XV]

Q.45 India, that is Bharat, shall be a:
a) Federation of States
b) Quasi federal
c) Union of States
d) Unitary State of a special type [AIBE-XV]

Q.46 The Supreme Court has legalized living wills and passive euthanasia subject to certain conditions in the case of:
a) Aruna Ramachandra Shanbaug Vs. Union of India (2011)
b) Common Cause Vs. Union of India (2018) 5 SCC 1
c) Gian Kaur Vs. State of Punjab (1996)
d) Chenna Jagadeeswar Vs. State of

A. P. (1988) [AIBE-XV]

Q.47 Article 310 of the Constitution mentions about:
a) Doctrine of immunities and instrumentalities with reference to civil servants
b) Doctrine of legitimate expectation with reference to civil servants
c) Doctrine of natural justice with reference to civil servants
d) Doctrine of pleasure with reference to civil servants
[AIBE-XV]

Q.48 Right to know the antecedents of the candidates in the election flow from:
a) Article 19(1)(a)
b) Article 20
c) Article 13
d) Article 14 [AIBE-XV]

Q.49 In the Preamble of the Indian Constitution, the expression 'liberty' is followed by the words:
a) Of status and opportunity
b) Of thought, expression, belief, faith and worship
c) Assuring the dignity of the individual
d) Justice, social economic and political [AIBE-XV]

Q.50 M. C. Mehta Vs. Union of India (1986) (Shriram food and Fertilizers case) relates to:
a) Oleum gas leak
b) Ganga water cleaning
c) Child labour
d) Bonded labour [AIBE-XV]

Q.51 The concept of 'curative petition' was introduced by the Supreme Court of India in the case of:
a) Rupa Ashok Hura Vs. Ashok Hura AIR 2002 SC 1771
b) M C Mehta Vs. Union of India AIR 1987 SC 1087
c) Krishna Swami Vs. Union of India (1992) 45 CC 605
d) Sheela Barse Vs. Union of India (1986) 35 CC 5962 [AIBE-XIV]

Q.52 Right to Free Legal Aid was recognized as a fundamental right under Art.21 of Indian Constitution in the case of:
a) Hussainara Khatoon Vs. State of Bihar AIR (1979) SC 1360
b) M H Hoskot Vs. State of Maharashtra AIR (1978) SC 1548
c) Madhu Mehta Vs. Union of India (1989) 4 SC 1548
d) Rudal Shah Vs. State of Bihar (1983) 45 SC 14 [AIBE-XIV]

Q.53 'Rule of Law' means:
a) Equality before the law
b) Supremacy of the law
c) Predominance of legal spirit
d) All of the above [AIBE-XIV]

Q.54 Supreme Court of India held that "it is permanent obligation of every member of medical profession, either government or private, to give medical aid to every injured person brought for treatment immediately without waiting for procedural formalities" in the case of:

a) Common Cause Vs. Union of India (1996) 1 SC 753

b) Peoples Union of India AIR 1983 SC 339

c) Parmanand Katara Vs. Union of India AIR 1989 SC 2039

d) Lakshmi Kant Pandey Vs. Union of India (1984) 25 SC 244

[AIBE-XIV]

Q.55 Residuary powers in India may be exercised by:

A: Parliament

b) State legislatures

c) President

d) Both (a) & (b) [AIBE-XIV]

Q.56 From which of the following countries, the Constitution of India has borrowed the 'Power of Judicial Review'?

a) Canada

b) United Kingdom

c) USA

d) Ireland [AIBE-XIV]

Q.57 Enforcement of which of the following Articles of the Constitution of India cannot be suspended even during the proclamation of Emergency?

a) 14 & 19

b) 20 & 21

c) 23 & 24

d) 21 & 22 [AIBE-XIV]

Q.58 Under which of the following Articles of the Indian Constitution, Parliament is empowered to legislate with respect to a matter in the State List in national interest?

a) Article 249

b) Article 250

c) Article 252

d) Article 253 [AIBE-XIV]

Q.59 In which of the following cases, the court has laid down that 'Right to life' does not include 'Right to die'?

a) State Vs. Sanjay Kumar Bhatia

b) Smt. Gian Kaur Vs. State of Punjab

c) R Vs. Holiday

d) P Rathinam Vs. UoI

[AIBE-XIV]

Q.60 The question whether a bill is a money bill or not is decided by:

a) The Prime Minister

b) The Finance Minister

c) The President

d) The Speaker, Lok Sabha

[AIBE-XIV]

Q.61 Decision under 10th Schedule is taken by:
a) President
b) Chief Justice of India
c) Prime Minister
d) **Presiding officers of Houses**
[AIBE-XIV]

Q.62 Which of the following is not a federal feature of any Constitution?
a) Written Constitution
b) Double set of Government
c) Rigid Constitution
d) Single Citizenship [AIBE-XIII]

Q.63 Parliament, in exercise of its power to amend under Article 368, may not amend:
a) Preamble
b) Fundamental Right
c) Supreme Court
d) Basic Structure [AIBE-XIII]

Q.64 Which article starts with 'Subject to public order, morality & health'?
a) Article 14
b) Article 15
c) Article 28
d) Article 25 [AIBE-XIII]

Q.65 The Supreme Court of India issued a number of directions for the prevention of women in various forms of prostitution and to rehabilitate their children through various welfare measures so as to provide them with dignity of person, means of livelihood and socio-economic development in the case of:
a) Vishakha Vs. State of Rajasthan AIR 1997 SC 3011
b) Gaurav Jain Vs. Union of India AIR 1997 SC 3021
c) Delhi Domestic Working Women's Forum Vs. Union of India (1998) 1 SC 14
d) Sheela Barse Vs. Union of India (1986) 35 SC 596 [AIBE-XIII]

Q.66 Right to Free Legal Aid was recognized as a fundamental right under Art.21 of Indian Constitution in the case of:
a) Hussainara Khatoon Vs. State of Bihar AIR 1979 SC 1360
b) M H Hoskot Vs. State of Maharashtra AIR 1978 SC 1548
c) Madhu Mehta Vs. Union of India (1989) 4 SC 1548
d) Rudul Sah Vs. State of Bihar (1983) 45 SC 14 [AIBE-XIII]

Q.67 Joint sitting of both Houses of Parliament may be called by the:
a) Speaker
b) Chairman
c) President
d) Prime Minister [AIBE-XIII]

Q.68 Ex-officio chairman of the Council of State is?

a) The President
b) Speaker, Lok Sabha
c) Vice President
d) None of the above [AIBE-XIII]

Q.69 Right to Property in India is:
a) Fundamental right
b) Constitutional right
c) Statutory right
d) Legal right [AIBE-XIII]

Q.70 Restrictions may not be imposed on freedoms provided under Article 19(1)(a) on this ground:
a) Defamation
b) Public Order
c) Sedition
d) Security of the State [AIBE-XIII]

Q.71 Right guaranteed to Citizen only is:
a) Article 21
b) Article 20
c) Article 19(1)(a)
d) Article 25 [AIBE-XIII]

Q.72 President can be removed on the ground of:
a) Proved misbehavior
b) Incapacity
c) Violation of Constitution
d) All of the above [AIBE-XIII]

Q.73 The First Constitutional amendment was enacted in:
a) 1950
b) 1951
c) 1967
d) 1975 [AIBE-XII]

Q.74 Doctrine of 'Pleasure' applies to:
a) Legislative
b) Civil Servants
c) Judges
d) Cabinet ministers [AIBE-XII]

Q.75 Article 361 provides:
a) Authority to Union government to dismiss the state governments
b) Authority to the state governments to pass legislation
c) Protection and immunities to the President and Governors from being prosecuted in courts
d) None of the above [AIBE-XII]

Q.76 Supreme Court decided in S. R. Bommai Vs. Union of India:
a) Relating to the President Rule in state
b) Relating to the illegal detention
c) Relating to the right to clean environment
d) None of the above [AIBE-XII]

Q.77 Supreme Court has decided in Kesavananda Bharati Vs. State of Kerala that:
a) Parliament can amend any provision of the Constitution
b) Parliament cannot amend any provision of the Constitution
c) Parliament can amend any provision of the Constitution but

not to alter the basic structure and basic feature of the Constitution
d) None of the above [AIBE-XII]

Q.78 Which is not the Private Right?
a) Rights of property
b) Right of freedom
c) Rights to Education
d) All of the above [AIBE-XII]

Q.79 Separation of Judiciary from Executive is guaranteed in Constitution under Article:
a) 19
b) 21
c) 48A
d) 50 [AIBE-XII]

Q.80 Article 213 empowers the Governor to promulgate ordinances:
a) When the state legislature is not in session
b) During the course of legislature session
c) On the recommendation of the state cabinet
d) With the permission of the union government [AIBE-XII]

Q.81 Financial Relations between the state and Centre are defined in Constitution:
a) Between Articles 245-255
b) Between Articles 256 -263
c) Between Articles 264 to 293
d) None of the above [AIBE-XII]

Q.82 'Rule of Law' is defined by:
a) Jeremy Bentham
b) Sir John Salmond
c) A V Dicey
d) Prof. Aristotle [AIBE-XII]

Q.83 Control over subordinate courts shall be vested in the:
a) High Court
b) Supreme Court
c) Chief Minister
d) Governor [AIBE-XII]

Q.84 Right to personal liberty includes:
a) Right against custodial violence
b) Right of under trials to separate them from convicted
c) Right against public hanging
d) All of the above [AIBE-XI]

Q.85 The Supreme Commander of the Defence Force of India is:
a) President
b) Prime Minister
c) The Defence Minister
d) Chief Marshal [AIBE-XI]

Q.86 Retirement age of Supreme Court Judges is:
a) 62 years
b) 60 years
c) 58 years
d) 65 years [AIBE-XI]

Q.87 The provision of establishing Public Service Commission is made under:
a) Article 310
b) Article 315
c) Article 320
d) Article 325 [AIBE-XI]

Q.88 Which one is not a fundamental right?
a) Right to Freedom of Assembly
b) Right to Property
c) Right to Equality
d) Right to Freedom of Speech and Expression [AIBE-XI]

Q.89 In Maneka Gandhi case, it was observed that:
a) Confiscation of passport was correct
b) Right to go abroad is not within the meaning of Article 21
c) Right to go abroad is within the ambit of Article 19(1)(a) but the confiscation of passport is not in accordance to the law
d) None of the above [AIBE-XI]

Q.90 Reasonable restrictions can be imposed on the right of free movement:
a) In the interest of general public
b) In the interest of political leaders
c) In the interest of women's safety
d) All of the above [AIBE-XI]

Q.91 Which of the following can claim Article 19 of Constitution?
a) A company
b) A corporation
c) Only citizens
d) Citizens and aliens [AIBE-XI]

Q.92 Clause (3) of Article 20(i) of the Indian Constitution says that no accused person shall be compelled to be:
a) An accused
b) A witness
c) A witness against himself
d) Hostile witness [AIBE-XI]

Q.93 Indra Sawhney Vs. Union of India is popularly known as:
a) Judges Transfer case
b) Illegal Detention case
c) Mandal Commission case
d) Constitutional case [AIBE-XI]

Q.94 Supreme Court in S P Gupta Vs. Union of India AIR 1982 SC 149 decided on:
a) Free legal aid
b) Bonded labourers
c) Judges transfer
d) Illegal detention [AIBE-XI]

Q.95 When a bill is passed by the Parliament and the President, what is the status of the same?
a) Bill approved
b) Law

c) Bill exercised for administration
d) Government procedures
[AIBE-X]

Q.96 *Minto-Morley reform* is associated with which Act?
a) Indian Council Act 1912
b) Indian Council Act 1856
c) Indian Council Act 1908
d) Indian Council Act 1909
[AIBE-X]

Q.97 In the Government of India Act 1935, which subjects are included in the concurrent list?
a) Marriage
b) Divorce & Arbitration
c) Criminal Law & Procedure
d) All of the above [AIBE-X]

Q.98 Under which Supreme Court judgement, action of the President to summon, prorogue and dissolve either of the houses of the Parliament, shall be unconstitutional if acted without advice of Council of Ministers?
a) Indira Gandhi Vs. Raj Narain AIR 1975 SC 2299
b) Anandan Vs. Chief Secretary AIR 1966 SC 657
c) Rao Vs. Indira Gandhi AIR 1971 SC 1002
d) None of the above [AIBE-X]

Q.99 What is the special constitutional position of Jammu and Kashmir?
a) It is above Indian Constitution
b) Indian laws are not applicable
c) It has its own constitution
d) It is not the integral parts of Indian Union [AIBE-X]

Q.100 Recently, in which case the Kerala High Court held that a University Grant Commission criterion which allowed certain relaxation in marks to reserved categories as violation of Article 16(1) of the Constitution?
a) Nair Service Society Vs. UGC; WP(C) No. 5190 of 2016
b) CBSE Vs. UGC; WP(C) No. 5190 of 2016
c) UGC Vs. State of Kerala; WP(C) No. 5190 of 2016
d) UGC Vs. Secretary of State; WP(C) No. 5190 of 2016 [AIBE-X]

Q.101 The Right of Equality before the law under Article 14 is subject to the restriction of:
a) Public order and morality
b) Reasonable classification
c) Reasonable restriction
d) Reasonable situations [AIBE-X]

Q.102 The provision relating to Abolition of Untouchability is given in:
a) Article 23
b) Article 24
c) Article 17

d) Article 15 [AIBE-X]

Q.103 The theoretical powers to amend the Constitution have been given to the Members of Parliament and State legislatures by:
a) Article 358
b) Article 368
c) Article 378
d) No such powers [AIBE-X]

Q.104 Directive Principles are:
a) Justifiable as fundamental rights
b) Justifiable but not as fundamental rights
c) Decorative portions of Indian Constitution
d) Not justifiable yet fundamental in the governance of the country [AIBE-IX]

Q.105 Who has the power to dissolve the Lok Sabha?
a) President
b) Prime Minister
c) Speaker of Lok Sabha
d) Council of Ministers [AIBE-IX]

Q.106 An amendment of the Constitution can be initiated by introduction of Bill for such purpose in:
a) Council of States
b) House of People
c) Either in Council of States or House of People
d) None of the above [AIBE-IX]

Q.107 Which of the following is true in respect of a Government contract which does not confirm to provisions of Article 299 of the Constitution?
a) They are not enforceable in court against the parties
b) They can be rectified by the Government
c) Both (a) and (b)
d) Neither (a) nor (b) [AIBE-IX]

Q.108 Which of the following are included in the concept of 'State' under Article 12?
a) Railway Board and Electricity Board
b) Judiciary
c) University
d) All of the above [AIBE-IX]

Q.109 The word *'procedure established by law'* in Article 21 means:
a) That due process of law must be followed
b) A procedure laid down or enacted by a competent authority
c) The same thing as due process of law
d) A law which is reasonable, just and fair [AIBE-IX]

Q.110 The entry on forests and protection of wild animals and birds was moved from _____ to the _____ by the 42nd Amendment to

the Constitution of India.
a) Centre List to State List
b) Centre List to Concurrent List
c) State List to Concurrent List
d) State List to Union List
[AIBE-IX]

Q.111 Entry No.22 of the Concurrent List deals with:
a) Social security and insurance, employment and unemployment
b) Industrial disputes concerning Union employees
c) Trade unions and industrial and labour disputes
d) Regulation of labour and safety in mines and oil fields [AIBE-VIII]

Q.112 Which Article under the Constitution of India talks about the participation of workers in the management of industries?
a) 43
b) 43A
c) 43B
d) 42 [AIBE-VIII]

Q.113 Selvi's daughter Kavita had married Shivakumar of a different caste against the wishes of her family. Shivakumar was brutally killed in 2004, and Selvi and two others became the suspects. Since the prosecution's case depended entirely on circumstantial evidence, it sought the Court's permission to conduct polygraphy and brain-mapping tests on the three persons. The Court granted permission and the tests were conducted. When the results of the polygraphy test indicated signs of deception, the prosecution sought the Court's permission to perform Narco Analysis on the three persons. The Magistrate directed the three to undergo Narco Analysis. All of them challenged this decision in the Karnataka High Court, but failed to get relief. They then went in appeal to the Supreme Court. The Court held:
a) Compulsory Brain-mapping and Polygraph tests and Narco Analysis were in violation of Articles 20(3) and 21 of the Constitution
b) Compulsory Brain-mapping and Polygraph tests and Narco Analysis were valid under Articles 20(3) and 21 of the Constitution
c) Compulsory Brain-mapping and Polygraph tests and Narco Analysis were in violation of Articles 20(1) and 21 of the Constitution
d) Compulsory Brain-mapping and Polygraph tests and Narco Analysis were in violation of Articles 14 and 21 of the Constitution [AIBE-VIII]

Q.114 According to Article 71, disputes arising in connection with the elections of a President or Vice-President are to be enquired into

and decided by:
a) The Supreme Court
b) High Court
c) Both by High Court and Supreme Court
d) Tribunal established for that purpose [AIBE-VIII]

Q.115 Article 48A and Article 51A(g) were inserted in the Constitution by:
a) The Constitution (42nd Amendment) Act 1978
b) The Constitution (42nd Amendment) Act 1976
c) The Constitution (43rd Amendment) Act 1978
d) The Constitution (44th Amendment) Act 1978 [AIBE-VIII]

Q.116 "If by imposing solitary confinement there is total deprivation of camaraderie (friendship) amongst co-prisoners coming and taking and being talked to, it would offend Article 21 of the Constitution. The liberty to move, mix, mingle, talk, Share Company with co-prisoners if substantially curtailed would be violative of Article 21." - This was held in the case of:
a) Sunil Batra Vs. Delhi Administration AIR 1978 SC 1675
b) Kishor Singh Vs. State of Rajasthan AIR1981 SC 625
c) D K Basu Vs. State of West Bengal AIR 1997 SC 610
d) Parmanand Katara Vs. Union of India AIR 1989 SC 2039
[AIBE-VIII]

Q.117 "Equality is a dynamic concept with many aspects and dimensions and it cannot be 'cribbed, cabined and confined' within traditional and doctrinaire limits. From a positivistic point of view, equality is antithetic to arbitrariness. In fact, equality and arbitrariness are sworn enemies." - this was stated in the case of:
a) Jespar, I Slang Vs. State of Meghalaya AIR 2004 SC 3533
b) Vajravelu Mudaliar Vs. Special Dty. Collector AIR 1965 SC 1017
c) E P Royappa Vs. State of T .N. AIR 1974 SC 555
d) Punjab Communications Ltd. Vs. Union of India 1999 (4) SCC 727
[AIBE-VIII]

Q.118 Right to freedom to acquire, hold and dispose-off property is abolished by:
a) 44th Amendment Act 1978
b) 43rd Amendment Act 1976
c) 50th Amendment Act 1950
d) 1st Amendment Act 1951
[AIBE-VII]

Q.119 Which one of the following is covered under the definition of State?

a) The Indian Statistical Institute
b) Indian Council of Agricultural Research
c) Sainik School Society
d) NCERT [AIBE-VII]

Q.120 The question whether the Fundamental Rights can be amended under Art.368 came for consideration first time in:
a) Shankari Prasad Vs. Union of India
b) Kesavananda Bharati Vs. Union of India
c) Golak Nath Vs. State of Punjab
d) None of the above [AIBE-VII]

Q.121 "A law which violates fundamental rights is not nullity or void-ab-initio but becomes only unenforceable" - this doctrine is called as:
a) Doctrine of severability
b) Doctrine of 3 points
c) Tornado doctrine
d) Doctrine of eclipse [AIBE-VII]

Q.122 Equality of opportunity admits discrimination with reasons. It was observed by apex court in:
a) State of Kerala Vs. N M Thomas
b) Indra Sawhney Vs. Union of India
c) Air India Vs. Nergesh Meerza
d) All of the above [AIBE-VII]

Q.123 New states are created under
a) Art.3 of the Indian Constitution
b) Art.4 of the Indian Constitution
c) Art.5 of the Indian Constitution
d) Art.370 of the Indian Constitution [AIBE-VI]

Q.124 Doctrine of pleasure with reference to civil servants is mentioned under:
a) Art.311 of the Indian Constitution
b) Art.308 of the Indian Constitution
c) Art.301 of the Indian Constitution
d) Art.310 of the Indian Constitution [AIBE-VI]

Q.125 Right to know flows from one of these articles of the Constitution:
a) Art.15
b) Art.19
c) Art.20
d) Art.23 [AIBE-VI]

Q.126 Freedom of trade, commerce and intercourse throughout the territory of India - is mentioned under:
a) Art.19(1)(g)
b) Art.300A
c) Art.301
d) Art.299 [AIBE-VI]

Q.127 Passive euthanasia under certain circumstance is permissible - held in the case of:

a) Aruna Ramchandra Shanbaug Vs. Union of India

b) Gian Kaur Vs. State of Punjab

c) State of Maharashtra Vs. Maruti Shripati Dubal

d) P Rathinam Vs. Union of India [AIBE-VI]

Q.128 It was held by the Supreme Court that the balance between Fundamental Rights and Directive Principles of State Policy is the bedrock and the basic structure of the Constitution - in which case?

a) Kesavanada Bharati Vs. State of Kerala

b) Minerva Mills Vs. UoI

c) Indira Nehru Gandhi Vs. Raj Narain

d) Kihota Hollohon Vs. Zachilhu [AIBE-VI]

Q.129 K C Gajapati Narayan Deo Vs. State of Orissa is often quoted with reference to:

a) Doctrine of eclipse

b) Doctrine of severability

c) Doctrine of colorable legislation

d) Doctrine of territorial nexus [AIBE-VI]

Q.130 Raja Ram Pal Vs. Hon'ble Speaker, Lok Sabha deals with:

a) Presidents' election

b) Privileges of the legislature

c) Pardoning power

d) Office of profit [AIBE-VI]

Q.131 Under Art.1 of the Constitution, India that is Bharat shall be:

a) Federation of states

b) Union of states

c) Democratic republic

d) Quasi federal [AIBE-VI]

Q.132 A Minister ceases to hold office if he does not become a member of the Legislature within six months - is mentioned under:

a) Art.164(4)

b) Art.164(1)

c) Art.164(2)

d) Art.164(3) [AIBE-VI]

Q.133 It was held by the Supreme Court of India that preamble was not a part of the Constitution in the case of .... and this has been overruled in the case of ....

a) In re: Berubari Union; Kesavananda Bharati Vs. State of Kerala

b) A K Gopalan Vs. State of Madras; Maneka Gandhi Vs. Union of India

c) Ajay Hasia Vs. Khalid Mujib; Som Prakash Vs. Union of India

d) I C Golaknath Vs. State of Punjab; Shankari Prasad Vs. Union of India [AIBE-V]

Q.134 By the Constitution (97th Amendment) Act 2011 the following word has been inserted under Art.19(1)(c):
a) Democratic societies
b) Registered societies
c) Cooperative societies
d) Cooperative managements
[AIBE-V]

Q.135 Doctrine of Legitimate Expectation was discussed in the following case:
a) Ram Krishna Dalmia Vs. Justice Tendolkar
b) M C Mehta Vs. Union of India
c) State of U. P. Vs. Deoman
d) **Food Corporation of India Vs. M/s. Kamdhenu Cattle Feed Industries** [AIBE-V]

Q.136 The Supreme Court in Selvi & Ors. Vs. State of Karnataka held that compulsory Brain Mapping and Polygraph tests and Narco Analysis were in violation of the following Articles of the Constitution:
a) Art.23 and 24
b) Art.15 and 16
c) Art.29 and 30
d) Art.20 and 21 [AIBE-V]

Q.137 "Passive Euthanasia is permitted in certain cases" - held in:
a) Aruna Ramachandra Shanbaug Vs. Union of India
b) Gian Kaur Vs. State of Punjab
c) P Rathinam Vs. Union of India
d) State of Maharashtra Vs. Chandrabhan [AIBE-V]

Q.138 *Equal pay for Equal work* can be enforced through
a) Art.39
b) Art.14 and 16
c) Art.311
d) Art.309 [AIBE-V]

Q.139 The executive power of every State shall be so exercised as to ensure compliance with the laws made by Parliament and any existing laws - mentioned under:
a) Art.352
b) Art.256
c) Art.254
d) Art.301 [AIBE-V]

Q.140 Justice Ram Nandan Committee relates to:
a) Union State relations
b) Creamy layer
c) Finance Commission
d) Elections [AIBE-V]

Q.141 Original Jurisdiction of the Supreme Court is dealt under:
a) Art.226
b) Art.130
c) Art.131
d) Art.124 [AIBE-V]

Q.142 Laws declared by the Supreme Court shall be binding on all courts - mentioned under
a) Art.142
b) Art.143
c) Art.136
d) Art.141 [AIBE-V]

Q.143 A seven-member bench of the Supreme Court unanimously struck down clauses 2(d) of Art.323 A and Clause 3(d) of Art.323B of the Constitution relating to tribunals which excluded the jurisdiction of High Court and Supreme Court. The court held that power of judicial review over legislative action is vested in the High Court under Art.226 and in the Supreme Court under Art.32. This is an integral part of the basic structure of the Constitution. Name the case.
a) L Chandra Kumar Vs. Union of India
b) Kihota Hollohon Vs. Zachilhu
c) Nagaraj Vs. State of A. P.
d) Rajendra Singh Rana Vs. Swami Prasad Maurya [AIBE-V]

Q.144 The father of which of the leader has been the Deputy Prime Minister of India?
a) Kumari Mayawati
b) Mrs. Meira Kumar
c) Mrs. Pratibha Devi Singh Patil
d) Mrs. Vasundhara Raje [AIBE-IV]

Q.145 Who was the Constitutional Advisor to the Constituent Assembly of India?
a) Dr. Rajendra Prasad
b) Dr. B R Ambedkar
c) B N Rao
d) Jawaharlal Nehru [AIBE-IV]

Q.146 The concept of 'Judicial Review' in India is based on:
a) Procedure established by law
b) Due process of law
c) Rule of law
d) International treaties and convention [AIBE-IV]

Q.147 Protection of environment is a:
a) Constitutional Duty
b) Directive Principle
c) Fundamental Duty
d) Both (b) & (c) [AIBE-IV]

Q.148 The item 'Education' belongs to the:
a) Union List
b) State List
c) Concurrent List
d) Residuary subjects [AIBE-IV]

Q.149 While interpreting the phrase 'equality before the law' contained in Article 14 of the Constitution, the Supreme Court constantly maintained that equality means:

a) Absolute equality among human beings
b) Equal treatment to all persons
c) Among equals, the law should be equal and should be equally administered
d) Both (b) & (c) [AIBE-IV]

Q.150 The number of Fundamental Rights available in Constitution of India is:
a) Six
b) Seven
c) Eight
d) Ten [AIBE-IV]

Q.151 Which one of the following Fundamental Rights was described by Dr. B. R. Ambedkar as 'the heart and soul of the Constitution'?
a) Rights to equality
b) Rights to Freedom of Religion
c) Rights to Constitutional Remedies
d) All of the above [AIBE-IV]

Q.152 What is the period of appointment of the Comptroller and Auditor General of India?
a) 6 years
b) Up to 65 years of age
c) 6 years or 65 years of age whichever is earlier
d) Up to 62 years of age [AIBE-IV]

Q.153 Which of the following writs is a bulwark of personal freedom?
a) Quo Warranto
b) Mandamus
c) Habeas Corpus
d) Certiorari [AIBE-IV]

Q.154 'Supremacy of law', 'Equality before law' and 'Predominance of legal spirit' are the basic principles of doctrine of:
a) Colorable Legislation
b) Doctrine of 'Separation of Powers'
c) Doctrine of 'Rule of Law'
d) Doctrine of 'Excessive delegation' [AIBE-IV]

Q.155 "Rule of Law is the antithesis of arbitrariness in all civilized societies. It has come to be regarded as mark of a free society. It seeks to maintain the balance between the opposite notions of individual liberty and public order." - This was opined by whom in famous 'Habeas Corpus' case?
a) Justice H R Khanna
b) Chief Justice Ray
c) Justice Chandrachud
d) Justice Bhagwati [AIBE-IV]

TOPIC 2: CODE OF CIVIL PROCEDURE

(10 questions are, generally, asked from this subject)

Q.1 A suit is pending in District Court A, but one of the parties, Meera, requests its transfer to District Court B, claiming that the judge in Court A is biased. The opposing party, Ravi objects, stating that the request is baseless. Who has the authority to decide whether the suit can be transferred ?

(A) The District Court A where the suit is currently pending.

(B) The High Court or the Supreme Court

(C) The Civil Judge in District Court B

(D) A committee of local advocates [AIBE-XIX]

Q.2 Maya files a suit in Court A for the recovery of a sum of money from her neighbour, Neha. During the proceedings, Neha requests that a third party, Seema, be added to the suit, as Seema is allegedly liable for the debt. Maya objects, claiming that Seema is not a necessary party. Court A then reviews the application and decides that Seema should indeed be included as a defendant.

Which principle of the CPC is applied in this situation ?

(A) Order 1, Rule 10 - Joinder and Substitution of Parties

(B) Order 7, Rule 11 - Rejection of Plaint

(C) Order 5 - Service of Summons

(D) Order 6, Rule 17 - Amendment of Pleadings [AIBE-XIX]

Q.3 Which section of the CPC allows for the appeal from original decrees?

(A) Section 96

(B) Section 100

(C) Section 115

(D) Section 104 [AIBE-XIX]

Q.4 Under the CPC, what is the maximum time limit for filing a written statement in a suit ?

(A) 30 Days

(B) 60 Days

(C) 120 Days

(D) 90 Days [AIBE-XIX]

Q.5 Which section of the CPC provides exemption of the President of India and the Governors of states from personal appearance in court ?

(A) Section 132

(B) Section 133

(C) Section 128

(D) Section 130 [AIBE-XIX]

Q.6 What is the term used for a

court's power to transfer a case from one court to another under the Code of Civil Procedure ?
(A) Res Judicata
(B) Reference
(C) Review
(D) Transfer of suits [AIBE-XIX]

Q.7 Under which order of the CPC the procedure for summary suits is provided ?
(A) Order XXXV
(B) Order XXXVII
(C) Order XXXIV
(D) Order XXXVI [AIBE-XIX]

Q.8 Which section of the CPC deals with the principle of "res judicata" ?
(A) Section 11
(B) Section 10
(C) Section 12
(D) Section 9 [AIBE-XIX]

Q.9 .... of the CPC provides for an interpleader suit.
(A) Section 88
(B) Section 89
(C) Section 92
(D) Section 86 [AIBE-XIX]

Q.10 Which section of the CPC provides for the payment of compensatory costs ?
(A) Section 35
(B) Section 35(A)
(C) Section 35(B)
(D) Section 36 [AIBE-XIX]

Q.11 Which of the following is material for deciding the jurisdiction of the Civil Court in the light of the Code of Civil Procedure, 1908?
a) Averments made in the plaint
b) Averments made in the written statement
c) Both (A) & (B)
d) Neither (A) nor (B)
[AIBE-XVIII]

Q.12 Which of the following cannot be considered as the suit of civil nature for Section 9 of the Code of Civil Procedure,1908?
a) Suit for recovery of voluntary payments or offerings
b) Suit for rights of franchise
c) Suit for specific reliefs
d) Suit relating to rights of worship [AIBE-XVIII]

Q.13 Which of the following provisions of the Code of Civil Procedure, 1908 makes the doctrine of *res judicata* applicable in representative suit?
a) Section 11, Explanation V
b) Section 11, Explanation VI
c) Section 11, Explanation VII
d) Section 11, Explanation VIII
[AIBE-XVIII]

Q.14 In which of the following situations, a court will not issue summons for personal appearance

to the defendant?
a) If the defendant resides within the local limit of the court's jurisdiction
b) If the defendant resides within 40 miles from the court
c) If the defendant resides 250 miles away from the court in an area having public conveyance available
d) A woman to whom Section 132 of the Civil Procedure Code, 1908 does not apply [AIBE-XVIII]

Q.15 In which of the following situations, plaintiff is precluded from bringing a fresh suit as per the Code of Civil Procedure, 1908?
a) Dismissal of suit where summons not served in consequence of plaintiff's failure to pay cost
b) Dismissal of suit because neither party appeared
c) Dismissal of suit because plaintiff did not appear
d) Dismissal of suit because plaintiff did not apply for fresh summons within a given time limit once it returned answered [AIBE-XVIII]

Q.16 How many times at max may an adjournment be granted to a party during hearing of the suit as per the Code of Civil Procedure, 1908?
a) Two times
b) Three times
c) Four times
d) No limit prescribed
[AIBE-XVIII]

Q.17 Which of the following Amendment Act made the provision in the Code of Civil Procedure, 1908 to produce a witness without a summons?
a) The Code of Civil Procedure (Amendment) Act, 1976
b) The Code of Civil Procedure (Amendment) Act, 1999
c) The Code of Civil Procedure (Amendment) Act, 2002
d) Such provision does not exist
[AIBE-XVIII]

Q.18 Which of the following is not included in the word 'costs' as provided under the Code of Civil Procedure, 1908?
a) The expenses of the witnesses incurred.
b) Legal fees and expenses incurred.
c) Fooding and lodging expenses incurred.
d) Any other expenses incurred in connection with the proceedings.
[AIBE-XVIII]

Q.19 What period is prescribed under the Code of Civil Procedure, 1908 for a defendant to enter an appearance for filing address for service of notice on him in case of a suit where summary procedure is to

be applied?
a) Seven days from the date of receiving summons
b) Ten days from the date of receiving summons
c) Fifteen days from the date of receiving summons
d) Thirty days from the date of receiving summons [AIBE-XVIII]

Q.20 Under which of the following provisions of the Code of Civil Procedure, 1908 the appellate court may remit an issue for trial to lower court?
a) Order XLI Rule 23
b) Order XLI Rule 23-A
c) Order XLI Rule 24
d) Order XLI Rule 25
[AIBE-XVIII]

Q.21 Which Order of Civil Procedure Code deals with Temporary Injunction and Interlocutory Injunction?
a) Order 38
b) **Order 39**
c) Order 40
d) Order 41 [AIBE-XVII]

Q.22 'A' is a tradesman in Ahmedabad. 'B' carries on business in Delhi. 'B', by his agent in Ahmedabad, buys goods of 'A' and requests 'A' to deliver them to the Western Roadways Transport Company. 'A' delivers the goods accordingly in Ahmedabad. 'A' may sue 'B' for the price of goods:
a) In Ahmedabad only
b) In Delhi only
c) **In either Ahmedabad or Delhi**
d) Anywhere in India [AIBE-XVII]

Q.23 Which of the following sections of Civil Procedure Code deals with the concept of Res Judicata?
a) Section 10
b) **Section 11**
c) Section 12
d) Section 13 [AIBE-XVII]

Q.24 Mr. X, Mr. Y and Mr. Z are jointly and severally liable for rupees 10,000 Under a decree obtained by Mr. A. Mr. Y obtains a decree for rupees 10,000 against Mr. A singly and applies for execution to the court in which the joint decree is being executed. Which of the following options is correct for Mr. A?
a) **Mr. A may treat his Joint Decree as Cross Decree under Order 21 Rule 18.**
b) Mr. A cannot treat his Joint Decree as Cross Decree under Order 21 Rule 18.
c) Mr. A cannot treat his Joint Decree as Cross Decree under Order 22 Rule 18.
d) None of these [AIBE-XVII]

Q.25 'A', 'B' and 'C' are coparceners of a Joint Hindu family. They jointly execute a mortgage in favour of 'Y'. 'Y' files suit against all of them. Summons are served to 'C', but not to 'A' and 'B' None of them appears and an ex parte decree is passed against all. 'A' and 'B' applied to set aside the ex parte decree. The decree will be set aside against:
a) Only 'C'
b) Only 'A' and 'B'
c) **'A', 'B' and 'C'**
d) None of these [AIBE-XVII]

Q.26 Which of the following provisions of Civil Procedure Code, 1908 deals with the Institution of Suits?
a) Section 22
b) Section 24
c) **Section 26**
d) Section 28 [AIBE-XVII]

Q.27 Defendant shall, within ___ days from the date of service of summon on him, present a Written Statement of his defence (Order VIII).
a) 15
b) **30**
c) 60
d) 45 [AIBE-XVII]

Q.28 Which of the following statements is incorrect?
a) First appeal can be on a question of fact or law or both.
b) Second appeal can be on substantial questions of law only.
c) **Second appeal can be on a question of fact or law or both.**
d) First appeal may or may not be in the High Court, second appeal has to be in the High Court.
[AIBE-XVII]

Q.29 As per Order VI, pleading shall mean:
a) Plaint
b) Written statement
c) **Both Plaint and Written statement**
d) None of these [AIBE-XVII]

Q.30 Which of the following order deals with "Death, Marriage and Insolvency of Parties"?
a) Order 20
b) Order 21
c) **Order 22**
d) Order 23 [AIBE-XVII]

Q.31 Which of the following sections of the Civil Procedure Code define the 'mesne profit':
a) Section 2(4)
b) Section 2(14)
c) Section 2(6)
d) **Section 2(12)** [AIBE-XVI]

Q.32 Under Civil Procedure Code 1908, "Foreign Court" means:

a) A court situated outside India
b) **A court situated outside India and not established under the authority of Government of India**
c) A court situated in India applying foreign law
d) All of the above [AIBE-XVI]

Q.33 Under Civil Procedure Code, find the incorrect match:
a) Section 5 - Revenue Court
b) Section 7 - Provincial Small Causes Court
c) **Section 9 - Pecuniary jurisdiction of Courts**
d) Section 8 - Presidency small cause Courts [AIBE-XVI]

Q.34 Recovery of Specific Immovable Property may be obtained by CPC within what period-
a) 7 months
b) **6 months**
c) 8 months
d) 10 months [AIBE-XVI]

Q.35 Provisions of Section 10 of CPC are:
a) **Directory**
b) Mandatory
c) None-Mandatory
d) Discretionary [AIBE-XVI]

Q.36 Constructive res-judicata is contained in which of the following:
a) Explanation III to Section 11
b) **Explanation IV to Section 11**
c) Explanation VI to Section 11
d) Explanation VIII to Section 11 [AIBE-XVI]

Q.37 If a party who obtained an order for leave to amend pleading does not amend the same, within how many days, he shall not be permitted to do that without the leave of the court?
a) Fifteen days
b) **Fourteen days**
c) Twenty days
d) Thirty days [AIBE-XVI]

Q.38 Provision for settlement of disputes outside court has been provided under Section ___ of Civil Procedure Code.
a) 91
b) **89**
c) 51
d) 151 [AIBE-XVI]

Q.39 A plaint has to be presented to the Court under Order IV, Rule 1 in:
a) Single copy
b) **Duplicate**
c) Triplicate
d) No fixed rule [AIBE-XVI]

Q.40 Omission to give notice under Order XXI, Rule 22 will:
a) **Render the execution null and void**

b) Render the execution irregular
c) Render the execution voidable
d) Not affect the execution [AIBE-XVI]

Q.41 Where a decree is passed against the Union of India or State for the Act done in the official capacity of the person concerned, under section 82 CPC, execution shall not be issued on any such decree unless the decree remains unsatisfied for a period of:
a) **3 months from the date of decree**
b) 6 months from the date of decree
c) 1 year from the date of decree
d) 2 years from the date of decree [AIBE-XVI]

Q.42 Which of the following statements hold true for de nova trials?
a) Omission or illegality in the procedure, even if does not affect the core of the case, can become a ground for calling de nova trials
b) **A de nova trial should be the last resort**
c) The court originally trying the case can order de nova trial
d) None of these [AIBE-XVI]

Q.43 Imposition of compensatory costs in respect of false or vexatious claims or defences is dealt under:
a) Section 33 of CPC
b) Section 35A of CPC
c) Section 30 of CPC
d) Section 35 of CPC [AIBE-XV]

Q.44 Which provision under the Code of Civil Procedure deals with substituted service of summons upon the defendant?
a) O.5 R.19A
b) O.5 R.19
c) O.5 R.20
d) O.5 R.21 [AIBE-XV]

Q.45 'decree holder' means:
a) Any person in whose favour a decree has been passed or an order capable of execution has been made
b) Any person in whose favour a decree has been passed or an order incapable of execution has been made
c) Any citizen in whose favour a decree has been passed or an order capable of execution has been made
d) Any corporation in whose favour a decree has been passed or an order capable of execution has been made [AIBE-XV]

Q.46 Suits by indigent persons is dealt under:
a) Order 44 of CPC
b) Order 33 of CPC
c) Order 55 of CPC
d) Order 22 of CPC [AIBE-XV]

Q.47 Provision regarding filing of

suits by an alien under the Code of Civil Procedure is dealt under:
a) Section 21A
b) Section 15
c) Section 21B
d) Section 83 [AIBE-XV]

Q.48 An order issued by court under Civil Procedure Code, 1908 as per order XXI, rule 46 for recovery of amount due to judgement creditor is known as:
a) IT order
b) Garnishee order
c) Decree Holder order
d) Bank order [AIBE-XV]

Q.49 Section 88 read with Order XXXV of the Code of Civil Procedure, 1908 deals with:
a) Interpleader suit
b) Interlocutory Order
c) Restitution Order
d) Attachment Order [AIBE-XV]

Q.50 The principle of *res judicata* is dealt under Section …. of CPC.
a) 9
b) 10
c) 11
d) 12 [AIBE-XV]

Q.51 Section 14 of the CPC deals with:
a) Presumption as to decisions of tribunals
b) Presumption as to foreign judgements
c) Presumption as to judgements of the lower court
d) Presumption as to judgements of High Court [AIBE-XV]

Q.52 'A', residing in Delhi, publishes in Kolkata statements defamatory of 'B'. 'B' may sue 'A':
a) Only in Delhi
b) Only in Kolkata
c) In both the place of Delhi and Kolkata
d) Either in Kolkata or in Delhi
[AIBE-XV]

Q.53 Which of the following is not a legal representative?
a) Executor and administrators
b) Hindu coparceners
c) Creditor
d) Intermeddler [AIBE-XIV]

Q.54 Which of the following is not an essential element of a decree?
a) Conclusive determination of the rights of the parties.
b) Formal expression of adjudication.
c) An adjudication from which an appeal lies as an appeal from an order.
d) The adjudication must have been given in a suit before the court.
[AIBE-XIV]

Q.55 Which order has been specially enacted to protect the interest of Minors and Unsound

Persons?
a) Order 31
b) Order 32
c) Order 33
d) Order 34 [AIBE-XIV]

Q.56 Which order of the CPC lays down general rules governing pleadings in a court?
a) Order 6
b) Order 7
c) Order 8
d) Order 9 [AIBE-XIV]

Q.57 Second appeal under Section 100 is applicable:
a) Substantial question of law as formulated by the High Court.
b) Substantial question of law as not formulated by the High Court
c) An appellate decree passed *ex parte*.
d) All of the above [AIBE-XIV]

Q.58 Which of the following is not a requirement for a foreign judgement to be conclusive?
a) It must be given on merits of the case
b) It must be pronounced by a Court of competent jurisdiction
c) It was not obtained by fraud
d) It is by a court in an enemy country [AIBE-XIV]

Q.59 A reference can be made during the pendency of the case:
a) The Subordinate Court refers the case to the High Court for the latter's opinion on a question of law.
b) The Subordinate Court refers the case to the High Court for the latter's opinion on a question of evidence.
c) The Subordinate Court refers the case to the High Court for the latter's opinion on a question of fact.
d) The Subordinate Court refers the case to the High Court for the Latter's opinion on a question of court procedure. [AIBE-XIV]

Q.60 A person can apply for review of judgement when:
a) He is aggrieved by a decree/order from which an appeal is allowed, but no appeal has been preferred.
b) He is aggrieved by a decree/order from which no appeal is allowed.
c) He is aggrieved by a decision on a reference from a Court of small causes.
d) All of the above [AIBE-XIV]

Q.61 In which of the following cases, the remedy of revision is not available?
a) Cases in which first appeal lies
b) Cases in which second appeal lies
c) Interlocutory orders
d) **All of the above** [AIBE-XIV]

Q.62 The term 'Suit of a Civil Nature' refers to:

a) Private rights and obligations of a citizen

b) Political, social and religious question

c) A suit in which principal question relates to caste or religion

d) All of the above [AIBE-XIII]

Q.63 The rule of *res sub-judice* implies:

a) Where the same subject matter is pending is a court of law for adjudication between the same parties, the other court is barred to entertain the case so long as the first suit goes on.

b) Where the same subject matter is pending in a court of law for adjudication between the different parties, the other court is barred to entertain the case so long as the first suit goes on.

c) Where the different subject matter is pending in a court of law for adjudication between the same parties, the other court is barred to entertain the case so long as the first suit goes on.

d) None of the above [AIBE-XIII]

Q.64 A suit was brought by a person to recover possession from a stranger of matth property claiming it as heir of the deceased Mahant. The suit was dismissed on his failure to produce the succession certificate. A second suit was filed by him as manager of the matth.

a) The second suit will be barred by res judicata.

b) The second suit will not be barred by res judicata.

c) The second suit will be barred by res sub-judice.

d) None of the above [AIBE-XIII]

Q.65 State of U. P. Vs. Nawab Hussain 1977 SCR (3) 428 relates to:

a) Res sub-judice

b) Res judicata

c) Constructive res judicata

d) Deemed res judicata

[AIBE-XIII]

Q.66 'X' is living in Pune and 'Y', his brother in Mumbai. 'X' wants to file a suit for partition of their joint property situated in Delhi and Bangalore:

a) The suit may be instituted in Delhi only

b) The suit may be instituted in Bangalore only

c) The suit maybe instituted either in Delhi or Bangalore

d) None of the above [AIBE-XIII]

Q.67 An immovable property held by 'Y' is situated at Bhopal and the wrongdoer personally works for

gain at Indore. A Suit to obtain compensation for wrong to the property may be instituted:
a) At Bhopal
b) At Indore
c) Either at Bhopal or at Indore
d) None of these [AIBE-XIII]

Q.68 'A' resides at Hyderabad, 'B' at Calcutta and 'C' at Delhi. 'A', 'B' and 'C' being together at Allahabad, 'B' and 'C' make a joint promissory note payable on demand, and delivered to 'A'. A may sue 'B' and 'C':
a) At Allahabad where the cause of action arises
b) At Calcutta, where B resides
c) At Delhi, where C resides
d) All of the above [AIBE-XIII]

Q.69 Section 25 empowers the Supreme Court to transfer any suit, appeal or other proceeding:
a) From one High Court to another High Court
b) Form one Civil Court in one state to another Civil Court in any other state
c) Both (a) and (b)
d) Only (a) [AIBE-XIII]

Q.70 In which of the following cases, can 'C' set-off the claim?
a) 'A' sues 'C' on a bill of exchange for Rs.500. 'C' alleges that A has wrongfully neglected to insure 'C''s goods and he is liable to pay compensation.
b) 'A' sues 'C' on a bill of exchange for Rs.500. 'C' holds a decree against 'A' for recovery of debt of Rs.1000.
c) 'A' sues 'B' and 'C' for Rs.1000; the debt is due to 'C' alone by 'A'.
d) 'A' and 'B' sue 'C' for Rs.1000; the debt is due to 'C' by alone.
[AIBE-XIII]

Q.71 A suit may be dismissed under Order IX:
i) Where the summons is not served upon the defendant in consequence of the plaintiff's failure to pay costs for service of summons (Rule 2)
ii) Where neither the plaintiff nor the defendant appears (Rule 3)
iii) Where plaintiff, after summons returned unserved, fails for 7 days to apply for fresh summons (Rule 5)
iv) Where, on the date fixed for hearing in a suit, only defendant appears and he does not admit the plaintiff's claim (Rule 8)
Codes:
a) i, ii and iii
b) i, iii and iv
c) ii, iii and iv
d) All of the above [AIBE-XIII]

Q.72 Who is garnishee?
a) A third party who is instructed by way of legal notice to

surrender money to settle a debt or claim
b) A borrower arrested for defaulting
c) A person who cannot repay a bank loan
d) A person who mortgaged his farm land [AIBE-XII]

Q.73 Section 10 of the CPC provides for:
a) Stay of the suit
b) Summoning of witness
c) Examination of witness
d) Sentencing the judgement [AIBE-XII]

Q.74 Clerical or arithmetical mistakes in judgements, decrees or orders etc. can be corrected:
a) Under Section 151 of CPC
b) Under Section 152 of CPC
c) Under Section 153 of CPC
d) Under Section 153A of CPC [AIBE-XII]

Q.75 Which of the following deals with plaint in interpleader suits in the Code of Civil Procedure?
a) Order 12, Rule 1
b) Order 17, Rule 10
c) Order 33, Rule 18
d) Order 35, Rule 1 [AIBE-XII]

Q.76 For a suit for compensation for false imprisonment, the period of limitation is:
a) 3 years from the date of sentencing the judgement
b) 3 years from the date of release from imprisonment
c) 3 years from the date of commencing the imprisonment
d) 1 year when the imprisonment ends [AIBE-XII]

Q.77 Which of the following is true of rules framed by the Supreme Court with reference to appeals to it?
a) They are a special law within Section 4 of the Code of Civil Procedure
b) They must take precedence over Section 114 or Order 47
c) Both (a) and (b)
d) None of these [AIBE-XII]

Q.78 Judgment should be delivered to the parties or to their pleaders in the open court:
a) By delivering the whole of the judgement
b) By reading out the whole of the judgement
c) By reading out the operative part of the judgement
d) All of the above [AIBE-XII]

Q.79 Section 34 of the CPC provides:
a) The Payment of fine imposed by the Court
b) Payment of compensation to the

other party
c) Payment of interest
d) None of the above [AIBE-XII]

Q.80 According to clauses (i), (ii) and (iii) of Section 145 of the Code of Civil Procedure, a surety:
a) May render himself personally liable
b) He may only give a change upon his property
c) He may undertake a personal liability and charge his property as further charge
d) All of these [AIBE-XII]

Q.81 The word 'case' used in Section 115 of the Code of Civil Procedure is of wide import and:
a) It means any state of facts juridically considered
b) It includes civil proceeding, other suits and is not restricted to anything contained in the Section to the entirety of the proceeding in a civil court
c) Both (a) and (b)
d) None of these [AIBE-XII]

Q.82 The words 'is not possessed of sufficient means' in Order 33 Rule 1 refer:
a) To dower debt due by the petitioner's husband
b) To property over which petitioner has actual control
c) To sufficient property and excludes sole means of livelihoods
d) None of these [AIBE-XII]

Q.83 Provision of Section 80 of CPC is binding on:
a) The High Court
b) The Court of Civil Judge
c) The District Judge
d) All of the above [AIBE-XI]

Q.84 Temporary Injunction can be granted:
a) Suo motu
b) Ex parte
c) Hearing both parties
d) None of the above [AIBE-XI]

Q.85 Right to Appeal is a:
a) Natural right
b) Inherent right
c) Statutory right
d) Delegated right [AIBE-XI]

Q.86 A decree can be:
a) Final
b) Preliminary
c) Only preliminary not final
d) Either preliminary or final
[AIBE-XI]

Q.87 Foreign Judgement is defined in CPC:
a) Under Section 2(6)
b) Under Section 2(7)
c) Under Section 2(8)
d) None of the above [AIBE-XI]

Q.88 Which of the following is not of civil nature?
a) Right to take out procession
b) Right to worship in a temple
c) Right to caste and religion
d) All of the above [AIBE-XI]

Q.89 In a suit where the doctrine of *res judicata* applies:
a) The suit is liable to be dismissed
b) The suit is liable to be stayed
c) Both (a) and (b)
d) None of the above [AIBE-XI]

Q.90 Under Section 16 CPC a suit relating to immovable property can be filed in a court:
a) Where the property is situated
b) Where the defendant voluntarily resides or carries on business
c) Both (a) and (b)
d) None of the above [AIBE-XI]

Q.91 Pleading means:
a) Plaint and written statement
b) Plaint only
c) Written statement
d) Oral statement by the pleader [AIBE-XI]

Q.92 On failure to file a written statement, under order VIII Rule 10 of CPC, the court may:
a) Pass any other order
b) Order for striking off the decree
c) May pronounce the judgement at once
d) Any of the above [AIBE-XI]

Q.93 'A' resides at Shimla, 'B' at Kolkata and 'C' at Delhi. 'A', 'B' & 'C' being together at Banaras, 'B' & 'C' make a joint promissory note payable on demand and delivered to 'A'. 'A' may sue 'B' & 'C':
a) At Banaras where the cause of action arose
b) At Kolkata where 'B' resides
c) At Delhi where 'C' resides
d) All of the above [AIBE-X]

Q.94 In a written statement, the defendant can claim:
a) Set-off
b) Counter plaint
c) Both (a) & (b)
d) None of the above [AIBE-X]

Q.95 In which of the following cases a *set-off* can be claimed?
a) 'A' owes the partnership firm of 'B' & 'C' Rs.1000. 'B' dies leaving 'C' surviving. 'A' sues 'C' for a debt of Rs.1500 due in his separate character. 'C' wants to set-off the debt of Rs.1000.
b) 'A' sues 'B' for Rs.20,000. 'B' wants to set-off the claim for damages for breach of contract for specific performance.
c) Both 'A' & 'B'
d) None of the above [AIBE-X]

Q.96 Under O.33, an indigent is allowed to prosecute any suit provided he satisfied certain conditions. Which of the following is not such a condition?

a) He is not possessed of sufficient means to enable him to pay the fees prescribed for the plaint in such suit

b) He is not entitled to property worth Rs.1000

c) He has no sufficient means for his livelihood

d) He may present the application for permission to sue as an indigent either himself or through an authorized agent [AIBE-X]

Q.97 A decree can be transferred for execution to another court:

a) If the judgement debtor actually and voluntarily resides or carries on business or personally works for gain, within the local limits of jurisdiction of such court

b) If the judgement debtor has property sufficient to satisfy the decree within the limits of that court

c) If the decree directs the sale or delivery of immoveable property situated outside the local limits of jurisdiction of the court which passed it

d) All of the above [AIBE-X]

Q.98 In which of the following cases, it was said that "unless a right of appeal is clearly given by statue it does not exist"?

a) Ramnarain Pvt. Ltd. Vs. Trading Corporation Ltd. AIR 1983 SC 786

b) Raja Himanshu Dhar Singh Vs. Addl. Registrar AIR 1982 ALL 439

c) Zair Hussain Khan Vs. Khurshed Jain (1906) ILR 28 ALL 545

d) Ganga Bai Vs. Vijay Kumar AIR 1974 SC 1126 [AIBE-X]

Q.99 A reference can be made during the pendency:

a) The subordinate court refers the case to the High Court for the latter's opinion on a question of law.

b) The subordinate court refers the case to the High Court for the latter's opinion on a question of evidence

c) The subordinate court refers the case to the High Court for the latter's opinion on a question of fact

d) The subordinate court refers the case to the High Court for the latter's opinion on a question of court procedure. [AIBE-X]

Q.100 Under Section 115, in the exercise of its revisional jurisdiction, a High Court can do which of the following things?

a) To call for the record of any case which has been decided by any court subordinate to the

High Court
b) To vary/reverse any decree or order against which an appeal lies to the High Court
c) Both (a) & (b)
d) None of the above [AIBE-X]

Q.101 Under Section 114, a person can apply for review of judgement when:
a) He is aggrieved by a decree/order from which an appeal is allowed, but no appeal is allowed
b) He is aggrieved by a decree/order from which no appeal is allowed
c) He is aggrieved by a decision on a reference from a court of small causes
d) All of the above [AIBE-X]

Q.102 Under which section of CPC, option for settlement of disputes is provided outside the court?
a) 80(1)
b) 89(2)
c) 89(1)
d) 80(2) [AIBE-X]

Q.103 Section 10 of CPC does not apply:
a) When the previous suit is pending in the same court
b) When the previous suit is pending in a foreign court
c) When the previous suit is pending in any other court of India
d) When the previous suit is pending in a court outside India established by the Central Government [AIBE-IX]

Q.104 Principle of *res judicata* is:
a) Mandatory
b) Directory
c) Discretionary
d) All of the above [AIBE-IX]

Q.105 Time which has begun to run can be stopped in case of:
a) Minority
b) Insanity
c) Idiocy
d) None of the above [AIBE-IX]

Q.106 Objection as to non-joinder or mis-joinder of parties under Order 1, Rule 13 of CPC:
a) Can be taken at any stage of the proceedings
b) Should be taken at the earliest possible opportunity or shall be invalid
c) Can be taken in appeal or revision for the first time
d) Either (a) or (c) [AIBE-IX]

Q.107 Objection as to the place of suing:
a) Can only be taken before the court of first instance at the earliest possible opportunity
b) Can also be taken before the Appellate Court for the first time

c) Can also be taken before the Court of Revision for the first time
d) All of the above [AIBE-IX]

Q.108 On the retirement, removal or death or a next friend under Order XXXII Rule 10 of CPC, the suit is liable to be:
a) Stayed
b) Dismissed
c) Rejected
d) Either (a) or (b) or (c) [AIBE-IX]

Q.109 Section 5 of the Limitation Act applies to:
a) Suits
b) Execution
c) Election petitions
d) None of the above [AIBE-IX]

Q.110 'A' is in possession of property claimed by 'B' and 'C' adversely. 'A' does not claim any interest in the property and is ready to deliver it to the rightful owner. A can institute .... suit.
a) Friendly suit
b) Caveat
c) Interpleader
d) Restitution [AIBE-VIII]

Q.111 What is the period of limitation prescribed for the suit instituted by a mortgagor to recover possession of immoveable property mortgaged?
a) 3 years
b) 10 years
c) 30 years
d) 12 years [AIBE-VIII]

Q.112 Sections 12-15 of the Limitation Act 1963 provide for exclusion of time in computing the period of limitation prescribed by law. Which of the following falls inside the ambit of exclusion?
a) Day on which judgement/order /award is pronounced
b) Time during which stay/injunction operated
c) Time during which the defendant had been out of India
d) All of the above [AIBE-VIII]

Q.113 Period of limitation for execution of the order of maintenance is .... from the date on which it becomes due:
a) 1 year
b) 5 years
c) 6 years
d) 15 years [AIBE-VIII]

Q.114 Where territorial jurisdiction of a Court is transferred after passing a decree, an execution application may be filed:
a) In the Court which had passed the decree
b) In the Court to which territorial jurisdiction was transferred only
c) In either of the Court under (a) or (b)

d) In any Court in India [AIBE-VIII]

Q.115 When a decree is transferred for execution to another Court and if the decree holder has reasons to apprehend that the judgement debtor will dispose of the property before it is attached by the other Court, he may apply to the Court which passed the decree to issue a ……. to attach the property at once.

a) Caveat

b) Restitution order

c) Attachment order

d) Precept [AIBE-VIII]

Q.116 Where the right to the discovery or the inspection sought depends on the determination of any issue in the suit, the court may try that issue as a ………… before deciding upon the right to discovery or inspection:

a) Special issue

b) Preliminary issue

c) Res judicata

d) Res sub-judice [AIBE-VIII]

Q.117 Identify a case where *Set-Off* can be pleaded:

a) Claim for unliquidated damages

b) Suit for recovery of ascertained sum of money

c) Suit for a sum legally non-recoverable

d) None of the above [AIBE-VIII]

Q.118 'A', a railway company is in possession of goods as a consignee. It does not claim any interest in the goods except lien of wharfage, demurrage and freight but rival claims have been made by 'B' and 'C' adversely to each other. 'A' can institute:

a) An application to decide the same

b) An interpleader suit

c) Friendly suit

d) None of the above [AIBE-VII]

Q.119 Period of limitation for execution of the order of maintenance is ………… from the date on which it becomes due.

a) 1 year

b) 5 years

c) 9 years

d) 15 years [AIBE-VII]

Q.120 What is the period of limitation to file a suit for compensation for false imprisonment?

a) 2 years

b) 3 years

c) 12 years

d) 1 year [AIBE-VII]

Q.121 As per S.19 of the Limitation Act 1963, if any payment is made on account of a debt before the

expiration of the prescribed period by the person liable to pay the debt or by his agent duly authorized in that behalf, a fresh period of limitation starts running from the:
a) Time when suit was filed
b) When the payment was made
c) When the creditor demands
d) None of the above [AIBE-VII]

Q.122 In the judgement of the Supreme Court in Salem Bar Association Vs. Union of India, the Supreme Court had requested this committee headed by …………… to prepare a case management formula.
a) Justice Bhagwati
b) Justice Muralidhar
c) Justice Raveendran
d) Justice Jagannadha Rao
[AIBE-VII]

Q.123 'A' resides at Delhi, and 'B' at Agra. 'B' borrows Rs.20,000 from 'A' at Benares and passes a promissory note to 'A' payable at Benares. 'B' fails to repay the loan. 'A' may sue 'B' at:
a) Benares or Agra
b) Benares only
c) Agra only
d) Benares, Agra and Delhi
[AIBE-VII]

Q.124 The general principle of waiver that provides that failure to raise objection in the court of the first instance and at the earliest opportunity shall prevent the defendant from raising such objection at a subsequent stage and the judgement would not be vitiated on the ground of absence of territorial or pecuniary jurisdiction is reflected in which provision of Civil Procedure Code:
a) S.15
b) S.16
c) S.51
d) S.21 [AIBE-VII]

Q.125 Claim made by the defendant in a suit against the plaintiff:
a) Cross claim
b) Cross suit
c) Counter claim
d) Cross decree [AIBE-VI]

Q.126 Interpleader suit is dealt with in which of the following sections of CPC?
a) Section 87
b) Section 88
c) Section 89
d) Section 90 [AIBE-VI]

Q.127 As required by S.80 CPC, the suit can be instituted after the expiry of ………. of notice.
a) 1 month
b) 2 months
c) 60 days
d) 30 days [AIBE-VI]

Q.128 Under S.2(2) of CPC, rejection of a plaint is:
a) Decree
b) Deemed decree
c) Cross decree
d) Cross appeal [AIBE-VI]

Q.129 Ratilal Vs. State of Bombay is a popular case on the point of:
a) Res judicata
b) Res sub-judice
c) Restitution
d) Doctrine of Cy-pres [AIBE-VI]

Q.130 Pick out the case u/s. 58(1)(a), in which arrest or detention in civil prison is not maintainable.
a) A judgement debtor, where decretal amount does not exceed Rs.5,000
b) A judgement debtor where decretal amount does not exceed Rs.2,500
c) A judgement debtor where decretal amount does not exceed Rs.2,000
d) A judgement debtor where decretal amount does not exceed Rs.1,000 [AIBE-VI]

Q.131 A precept seeks to .... of the judgement debtor.
a) Attach the property
b) Prevent alienation of property
c) Prevent attachment and alienation
d) None of the above [AIBE-VI]

Q.132 R.90 of Order 21 deals with:
a) Pre-sale illegalities committed in the execution
b) Post-sale irregularities causing substantial injury to judgement debtor
c) Both (a) and (b)
d) None of the above [AIBE-VI]
.

Q.133 The place of suing in a suit for partition will be:
a) Court within whose jurisdiction the person is residing
b) Court within whose jurisdiction the elder person of the family resides
c) Court within whose jurisdiction the entire property of the family is situated
d) Court within whose jurisdiction the immovable property is situated [AIBE-VI]

Q.134 Appeal against a decree or order can be filed in a High Court within:
a) 60 days
b) 30 days
c) 90 days
d) 91 days [AIBE-VI]

Q.135 Where, before the expiration of the prescribed period for a suit or application in respect of any property or right, an acknowledgement of liability in respect of such property or right has been made in writing signed by the party against whom such property or right is claimed, or by any person through whom he derives his title or liability:

a) a fresh period of limitation shall be computed from the time when the acknowledgement was so signed.

b) limitation shall be computed from the time when originally the signature has been given.

c) a fresh period of limitation shall not be computed from the time when the acknowledgement was so signed.

d) None of the above [AIBE-VI]

Q.136 The period of limitation for an action by a principal against his agent for movable property received by the latter and not accounted for is:

a) 12 years

b) 3 years

c) 5 years

d) No limitation [AIBE-VI]

Q.137 Existence of two suits, by parties litigating under same title, one previously instituted which is pending at present and the other filed later, wherein a matter in issue in the subsequently filed suit is directly and substantially in issue in the other and the relief claimed in the subsequent suit can effectively be passed by the court of previous instance. Which section of CPC decides the fate of the subsequently filed suit and its proceeding?

a) S.11

b) S.9

c) S.10

d) S.12 [AIBE-V]

Q.138 Where there are mutual debts between the plaintiff and the defendant, one debt may be settled against another. This can be a statutory defence to a plaintiff's action and it is called as:

a) cross-claim

b) set-off

c) cross-demands

d) cross-decrees [AIBE-V]

Q.139 An attachment before judgement order takes away:

a) Right to ownership

b) Right to file suit

c) Power to alienate the property

d) Capacity of execution of a decree [AIBE-V]

Q.140 The three pillars on which foundation of every order of injunction rests:

a) prima facie case, injury with damage and balance of

inconvenience
b) prima facie case, repairable injury and balance of convenience
c) prima facie case, irreparable injury and balance of convenience
d) prima facie case, damage without injury and balance of convenience
[AIBE-V]

Q.141 …… is to enable subordinate courts to obtain in non-appealable cases the opinion of the High Court in the absence of a question of law and thereby avoid the commission of an error which could not be remedied later on.
a) Review
b) Reference
c) Appeal
d) Revision [AIBE-V]

Q.142 Who decides as to which of the several modes he/she will execute the decree?
a) Plaintiff
b) Court
c) Judgment debtor
d) Decree holder [AIBE-V]

Q.143 Where a party to a suit requires information as to facts from the opposite party, he may administer to his adversary a series of questions. It is called as:
a) Question petition
b) Question pamphlet
c) Interrogatories
d) Discovery [AIBE-V]

Q.144 ……. is a suit filed by or against one or more persons on behalf of themselves and others having the same interest in the suit.
a) Joint suit
b) Representative suit
c) Collusive suit
d) Collective suit [AIBE-V]

Q.145 A person appointed by the court to protect, preserve and manage the property during the pendency of the litigation:
a) Amicus curiae
b) Preserver
c) Protector
d) Receiver [AIBE-V]

Q.146 The provision under CPC that relates to suit by indigent persons:
a) O.32
b) O.34
c) O.35
d) O.33 [AIBE-V]

Q.147 S.5 of the Limitation Act 1963 enables the court to condone delay in filing .... on sufficient satisfaction of sufficient cause.
a) appeal or application
b) appeal, suit and application
c) appeal, petition and counter

petition
d) appeal, petition, suit and counter petition [AIBE-V]

Q.148 Limitation period prescribed in filing a suit by a mortgagor to recover possession of immoveable property mortgaged:
a) 20 years
b) 12 years
c) 10 years
d) 30 years [AIBE-V]

Q.149 *Foreign Court* under Section 2(5) of CPC means:
a) A court situation outside India
b) A court situated outside India the authority of Government of India
c) A court situated in India applying foreign law
d) All of these [AIBE-IV]

Q.150 Judgment under Section 2(9) means:
a) A decree
b) Dismissal of an appeal
c) Statement of grounds of an order or decree
d) All of the above [AIBE-IV]

Q.151 Principle of *res sub-judice* is provided in:
a) Section 10 of CPC
b) Section 11 of CPC
c) Section 13 of CPC
d) Section 14 of CPC [AIBE-IV]

Q.152 Doctrine of *res judicata* as contained in Section 11 of CPC is based on the maxim:
a) Nemo debet bis vexari pro una et eadem causa
b) Interest rei publicae ut sit finis litium
c) Both (a) & (b)
d) Either (a) or (b) [AIBE-IV]

Q.153 Principle of *res judicata* applies:
a) Between Co-defendants
b) Between Co-plaintiffs
c) Both (a) & (b)
d) Neither (a) nor (b) [AIBE-IV]

Q.154 Validity of a Foreign Judgement can be challenged under Section 13 of CPC:
a) In a Civil Court only
b) In a Criminal Court only
c) In both Civil and Criminal Court
d) Neither in Civil nor in Criminal Court [AIBE-IV]

Q.155 Under Section 15 of CPC, every suit shall be instituted in:
a) The District Court
b) The Court of the lowest grade
c) The Court of higher grade
d) All of the above [AIBE-IV]

Q.156 'X', residing in Delhi, publishes statements defamatory to 'Y' in Calcutta. 'Y' can sue 'X' at:

a) Delhi
b) Calcutta
c) Anywhere in India
d) Either in Delhi or in Calcutta [AIBE-IV]

Q.157 A suit for damages for breach of contract can be filed at a place:
a) Where the contract was made
b) Where the contract was to be performed or breach occurred
c) Anywhere in India
d) Both (a) and (b) [AIBE-IV]

Q.158 In every plaint under Section 26 of CPC, facts should be proved by:
a) Oral evidence
b) Affidavit
c) Document
d) Oral evidence as well as document [AIBE-IV]

Q.159 The existence of statutes of limitation is due to:
a) Long dormant claims have more of cruelty than justice in them
b) The defendant may have lost the evidence to dispute the state claim
c) Persons with good causes of action should pursue them with reasonable diligence
d) All of the above [AIBE-IV]

Q.160 Limitation Act is applicable to:
a) Civil suits
b) Criminal cases
c) Both of the following is correct
d) All of the above [AIBE-IV]

TOPIC 3: CRIMINAL PROCEDURE CODE

(10 questions are, generally, asked from this subject)

Q.1 Consider the following statements and answer the question given below:

Mr. Patel being a police officer receives a complaint and information that Raju was involved in a robbery of bank and has also helped to hide the valuable properties in his farm, as stated by two villagers. With this regard, consider the following:

The Police Officer Mr. Patel may arrest Raju without warrant when -

(1) Raju can be arrested only if he commits a non-cognizable offence in the presence of Mr. Patel.

(2) Since the reasonable complaint against Raju has been received and there is a strong suspicion exists due to the testimony of villagers, he can be immediately arrested.

(3) Raju can be arrested only when he tries to escape or run away.

(4) Raju can be arrested so as to prevent him from making any inducement, threat or promise to any person acquainted with facts and circumstances.

Which of the above is/are the correct statement ?

(A) (1) and (3)

(B) (2) and (4)

(C) Only (4)

(D) Only (2) [AIBE-XIX]

Q.2 BNSS introduced the provision of registration of FIR relating to commission of cognizable offense irrespective of area where the offense is committed. This FIR is known as:

(A) NCR

(B) Zero FIR

(C) False FIR

(D) Counter FIR [AIBE-XIX]

Q.3 The BNSS mandates a forensic team to visit the crime scenes to collect evidence for offenses punishable with imprisonment for at least .... years.

(A) 2

(B) 4

(C) 7

(D) 5 [AIBE-XIX]

Q.4 Which section of the BNSS allows for trials in absentia of proclaimed offenders ?

(A) 251

(B) 349

(C) 356

(D) 366 [AIBE-XIX]

Q.5 Which section of BNSS facilitates trials and proceedings to be held in electronic mode ?

(A) 532

(B) 330
(C) 430
(D) 530 [AIBE-XIX]

Q.6 Which section of BNSS repeals the Code of Criminal Procedure, 1973?
(A) 531
(B) 101
(C) 2
(D) 1 [AIBE-XIX]

Q.7 Which section mandates State Government prepare and notify a witness protection scheme for the state with a view to ensure the protection of witnesses ?
(A) 98
(B) 198
(C) 298
(D) 398 [AIBE-XIX]

Q.8 Which section of BNSS mandates the appointment of a designated police officer in each district and police station to provide information about arrested individuals to the general public ?
(A) 25
(B) 35
(C) 37
(D) 45 [AIBE-XIX]

Q.9 Which section of BNSS introduces provisions for identifying, attaching, and forfeiting the property of proclaimed offenders located outside India ?
(A) 74
(B) 76
(C) 84
(D) 86 [AIBE-XIX]

Q.10 Which section of BNSS places restrictions on the adjournment of trials, ensuring the expeditious resolution of cases ?
(A) 146
(B) 246
(C) 346
(D) 356 [AIBE-XIX]

Q.11 Which of the following sentences is an Assistant Sessions Judge authorised to pass as per the Code of Criminal Procedure, 1973?
a) Sentence of death
b) Sentence of imprisonment for life
c) Sentence of imprisonment for a term not exceeding 10 years
d) Sentence of imprisonment for a term exceeding 10 years
[AIBE-XVIII]

Q.12 A person arrested by a private person for committing a non-bailable and cognizable offence shall be re-arrested by a police officer if such person comes under which of the following provisions of the Code of Criminal Procedure, 1973?
a) Section 41

b) Section 41A
c) Section 42
d) Section 43 [AIBE-XVIII]

Q.13 Under which of the following situations is the wife not entitled for maintenance under Section 125 of the Code of Criminal Procedure, 1973?
a) Husband presumes that the wife is living in adultery.
b) Voluntarily, the wife refuses to live with husband.
c) Wife lives separately as the husband keeps a mistress.
d) Wife is forcefully removed from the house. [AIBE-XVIII]

Q.14 Which of the following procedures is dealt under Section 164-A of the Code of Criminal Procedure, 1973?
a) Medical examination of the victim of rape
b) Attendance of witness by police officer
c) Recording of confession statement
d) Recording of First Information Report by police officer
[AIBE-XVIII]

Q.15 Which of the following is incorrect with respect to the diary of proceedings in investigation as per the Code of Criminal Procedure, 1973?
a) The statements of witnesses recorded during investigation shall be inserted in the diary.
b) The diary should be duly paginated.
c) The diary may be used as evidence.
d) The diary can be used by the police officers to refresh memory.
[AIBE-XVIII]

Q.16 In which of the following cases, manner of committing offence is not required to be mentioned in the charge as per the code of criminal procedure 1973?
a) A is accused of the theft of a certain article at a certain time and place.
b) A is accused of cheating B at a given time and place.
c) A is accused of disobeying a direction of the law with intent to save B from punishment.
d) A is accused of giving false evidence at a given time and place.
[AIBE-XVIII]

Q.17 Which of the following offences may be tried summarily as per the Code of Criminal Procedure, 1973?
a) Offence under Section 454 of the IPC
b) Offence under Section 504 of the IPC

c) Offence punishable with imprisonment for a term not exceeding two years
d) Offence punishable with life imprisonment [AIBE-XVIII]

Q.18 Which of the following sections of the Code of Criminal Procedure, 1973 provides for reference to the High Court?
a) Section 275
b) Section 325
c) Section 383
d) Section 395 [AIBE-XVIII]

Q.19 A person accused of the following offence may not be granted bail under section 438 of the Code of Criminal Procedure, 1973:
i. Accused of offence under Section 376AB of the IPC.
ii. Accused of offence under Section 376DA of the IPC.
iii. Accused of offence under Section 376DB of the IPC.
a) i & ii
b) ii & iii
c) iii & i
d) i, ii & iii [AIBE-XVIII]

Q.20 Which of the following acts, if done by any magistrate, even in good faith without being empowered, shall vitiate the proceedings as per the Code of Criminal Procedure, 1973?
a) Tender of pardon under Section 306 of CrPC
b) Recall a case and try it under Section 410 of the CrPC
c) Attaches property under Section 83 of the CrPC
d) Hold an inquest under Section 176 of the CrPC [AIBE-XVIII]

Q.21 The provision of 'Plea Bargaining' under chapter XXIA of CRPC are not applicable if the offence is committed against a child below the age of:
a) 12 years
b) **14 years**
c) 16 years
d) 18 years [AIBE-XVII]

Q.22 "Section 125 of the Criminal Procedure Code is SECULAR in character" was observed in which of the following cases?
a) Lalita Kumari Vs state of Uttar Pradesh
b) Arnesh Kumar's case
c) **Mohd. Ahmed Khan Vs Shah Bano Begum**
d) Selvy Vs State of Karnataka
[AIBE-XVII]

Q.23 Who has the power of summary trial of a case?
a) Chief Judicial Magistrate
b) Metropolitan Magistrate
c) Any magistrate of first class, specially empowered by the High

Court
d) **All of these** [AIBE-XVII]

Q.24 Which sections deal with the processes to compel appearance under Code of Criminal Procedure 1973?
a) **Sections 61 to 90**
b) Sections 154 to 173
c) Sections 211 to 219
d) Sections 274 to 282
[AIBE-XVII]

Q.25 An offence for which a police officer may arrest a person without warrant is known as:
a) Non-cognizable offence
b) **Cognizable offence**
c) Bailable offence
d) None of these [AIBE-XVII]

Q.26 In a summons trial case instituted on a complaint wherein the summons has been issued to the accused, the non-appearance or death of the complainant shall entail _____.
a) Discharge of the accused
b) **Acquittal of the accused**
c) Either discharge or acquittal, depending on the facts and circumstances of the case
d) None of these [AIBE-XVII]

Q.27 Suppose FIR is not registered by the Station House Officer. What are the options that the complainant has?
a) Approach Superintendent of Police
b) Approach the Magistrate by filing a private complaint
c) None of these
d) **Both (Approach Superintendent of Police) & (Approach the Magistrate by filing a private complaint**
[AIBE-XVII]

Q.28 Any police officer making an investigation under section 160 of CRPC cannot require the attendance of a male at a place other than the place of his residence, who is:
a) Under the age of 15 years and above the age of 60 years
b) Under the age of 18 years and over the age of 60 years
c) **Under the age of 15 years and above the age of 65 years**
d) Under the age of 18 years and above the age of 65 years
[AIBE-XVII]

Q.29 If someone lies before the court on affidavit, how can it be tackled by the Advocate/s?
a) **Perjury application can be filed**
b) Withdraw from the case
c) File application to support that
d) Pay the fine for the same
[AIBE-XVII]

Q.30 Proclamation for person absconding shall be published as follows:
(i) It shall be publicly read in some conspicuous place of the town or village in which such person ordinarily resides.
(ii) It shall be affixed to some conspicuous part of the house or homestead in which such person ordinarily resides, or to some conspicuous place of such town or village.
(iii) A copy thereof shall be affixed to some conspicuous part of the court-house.
(iv) The Court may also, if it thinks fit, direct a copy of the proclamation to be published in a daily newspaper circulating in the place in which such person ordinarily resides.
a) Only ii, iii and iv are correct
b) Only ii and iii are correct
c) Only i, iii and iv are correct
d) **All i, ii, iii and iv are correct**
[AIBE-XVII]

Q.31 A Chief Judicial Magistrate may pass a sentence of imprisonment:
a) **Not exceeding seven years**
b) Exceeding seven years
c) For life
d) None of the above [AIBE-XVI]

Q.32 The Bond under Section 109 Cr.P.C. as security for good behaviour from suspected person can be executed for a period not exceeding:
a) Six months
b) Two years
c) **One year**
d) Three months [AIBE-XVI]

Q.33 The maximum limit of Rs. 500 that could be paid to the wife as maintenance under Section 125 of the Cr.P.C. 1973 was removed in:
a) 1973
b) 1989
c) **2001**
d) 2007 [AIBE-XVI]

Q.34 Under the head subsequent conduct, which of the following types of conduct would be material?
a) Change of life
b) Evasion of justice
c) Fear, trembling
d) **All of them** [AIBE-XVI]

Q.35 Under Criminal Procedure Code 1973, who shall record the information of rape being given by a rape victim?
a) Officer-in-charge of the police station
b) Deputy Superintendent of police
c) Officer not below the rank of Sub inspector
d) **Woman police officer or any**

woman officer [AIBE-XVI]

Q.36 Under the provision of the Code of Criminal Procedure, 1973:
a) Summons can be oral
b) Summons cannot be served on corporate entities
c) **Summons are either for appearance or for producing a document thing**
d) Summons can be served to servants in case the person on whose name summons are made cannot be found [AIBE-XVI]

Q.37 Any private person may arrest any person who:
a) Commits non bailable offence in his presence.
b) Commits non bailable offence and cognizable offence in his presence.
c) Commits Compoundable offence in his presence.
d) **Commits offence in his presence, or is a proclaimed offender.** [AIBE-XVI]

Q.38 How long a warrant of arrest shall remain in force?
a) 6 years
b) 10 years
c) 12 years
d) **Until executed or cancelled** [AIBE-XVI]

Q.39 Under the scheme of Criminal Procedure Code, non-cognizable offences are:
a) Public wrongs
b) **Private wrongs**
c) Both public and private wrongs
d) None of the above [AIBE-XVI]

Q.40 Which of the following cases can be cured under section 465 of the Code of Criminal Procedure, 1973?
a) Entertaining of complaint without complying with Section 195 and 340 of the Cr.P.C.
b) **The reading and recording of the evidence taken in one case into another companion case.**
c) The examination of witness in absence of the accused.
d) Non-compliance with 235(2) [AIBE-XVI]

Q.41 Section 265A to 265L, Chapter XXIA of the Criminal Procedure Code deals with the concept of:
a) Unlawful Assembly
b) Arrest without warrant
c) Search and seizures
d) Plea Bargaining [AIBE-XV]

Q.42 Security for good behaviour from habitual offenders is dealt under:
a) Section 109 of CrPC
b) Section 110 of CrPC
c) Section 111 of CrPC

d) None of the above [AIBE-XV]

Q.43 The *'Plea Bargaining'* is applicable only in respect of those offences for which punishment of imprisonment is up to a period of:
a) 7 years
b) 10 years
c) 11 years
d) 14 years [AIBE-XV]

Q.44 "From a plain reading of Section 195 CrPC, it is manifest that it comes into operation at the stage when the Court intends to take cognizance of an offence under Section 190(1) CrPC; and it has nothing to do with the statutory power of the Police to investigate into an F.I.R. which discloses a cognizable offence. In other words, the statutory power of the Police to investigate under the Code is not in any way controlled or circumscribed by Section 195 CrPC." - This was held by the Supreme Court in the case of:
a) Nalini Vs. State of Tamil Nadu
b) Raj Singh Vs. State (1998)
c) Shamsher Singh Vs. State of Punjab
d) State of Himachal Pradesh Vs. Tara Dutta [AIBE-XV]

Q.45 Which provision under Criminal Procedure Code, 1973 deals with the procedure to be adopted by the Magistrate to record confessions and statements?
a) Section 162
b) Section 164
c) Section 163A
d) Section 165 [AIBE-XV]

Q.46 Attachment of property of person absconding can be done under Section .... of CrPC.
a) 83
b) 82
c) 85
d) 86 [AIBE-XV]

Q.47 Magistrate may dispense with personal attendance of accused under Section .... of CrPC.
a) 201
b) 204
c) 205
d) 200 [AIBE-XV]

Q.48 Section 105H of CrPC deals:
a) Forfeiture of property in certain cases
b) Notice of forfeiture of property
c) Management of properties seized or forfeited
d) Identifying unlawfully acquired property [AIBE-XV]

Q.49 Bar to taking cognizance after lapse of the period of limitation is dealt under:
a) Section 178 of CrPC
b) Section 469 of CrPC
c) Section 478 of CrPC
d) Section 168 of CrPC

[AIBE-XV]

Q.50 Under Section 29 of CrPC, the court of a Chief Judicial Magistrate may pass any sentence authorized by law except:
a) A sentence of death
b) Imprisonment for life
c) Imprisonment for a term exceeding seven years
d) All of the above [AIBE-XV]

Q.51 Which one of the following sections of CrPC deals with irregularities which vitiate proceedings?
a) Section 460
b) Section 461
c) Section 462
d) Section 468 [AIBE-XIV]

Q.52 Under which of the following sections of CrPC, provisions relating to police report is given?
a) Section 173(2)(i)
b) Section 177
c) Section 174(2)(i)
d) Section 175 [AIBE-XIV]

Q.53 Which one of the following provisions of CrPC deals with anticipatory bail?
a) Section 437
b) Section 438
c) Section 439
d) None of the above [AIBE-XIV]

Q.54 The provisions relating to cancellation of bond and bail bond is given under:
a) Section 446A
b) Section 446
c) Section 447
d) Section 450 [AIBE-XIV]

Q.55 Under which one of the following section of CrPC, Police Officer is under obligation to inform the accused ground of right to bail?
a) Section 49
b) Section 50
c) Section 57
d) Section 60 [AIBE-XIV]

Q.56 Under what circumstances, court can issue an order for the attachment of property of person absconding?
a) Where the person to whom proclamation is issued is about to dispose of the whole of his property
b) Where the person to whom proclamation is issued is about to dispose of any part of his property
c) Where the person to whom proclamation is issued is about to remove the whole or any part of his property from the local jurisdiction of the court
d) All of the above [AIBE-XIV]

Q.57 Inherent Power under Section 482 CrPC can be exercised by:
a) The Supreme Court

b) The Court of Session
c) The High Court
d) All of the above [AIBE-XIV]

Q.58 Which of the following sentences can the Court of Session pass?
a) Death Sentence
b) Rigorous Imprisonment
c) Simple Imprisonment
d) Any sentence authorized by law, but Death Sentence must be confirmed by the High Court
[AIBE-XIV]

Q.59 Under which one of the following sections of CrPC, Police Officer can arrest an accused without warrant?
a) Section 40
b) Section 41
c) Section 42
d) Section 43 [AIBE-XIV]

Q.60 The FIR gives information of:
a) Report to the Magistrate about the inquiry conducted by a Police Officer
b) Report submitted to the court by the investigation officer in a criminal case
c) The commission of a cognizable crime
d) None of the above [AIBE-XII]

Q.61 Which one of the following courts, under Criminal Procedure Code, 1973 can try a murder case?
a) Judicial Magistrate 1st Class
b) Chief Judicial Magistrate
c) Court of Sessions
d) None of the above [AIBE-XIV]

Q.62 Which one of the following sections of CrPC deals with compoundable offence?
a) Section 319
b) Section 320
c) Section 321
d) Section 324 [AIBE-XIII]

Q.63 What is the time limit under Section 468 of CrPC for taking cognizance?
a) One year
b) Two years
c) Three years
a) No limit [AIBE-XIII]

Q.64 The provision relating to free legal aid is given under:
a) Section 301
b) Section 304
c) Section 303
d) Section 305 [AIBE-XIII]

Q.65 Under which one of the following provisions of CrPC, Police Officer is under an obligation to produce the person arrested before a Magistrate within 24 hours of the arrest?
a) Section 56
b) Section 57

c) Section 60
d) Section 70 [AIBE-XIII]

Q.66 Who may record confessional statement under Section 164 of the CrPC?
a) Police officer
b) Judicial officer
c) Both (a) and (b)
d) Judicial Magistrate having jurisdiction only [AIBE-XIII]

Q.67 The provision relating *'Plea Bargaining'* is not applicable in following offence:
a) Socio-economic offence
b) Offence against women
c) Both (a) and (b)
d) None of the above [AIBE-XIII]

Q.68 Which one of the following section deals with form of summons?
a) Section 60
b) Section 61
c) Section 62
d) Section 64 [AIBE-XIII]

Q.69 Under CrPC, provisions relating to prosecution of judge are provided under:
a) Section 196
b) Section 197
c) Section 198
d) Section 199 [AIBE-XIII]

Q.70 Which one of the following sections of CrPC deals with examination of person accused of rape by medical practitioner?
a) Section 54A
b) Section 55A
c) Section 53A
d) Section 60A [AIBE-XIII]

Q.71 According to Section 167 of the CrPC, an accused person can be remanded to police custody for not more than:
a) 7 days at one time
b) 30 days at one time
c) 15 days at one time
d) 60 days at onetime [AIBE-XIII]

Q.72 Examination in Chief is conducted by the:
a) Chief Examiner of the Court
b) A lawyer appointed by the accused
c) A lawyer appointed by the government
d) Presiding Judge in the Court
[AIBE-XII]

Q.73 Under Section 320(1) CrPC, for criminal intimidation which section of IPC is applicable?
a) 503
b) 504
c) 505
d) 506 [AIBE-XII]

Q.74 Under which of the following sections of the Code of Criminal

Procedure, Police can arrest an accused without warrant?
a) Section 40
b) Section 41
c) Section 42
d) Section 37 [AIBE-XII]

Q.75 Which one of the following is true of summons under Section 61 CrPC?
a) It is milder form of process
b) It is for appearance
c) It is for producing documents or thing
d) All of them [AIBE-XII]

Q.76 Under Section 239 CrPC, the Magistrate can:
a) Frame charges against the accused person
b) Discharge the accused if charges are groundless
c) Open trial for evidence
d) Convict the accused if pleaded guilty [AIBE-XII]

Q.77 A person arrested should not be detained more than:
a) 48 hours
b) 24 hours
c) 14 days
d) 90 days [AIBE-XII]

Q.78 In which of the following, under Section 59 CrPC, the discharge of the arrested person by a Police Officer can take place?
a) On his own bond
b) On bail
c) Under special order of the Magistrate
d) All of them [AIBE-XII]

Q.79 Police can seek a bond for good behaviour u/s. 109 and 110 of CrPC from:
a) Habitual offenders
b) White collar criminals
c) Jail inmates
d) None of the above [AIBE-XII]

Q.80 What is the time prescribed for filing an FIR?
a) Within 24 hours
b) Within 48 hours
c) Within 14 days of the offence
d) No time limit is specified [AIBE-XII]

Q.81 Which of the following deals with the evidence for prosecution?
a) Section 242 CrPC
b) Section 264 CrPC
c) Section 237 CrPC
d) Section 235 CrPC [AIBE-XII]

Q.82 Criminal Procedure Code is a subject of:
a) Concurrent list
b) State list
c) Union list
d) None of the above [AIBE-XI]

Q.83 'Bailable' and 'Non-Bailable'

offence has been defined in:
a) Section 2(a) of CrPC
b) Section 2(b) of CrPC
c) Section 2(c) of CrPC
d) Section 20 of IPC [AIBE-XI]

Q.84 Under Section 21 of CrPC, Special Executive Magistrate may be appointed by:
a) Central Government
b) High Court
c) Supreme Court
d) State Government [AIBE-XI]

Q.85 Police may carry out personal search on an arrested person:
a) U/s. 49 CrPC
b) U/s. 50 CrPC
c) U/s. 51 CrPC
d) U/s. 52 CrPC [AIBE-XI]

Q.86 The Special Court is:
a) Not subordinate to High Court
b) Superior to High Court
c) Supplement to High Court
d) Equal to Supreme Court
[AIBE-XI]

Q.87 The powers under Section 159 of CrPC can be exercised by a Magistrate:
a) When the Police decide not to investigate the case
b) When the investigation is still going on
c) Both (a) and (b)
d) None of the above [AIBE-XI]

Q.88 Statement recorded during investigation u/s. 161 can be used in trial:
a) For contradicting the witness
b) For corroborating the witness
c) Incorporating in the charge sheet
d) Discharging the accused
[AIBE-XI]

Q.89 Power of taking cognizance of offence by a Magistrate of First class or Second Class is provided:
a) Under Section 173 of Criminal Procedure Code
b) Under Section 190 of Criminal Procedure Code
c) Under Section 190 of Indian Penal Code
d) None of the above [AIBE-XI]

Q.90 Additions or alteration of charges is provided in CrPC:
a) U/s. 214
b) U/s. 215
c) U/s. 216
d) U/s. 210 [AIBE-XI]

Q.91 Which is the authority that determines the language of the Court other than High Court within a given State, under Section 271 of CrPC?
a) State Government
b) Central Government
c) Supreme Court of India
d) Both (a) and (b) [AIBE-XI]

Q.92 A warrant of arrest may be extended:
a) To that place where the offender has committed the offence
b) At any place within India
c) To the place specified under the Criminal Procedure Code
d) None of the above [AIBE-X]

Q.93 Which of the following section deals with search warrant?
a) 93
b) 94
c) 95
d) 96 [AIBE-X]

Q.94 Which case is leading case on arrest?
a) Joginder Kumar Vs. State of U. P.
b) State of W. B. Vs. D K Basu
c) Both (a) and (b)
d) None of the above [AIBE-X]

Q.95 The concept of '*Plea Bargaining*' is not applicable to the offences committed against:
a) A women
b) A child
c) Both (a) and (b)
d) None of the above [AIBE-X]

Q.96 Under which section of CrPC, the Assistant Public Prosecutor is appointed?
a) 13
b) 20
c) 24
d) 25 [AIBE-X]

Q.97 Which of the following sections deals with the provisions relating to maximum period for which an under-trial prisoner can be detained?
a) 436
b) 436A
c) 437A
d) 437 [AIBE-X]

Q.98 To make the criminal harmless by supplying him those things which he lacks and to cure him of those drawbacks which made him to commit crime is known as:
a) Expiatory or penance theory of punishment
b) Deterrent theory or preventive theory of punishment
c) Reformative or rehabilitative or corrective theory of punishment
d) Retributive theory of punishment
[AIBE-X]

Q.99 Which of the following sections enables the Court to cancel the bond and bail bond?
a) 446A
b) 446
c) 448
d) 450 [AIBE-X]

Q.100 In which of the following cases, the Supreme Court of India opined that 'bail is the surety and jail is an exception'?
a) Joginder Kumar Vs. State of U. P.
b) Moti Ram Vs. State of M. P.
c) Maneka Gandhi Vs. Union of India
d) State of W. B. Vs. D K Basu
[AIBE-X]

Q.101 Where a Magistrate of the First Class passes only a sentence of fine not exceeding Rs.100, against this order where an appeal shall lie?
a) In the court of Chief Judicial Magistrate
b) In the court of Chief Metropolitan Magistrate
c) Both (a) and (b)
d) None of the above [AIBE-X]

Q.102 In a bailable offence, bail is granted as a matter of right:
a) By the Police Officer
b) By the court
c) Both by the Police Officer and the court
d) Either (a) or (b) [AIBE-IX]

Q.103 A proclaimed person whose property has been attached can claim the property or the sale proceeds on appearance:
a) Within 6 months of attachment
b) Within 2 years of attachment
c) Within 3 years of attachment
d) Within 1 year of attachment
[AIBE-IX]

Q.104 Where the Police submit a final report under Section 173(2) or CrPC for dropping of proceedings to a Magistrate, the Magistrate:
a) May accept the same
b) May reject the same
c) May reject the same and order further investigation
d) Any of the above [AIBE-IX]

Q.105 The orders under Section 125 of CrPC are:
a) Summary in nature but finally determine the rights and obligations of the parties
b) Summary in nature and do not finally determine the rights and obligations or the parties which are to be finally determined by a Civil Court
c) Substantive in nature and finally determine the rights and obligations of the parties
d) Substantive in nature and are not subject to determination of a right of the parties by a Civil Court
[AIBE-IX]

Q.106 In a cognizable case under IPC, Police have the:
a) Authority to arrest a person without warrant
b) Authority to investigate the

offence without permission of the Magistrate
c) Both (a) and (b)
d) Either (a) or (b) [AIBE-IX]

Q.107 During investigation, a search can be conducted without warrant by:
a) Any Police Officer
b) By the Investigating Officer
c) Both (a) and (b)
d) Either (a) or (b) [AIBE-IX]

Q.108 Committal proceedings under Section 209 of CrPC are in the nature of:
a) Aid in investigation
b) Inquiry
c) Trial
d) Either inquiry or trial [AIBE-IX]

Q.109 Recording of pre-summoning evidence may be dispensed with under Section 200 of CrPC:
a) If the complaint is supported by the affidavit of the complainant
b) If the complaint is made in writing by a public servant in the discharge of his official duties
c) Both (a) and (b) are correct
d) Only (a) is correct but (b) is incorrect [AIBE-IX]

Q.110 An Executive Magistrate may require security for keeping good behavior from habitual offenders for a period not more than:
a) 6 months
b) 3 months
c) 1 year
d) 3 years [AIBE-VIII]

Q.111 The Police Officer executing the warrant may use adequate force to access the place where search is to be conducted when:
a) A free ingress is not possible
b) The occupant of the place is a hardened criminal and there is possibility to escape
c) The area is in such a nature that problem may arise at any time
d) None of these [AIBE-VIII]

Q.112 As per the provisions of the Code of Criminal Procedure, in case of merger of the complaint with the police report, the procedure to be followed for the trial shall be of:
a) The complaint case
b) The case instituted on the police report
c) Both as per the convenience during the trial
d) None of these [AIBE-VIII]

Q.113 Special Summons under Section 206 of the Criminal Procedure Code can be issued by:
a) A Magistrate only
b) A Magistrate as well as the Court of Sessions
c) The Court of Sessions

d) The High Court [AIBE-VIII]

Q.114 Section 41B is incorporated into the Criminal Procedure Code on the basis of which of the following decisions?
a) Nandini Satpathy Vs. PL Dani
b) Sunil Batra Vs. Delhi Administration
c) Prem Shankar Shukla Vs. Delhi Administration
d) D K Basu Vs. State of West Bengal [AIBE-VIII]

Q.115 Chapter dealing with *'Plea Bargaining'* has been inserted by:
a) The Criminal Law (Amendment) Act 1993
b) The Criminal Law (Amendment) Act 2005
c) The Code of Criminal Procedure (Amendment) Act 2001
d) The Code of Criminal (Amendment) Act 1993
[AIBE-VIII]

Q.116 As per the Criminal Procedure Code, during investigation a search can be conducted without warrant by:
a) Judicial officer
b) Any person
c) The Investigating Officer
d) Any Police Officer [AIBE-VIII]

Q.117 Which provision under the Criminal Procedure Code reflects the principle of autrefois acquits / autrefois convict?
a) Sec.300
b) Sec.305
c) Sec.306
d) Sec.311 [AIBE-VIII]

Q.118 As per the provisions of the Criminal Procedure Code, the word 'inspection' used in S.93(1)(c) refers to:
a) Things or documents
b) Documents only
c) Locality and place
d) None of the above [AIBE-VII]

Q.119 Statement recorded during investigation under S.161 of CrPC can be used during trial for:
a) Corroborating the witness
b) Contradicting the witness
c) Both (a) and (b)
d) Neither (a) nor (b) [AIBE-VII]

Q.120 "If an accused is charged of a major offence but is not found guilty thereunder, he can be convicted of minor offence if the facts established indicate that such minor offence has been committed." - It was so upheld in which case?
a) Sangarabonia Sreenu Vs. State of Andhra Pradesh
b) State of Himachal Pradesh Vs. Tara Dutt
c) Shamsher Singh Vs. State of

Punjab
d) Nalini Vs. State of Tamil Nadu [AIBE-VII]

Q.121 If a Court, lower to the Sessions Court, tries a murder case that Court is called as:
a) Coram sub judice
b) Coram non judice
c) Coram non-sub-judice
d) Coram judice [AIBE-VII]

Q.122 An Executive Magistrate may require security for keeping good behavior from habitual offenders for a period not more than:
a) 6 months
b) 1 year
c) 2 years
d) 3 years [AIBE-VII]

Q.123 S.167 of the Criminal Procedure Code provides that the nature of custody can be altered from judicial custody to police custody and vice-versa. This alteration can be done during the period of first:
a) 15 days
b) 16 days
c) 14 days
d) 12 days [AIBE-VII]

Q.124 Under which provision of the Code of Criminal Procedure, it is mandatory for a Police Officer to inform the person arrested the grounds of arrest and right of bail, if the offence is not non-bailable?
a) S.150
b) S.105
c) S.50
d) S.510 [AIBE-VII]

Q.125 S.41B is inserted into the Criminal Procedure Code on the basis of which among the following decisions?
a) Nandini Satpathy Vs. PL Dhani
b) Sunil Batra Vs. Delhi Administration
c) Prem Shankar Shukla Vs. Delhi Administration
d) D K Basu Vs. State of West Bengal [AIBE-VII]

Q.126 Civil Surgeon shall refer unsound minded person to a clinical Psychologist / Psychiatrist. However, by virtue of S……. the aggrieved accused may prefer appeal before Medical Board consisting of head of Psychiatry and faculty of Medical College:
a) 328
b) 328 (1A)
c) 328(2)
d) 346 [AIBE-VII]

Q.127 Procedure of investigation of criminal cases under the Criminal Procedure Code is contained in Chapter:
a) XI

b) XII
c) X
d) IX [AIBE-VII]

Q.128 The Criminal Procedure Code ensures that:
a) Principle of separation of powers of each limb of the State is not breached
b) Principle of combined of powers of each limb of the State is not breached
c) (a) and (b)
d) Principle of separation of powers of each limb of the State is breached [AIBE-VI]

Q.129 Section 6 of the CrPC defines:
a) Classes of Criminal Courts
b) Classes of District Courts
c) Classes of Municipal Courts
d) Classes of Civil Courts
[AIBE-VI]

Q.130 When an offence is bailable:
a) A person has no right to be released on bail upon arrest
b) A person has a right to be released on bail upon arrest
c) A right to be released is dependent on the exercise of judicial discretion
d) A person shall be released within 24 hours [AIBE-VI]

Q.131 As per Section 273 of CrPC, how an evidence is to be taken?
a) In the presence of accused
b) When personal attendance of the accused is dispensed with, in the presence of his pleader.
c) In presence of Police
d) Both (a) and (b) [AIBE-VI]

Q.132 If a woman sentenced to death is found to be pregnant, the High Court shall order the execution of the sentence:
a) To be postponed
b) If thinks fit commute the sentence to imprisonment for life
c) Sent for medical assistance
d) Non-judicial mandate of powers
[AIBE-VI]

Q.133 Under which section of the CrPC, the procedure when investigation cannot be completed within twenty-four hours has been described?
a) Sec.165
b) Sec.167
c) Sec.166
d) Sec.164 [AIBE-VI]

Q.134 What is provided by the Code of Criminal Procedure, 1973?
a) The Code provides the procedure for the implementation of the criminal justice system
b) It provides the mechanism for the investigation into trial of offences

c) The Code provides the procedure for the implementation of the civil justice system
d) (a) and (b) [AIBE-VI]

Q.135 As per Section 2(c) a 'cognizable offence' is:
a) where a Police Officer may arrest without warrant
b) where a Police Officer may not arrest without warrant
c) where a Police Officer may arrest with permission of a court
d) Any person in the public can arrest [AIBE-VI]

Q.136 Section 100 of the CrPC refers to:
a) Seizure
b) Search
c) Summons
d) Search warrants [AIBE-VI]

Q.137 Is there any maximum period for which an under-trial can be detained under Section 436 A of the CrPC?
a) Yes, half of the Maximum period of imprisonment specified for that offence
b) No period is prescribed
c) Court can decide
d) Maximum 90 days [AIBE-VI]

Q.138 Which provision under Criminal Procedure Code, 1973 deals with the procedure to be adopted by the Magistrate to record confessions and statements?
a) S.164
b) S.162
c) S.163
d) S.164A [AIBE-V]

Q.139 Any Police Officer may, without an order from a Magistrate and without a warrant, arrest any person who obstructs a Police Officer while in the execution of his duty, or who has escaped, or attempts to escape, from lawful custody under which section?
a) S.41(a)
b) S.41(c)
c) S.41(e)
d) S.41(d) [AIBE-V]

Q.140 The *'Plea Bargaining'* is applicable only in respect of those offences for which punishment of imprisonment is up to a period of:
a) 7 years
b) 2 years
c) 10 years
d) 5 years [AIBE-V]

Q.141 Which provision under the Code provides the indication as to the rule against double jeopardy?
a) S.300
b) S.305
c) S.309
d) S.311 [AIBE-V]

Q.142 "If an accused is charged of a major offence but is not found guilty thereunder, he can be convicted of minor offence if the facts established indicate that such minor offence has been committed." It was so upheld in which case?

a) Sangarabonia Sreenu Vs. State of Andhra Pradesh

b) State of Himachal Pradesh Vs. Tara Dutt

c) Shamsher Singh Vs. State of Punjab

d) Nalini Vs. State of Tamil Nadu [AIBE-V]

Q.143 "Provisions of S.195 of the Code are mandatory and non-compliance of it would initiate the prosecution and all other consequential orders." In which case the court upheld so?

a) C Muniappan Vs. State of Tamil Nadu

b) Kishun Singh Vs. State of Bihar

c) State of Karnataka Vs. Pastor P Raju

d) None of the above [AIBE-V]

Q.144 Order granting anticipatory bail becomes operative:

a) On arrest

b) On passing of the order by the court

c) Prior to arrest

d) None of the above [AIBE-V]

Q.145 Compensation to victims of crime under Criminal Law relates to:

a) S.336

b) S.331

c) S.335

d) S.357 [AIBE-V]

Q.146 What persons may be charged jointly and tried together under S.223 of CrPC:

a) Persons accused of the same offence committed in the course of the same transaction

b) Persons accused of an offence and persons accused of abetment of or attempt to commit such offence

c) Persons accused of different offences committed in the course of the same transaction

d) All of the above [AIBE-V]

Q.147 The investigating officer during the investigation records the statements of a witness under:

(a) Section 160 of CrPC

(b) Section 162 of CrPC

(c) Section 161 of CrPC

(d) Section 164 of CrPC [AIBE-IV]

Q.148 In a bailable offence, the bail is granted as a matter of right:

(a) By the police officer

(b) By the court

(c) Both by the police officer & the court

(d) Either (a) or (b) [AIBE-IV]

Q.149 Non-cognizable offence has been defined:
(a) Under section 2(a)
(b) Under section 2(e)
(c) Under section 2(f)
(d) Under section 2(i) [AIBE-IV]

Q.150 Section 91 of CrPC does not apply to:
(a) The complainant
(b) The accused
(c) The Witness
(d) A person who is neither a complainant nor an accused nor a witness [AIBE-IV]

Q.151 Cognizable offence under CrPC has been defined:
(a) Under section 2(a) of CrPC
(b) Under section 2(c) of CrPC
(c) Under section 2(f) of CrPC
(d) Under section 2(1) of CrPC
[AIBE-IV]

Q.152 It is mandatory to produce the person arrested before the Magistrate within 24 hours of his arrest under:
(a) Section 56 of CrPC
(b) Section 57 of CrPC
(c) Section 58 of CrPC
(d) Section 59 of CrPC [AIBE-IV]

Q.153 A refusal to answer questions put to a witness under section 161 of CrPC is an offence under:
(a) Section 176 IPC
(b) Section 179 IPC
(c) Section 187 IPC
(d) Neither (a) nor (b) nor (c)
[AIBE-IV]

Q.154 A statement of a witness recorded under section 161 of CrPC in writing during investigation & is signed by the person making the statement or any record thereof.
(a) Section 161(2) of CrPC
(b) Section 161(3) of CrPC
(c) Section 162(1) of CrPC
(d) Section 162(2) of CrPC
[AIBE-IV]

Q.155 Which classification of offence comes under Criminal Procedure Code?
(a) Cognizable & non-cognizable
(b) Bailable & non-bailable
(c) Summons cases & warrant cases
(d) All of the above [AIBE-IV]

Q.156 Complaint as provided under Sec.2(d) of CrPC:
(a) Can be in writing only
(b) Can be oral
(c) Either in writing or oral
(d) Can be by gestures [AIBE-IV]

TOPIC 4: INDIAN PENAL CODE

(8 questions are, generally, asked from this subject)

Q.1 Bhartiya Nyaya Sanhita, 2023 considers force to be "Criminal Force":

(A) When it is used unintentionally.

(B) When intentionally uses force only.

(C) When it is used intentionally without consent, causing injury, fear or annoyance.

(D) When it is used in self-defense.

[AIBE-XIX]

Q.2 According to Bhartiya Nyaya Sanhita, 2023, what is the maximum fine for making or use a document that resembles a currency note or a bank note under Section 182(1) ?

(A) One hundred rupees

(B) Five hundred rupees

(C) Three hundred rupees

(D) One thousand rupees

[AIBE-XIX]

Q.3 According to the provisions of the Bhartiya Nyaya Sanhita, 2023, the right of private defence of property extends to the voluntary causing of death or of any other harm to the wrong-doer in which of the offences committed or attempting to be committed ?

(1) Robbery (2) House-breaking after sunset

(3) Theft, mischief or house trespass

(A) (1) only

(B) (1) and (3) both

(C) (1) and (2) both

(D) (1), (2) and (3) [AIBE-XIX]

Q.4 Rajesh, in a heated argument with Sunil, strikes him with a heavy iron rod. The blow fractures Sunil's arm, and he is unable to use it for several weeks. The medical report confirms that the fracture amounts to grievous hurt. Which of the following offenses has Rajesh committed ?

(A) Simple hurt under Section 323 of IPC

(B) Voluntarily causing grievous hurt under Section 325 of IPC

(C) Voluntarily causing hurt under Section 324 of IPC

(D) Attempt to commit culpable homicide under Section 308 of IPC

[AIBE-XIX]

Q.5 Amit, intending to cause the death of Vijay, attacks him with a knife. Vijay sustains severe injuries and dies on the spot. The investigation reveals that Amit acted with the knowledge that his actions were likely to cause death. However, there is no evidence of premeditation or intent to murder Vijay. Which of the following offenses has Amit committed ?

(A) Murder under Section 302 of IPC

(B) Culpable homicide not amounting to murder under Section 304 of IPC

(C) Causing death by negligence under Section 304A of IPC

(D) Voluntarily causing grievous hurt under Section 325 of IPC

[AIBE-XIX]

Q.6 Amit and Rani decide to break into a house at night with the intent of stealing valuables. They use a crowbar to force open the door, but before they can take anything, the owner of the house, Vikram, unexpectedly arrives home. Amit and Rani panic and run away without stealing anything. The police arrest them the following morning based on a complaint from Vikram. Which of the following offenses under the BNS have Amit and Rani committed ?

(A) Attempt to commit theft

(B) House trespass with intent to commit theft

(C) Attempt to commit robbery

(D) Burglary

[AIBE-

XIX]

Q.7 Punishment for rape in cases where the victim is a woman below the age of 16 or 12 is included in which section of the BNS ?

(A) 64

(B) 65

(C) 63

(D) 72 [AIBE-XIX]

Q.8 A new offense of 'Snatching' has been introduced by the BNS. Which section of the BNS defines 'Snatching' as an offense?

(A) 308

(B) 303

(C) 305

(D) 304 [AIBE-XIX]

Q.9 In which of the following situations Indian Penal Code, 1860 may not apply?

i. An offence committed by Indians outside India

ii. An offence committed by any person on any ship registered in India

iii. Any person committing offence targeting computer resources located in any country

a) Only i

b) Only ii

c) Only iii

d) Only i & ii [AIBE-XVIII]

Q.10 How many types of punishment are currently existing under the Indian Penal Code, 1860?

a) 3

b) 4
c) 5
d) 6 [AIBE-XVIII]

Q.11 A and Z agree to fence with each other for amusement. In the course of such fencing, while playing fairly, A hurts Z severely. Which of the following offences is committed by A?
a) Hurt
b) Attempt to murder
c) Grievous hurt
d) No offence [AIBE-XVIII]

Q.12 In which of the following situations, right of private defence cannot extend to causing death?
a) In case when assault is causing apprehension of murder
b) In case when assault is reflecting intention of committing rape
c) In case when assault is reflecting intention of causing simple hurt
d) In case when assault is reflecting intention of gratifying unnatural lust [AIBE-XVIII]

Q.13 For which of the following sections of the Indian Penal Code, 1860 the word 'benefit' does not include pecuniary benefits?
a) Section 89
b) Section 155
c) Section 156
d) Section 370 [AIBE-XVIII]

Q.14 X intentionally pulls up a woman's veil without her consent intending to annoy her. As per the Indian Penal Code, 1860 which of the following offences has he committed?
a) Hurt
b) Criminal force
c) Assault
d) Grievous hurt [AIBE-XVIII]

Q.15 What punishment is prescribed under the Indian Penal Code, 1860 for a person who maims any minor in order that such minor may be used for the purpose of begging?
a) Imprisonment for 5 years and fine
b) Imprisonment for 7 years and fine
c) Imprisonment for 10 years and fine
d) Imprisonment for life and fine [AIBE-XVIII]

Q.16 X threatens to publish a defamatory libel concerning Y unless Y gives him money. Which of the following punishments may be given to X for the act committed by him, as per the Indian Penal Code, 1860?
a) Imprisonment up to 2 years, or with fine or with both
b) Imprisonment up to 3 years,

or with fine or with both
c) Imprisonment up to 5 years, or with fine or with both
d) Imprisonment up to 7 years, or with fine or with both
[AIBE-XVIII]

Q.17 Under section 82 and 83 of Indian Penal Code, an offence is punishable if it is done by a child
a) of below 7 years of age.
b) **of above 7 years of age, but below 12 years having attained sufficient maturity and understanding**.
c) of above 7 years of age, but below 10 years having attained sufficient maturity and understanding.
d) of above 7 years of age, but below 12 years not having attained sufficient maturity and understanding. [AIBE-XVII]

Q.18 Name two essential conditions of penal liability.
a) Guilty body and rightful act
b) Guilty intent and wrong motive
c) **Guilty mind and wrongful act**
d) Guilty motive and wrongful act
[AIBE-XVII]

Q.19 Provisions for Right of Private Defence is given between ___ of IPC.
a) Sections 74-84
b) **Sections 96-106**
c) Sections 107-120
d) Sections 141-160 [AIBE-XVII]

Q.20 The consent is not a valid consent under section 90 of IPC:
a) If given under fear of injury or misconception of fact.
b) If given by a person of unsound mind.
c) If given by a child below 12 years of age.
d) **All of these** [AIBE-XVII]

Q.21 Causing the death of a child in the mother's womb is not homicide as provided under:
a) Explanation III to Section 300
b) **Explanation III to Section 299**
c) Explanation III to Section 301
d) Explanation III to Section 302
[AIBE-XVII]

Q.22 Punishment for defamation under Indian Penal Code is simple imprisonment for a term which may extend it to _____ or with fine, or with both.
a) **2 years**
b) 3 years
c) 4 years
d) 5 years [AIBE-XVII]

Q.23 Assault or criminal force to women with intent to outrage her modesty under IPC is which kind of offence?
a) Non-cognizable and bailable

b) Cognizable and bailable
c) **Cognizable and non-bailable**
d) Non-cognizable and non-bailable [AIBE-XVII]

Q.24 'A' places men with firearms at the outlets of a building and tells 'Z' that they will fire at 'Z' if 'Z' attempts to leave the building. 'A' is guilty of:
a) **Wrongful confinement**
b) Wrongful restraint
c) Both wrongful confinement and wrongful restraint
d) None of these [AIBE-XVII]

Q.25 "Casting Couch" in Bollywood, the Indian film industry, is an example of-
a) sexual assault
b) **sexual harassment**
c) both (a) and (b)
d) None of the above [AIBE-XVI]

Q.26 Harbouring an offender who has escaped from custody or whose apprehension has been ordered, if the offence be capital is dealt under:
a) Section 215 of IPC
b) **Section 216 of IPC**
c) Section 217 of IPC
d) Section 218 of IPC [AIBE-XVI]

Q.27 The maxim '*actus non facit reum nisi mens sit rea*' means:
a) **There can be no crime without a guilty mind**
b) Crime has to be coupled with guilty mind
c) Crime is the result of guilty mind
d) In crime, intention is relevant, motive is irrelevant [AIBE-XVI]

Q.28 The famous pronouncement of Delhi High Court regarding constitutional validity of section 377 Indian Penal Code reversed by Supreme Court in:
a) NALSA Vs Union of India
b) Naz Foundation Vs Government of NCT of Delhi
c) Shabnam Hasmi Vs Union of India
d) **Suresh Kaushal Vs Naz Foundation** [AIBE-XVI]

Q.29 Under which section of IPC, Professional Negligence is often invoked against medical professionals in cases alleging professional negligence?
a) 303A
b) **304A**
c) 302
d) 305 [AIBE-XVI]

Q.30 A offers a bribe to B, a public servant, as a reward for showing A some favour in the exercise of B's official functions. B accepts the bribe.
a) A has abetted the offence defined in Section 160, IPC
b) **A has abetted the offence**

defined in Section 161, IPC
c) A has abetted the offence defined in Section 162, IPC
d) A has abetted the offence defined in Section 163, IPC
[AIBE-XVI]

Q.31 The Committee, which led to the passing of the Criminal Law Amendment Act 2013, was headed by:
a) Justice Dalveer Bhandari
b) Justice Altamas Kabir
c) **Justice J.S. Verma**
d) Justice A.S. Anand [AIBE-XVI]

Q.32 'Z', under the influence of madness, attempts to kill 'X'. Is 'Z' guilty of an offence? Has 'X' the same right of private defence, which he would have if 'Z' were sane?
a) **'Z' has not committed any offence as per section 98 of IPC and same right of private defence to 'X' if 'Z' is mad**
b) As per Section 98 of IPC, 'X' has committed an offence and no right of private defence to 'X'
c) 'Z' has committed an offence for not using his mind
d) None of the above [AIBE-XVI]

Q.33 As per section 53 of IPC, the word "injury" denotes any harm whatever illegally caused to any person's:
a) Body
b) Mind
c) Reputation
d) **All of the above** [AIBE-XVI]

Q.34 The provisions of Indian Penal Code apply also to any offence committed by:
a) Any citizen of India in any place without and beyond India
b) Any person on any ship or aircraft registered in India wherever it may be
c) Any person in any place without and beyond India committing offence targeting a computer resource located in India
d) All of the above [AIBE-XV]

Q.35 Voluntarily throwing or attempting to throw acid is an offence punishable under:
a) Section 326B of the Indian Penal Code
b) Section 120B of the Indian Penal Code
c) Section 509 of the Indian Penal Code
d) Section 295B of the Indian Penal Code [AIBE-XV]

Q.36 'A' is at work with a hatchet; the head flies off and kills a man who is standing by. Here, if there was no want of proper caution on the part of 'A', his act is:
a) An offence of murder
b) An offence of culpable homicide
c) Not an offence

d) An offence of causing grievous hurt [AIBE-XV]

Q.37 'A', with the intention of causing 'Z' to be convicted of a criminal conspiracy, writes a letter in imitation of 'Z''s handwriting, purporting to be addressed to an accomplice in such criminal conspiracy, and puts the letter in a place which he knows that the officers of the Police are likely to search. 'A' has committed an offence under:
a) Section 256 of IPC
b) Section 192 of IPC
c) Section 195A of IPC
d) Section 201 of IPC [AIBE-XV]

Q.38 In which of the following cases, the offence of sedition was in issue:
a) Queen Empress Vs. Bal Gangadhar Tilak
b) Niharendu Dutt Mazumdar Vs. Emperor
c) Kedar Nath Singh Vs. State of Bihar
d) All of the above [AIBE-XV]

Q.39 Deliberate and malicious acts, intended to outrage religious feelings of any class by insulting its religion or religious beliefs - is an offence under:
a) Section 295
b) Section 295A
c) Section 265A
d) Section 276 [AIBE-XV]

Q.40 Under Section 82 of the Indian Penal Code, nothing is an offence which is done by a child under the age of:
a) 14 years
b) 7 years
c) 18 years
d) 21 years [AIBE-XV]

Q.41 R Vs. Dudley & Stephen stands for the principle that:
a) Killing an innocent life to save his own is not a defence and necessity cannot be pleaded as a defence against murder.
b) Necessity can be pleaded as a defence against murder, killing an innocent life to save his own may become inevitable.
c) Killing out of mercy is a defence and necessity cannot be pleaded as a defence against murder.
d) None of the above [AIBE-XV]

Q.42 The provisions relating to dowry is given under:
a) Section 304B of the IPC
b) Section 304A of the IPC
c) Section 304 of the IPC
d) Section 305B of the IPC
[AIBE-XIV]

Q.43 Which of the following section is designed to curb infanticide?

A: Section 317 of the IPC
b) Section 313 of the IPC
c) Section 318 of the IPC
d) Section 315 of the IPC
[AIBE-XIV]

Q.44 If a person, undergoing life imprisonment, attempts to commit murder and hurt is caused thereby, he may be punished with:
a) Life Imprisonment
b) Death
c) Imprisonment
d) All of the above [AIBE-XIV]

Q.45 The punishments to which offenders are liable under the provision of IPC are?
a) Death and imprisonment for life
b) Rigorous imprisonment and simple imprisonment
c) Forfeiture of property and fine
d) All of the above [AIBE-XIV]

Q.46 M'Naghten rules form the basis of the law of:
a) Infancy
b) Insanity
c) Ignorance of fact
d) Mistake [AIBE-XIV]

Q.47 'A' places men with firearms at the outlets of a building and tells 'Z' that they will fire at 'Z' if 'Z' attempts to leave the building. 'A':
a) Wrong fully restrains Z
b) Wrong fully confines Z
c) Both (a) & (b)
d) None of the above
[AIBE-XIV]

Q.48 'A' incites a dog to spring upon 'Z', without Zs' consent. If 'A' intends to cause injury, fear or annoyance to 'Z':
a) 'A' uses force to 'Z'
b) 'A' assaulted 'Z'
c) 'A' uses criminal force to 'Z'
d) None of the above
[AIBE-XIV]

Q.49 'A' causes cattle to enter upon the field belonging to 'Z', intending to cause and knowing that he is likely to cause damage to 'Z''s crop. 'A' has committed:
a) Mischief
b) Criminal trespassing
c) Criminal breach of trust
d) Extortion [AIBE-XIV]

Q.50 'X' strikes 'A'. 'A' is, by this provocation, excited to violent range. 'Y', a bystander, intending to take advantage of 'A's rage and to cause him kill 'X', gives a revolver into 'A''s hand for that purpose. 'A' kills 'X' with the revolver:
a) 'A' is liable for committing murder and 'Y' is liable for abetting murder.
b) 'A' is liable for committing culpable homicide and 'Y' is not liable.

c) 'A' is liable for committing culpable homicide and 'Y' is liable for abetting culpable homicide not amounting to murder.
d) 'A' is not liable and 'Y' is liable for abetting murder. [AIBE-XIII]

Q.51 'A' and 'B' agree to fence with each other for amusement. This agreement implies the consent of each to suffer any harm which in the course of fencing, may be caused without foul play and if 'A', while playing fairly, hurts 'B', 'A' commits no offence. The provisions are given under:
a) Section 87
b) Section 85
c) Section 86
d) Section 88 [AIBE-XIII]

Q.52 The provisions of the right of private defence are given:
a) Under sections 96-108 of the Indian Penal Code
b) Under sections 94-106 of the Indian Penal Code
c) Under sections 96-106 of the Indian Penal Code
d) Under sections 95-106 of the Indian Penal Code [AIBE-XIII]

Q.53 When two or more persons agree to do an illegal act or an act which is not illegal by illegal means, such an agreement is designated as:
a) Abetment by conspiracy
b) Abetment by aid
c) Criminal conspiracy
d) Abetment [AIBE-XIII]

Q.54 The provisions regarding sedition are given:
a) Under Section 124 of the IPC
b) Under Section 124A of the IPC
c) Under Section 121A of the IPC
d) Under Section 130 of the IPC
[AIBE-XIII]

Q.55 When two or more persons, by fighting in a public place, disturb the public peace, they are said to commit:
a) A riot
b) An affray
c) An assault
d) None of the above [AIBE-XIII]

Q.56 Promotion of 'class hatred' in given under:
a) Section 153A of the IPC
b) Section 153AA of the IPC
c) Section 153B of the IPC
d) Section 144 of the IPC
[AIBE-XIII]

Q.57 The distinction between sections 299 and 300 was made clear by Melvill J. in:
a) Reg Vs. Gorachand Gope
b) Reg Vs. Govinda
c) Govinda Vs. Reg
d) Reg Vs. Hayward [AIBE-XIII]

Q.58 A person instigates any person to do an offence or illegal act or omission attracts:

a) Section 107 IPC

b) Section 120B of IPC

c) Section 114 of IPC

d) Section 144 of IPC [AIBE-XII]

Q.59 Uttering of words with deliberate intention to wound religious sentiments will be dealt with:

a) Section 298 of IPC

b) Section 296 of IPC

c) Section 297 of IPC

d) None of the above [AIBE-XII]

Q.60 'A' is at work with a hatchel. The head flies off and kills a man who is standing by. If there was no want of a proper caution on the part of 'A', his act is excusable and not an offence. It is contained in:

a) Section 80 of IPC

b) Section 84 of IPC

c) Section 81 of IPC

d) Section 85 of IPC [AIBE-XII]

Q.61 In-camera trial is conducted in the cases charged under Section:

a) 302 IPC

b) 307 IPC

c) 376 IPC

d) 498A IPC [AIBE-XII]

Q.62 Mahatma Gandhi was jailed and prosecuted by British regime in 1922 at Ahmadabad u/s. 124(A) of IPC for:

a) Calling Hartal

b) Breaching public peace and tranquility

c) Sedition and disaffection to the government

d) None of the above [AIBE-XII]

Q.63 Abetting the commission of Suicide is given under:

a) Section 9 of IPC

b) Section 8 of IPC

c) Section 7 of IPC

d) None of the above [AIBE-XII]

Q.64 'A' finds a purse with money not knowing to whom it belongs, he afterwards discovers that it belongs to 'B' and appropriates to his own use. 'A' is guilty of:

a) Criminal breach of trust

b) Cheating

c) Criminal misappropriation

d) Theft [AIBE-XII]

Q.65 Who is lawful guardian?

a) A person who in law represents the minor

b) A person who has been appointed by the Court

c) A person who has been authorized to represent an unmarried daughter

d) All of the above [AIBE-XII]

Q.66 What is meant by Homicide?

a) Suicide by human being not at home
b) Suicide at home
c) Killing of human being by another human being
d) Killing of human being by animal [AIBE-XI]

Q.67 Adulteration of food or drink is a punishable offence:
a) Under Section 274-276 of IPC
b) Under Section 277-278 of IPC
c) Under Section 272-273 of IPC
d) None of the above [AIBE-XI]

Q.68 Maximum punishment for waging a war against the Government of India under IPC is:
a) Rigorous imprisonment up to 5 years
b) Rigorous imprisonment up to 10 years
c) Rigorous imprisonment for life term
d) Death sentence [AIBE-XI]

Q.69 Offences relating to elections are:
a) Contained in the IPC as originally enacted
b) Are introduced in the IPC by a subsequent amendment
c) Are not covered by IPC
d) None of the above [AIBE-XI]

Q.70 Rupan Bajaj Vs. K P S Gill is a famous case which the Supreme Court decided on:
a) Wrongful restraint
b) Wrongful confinement
c) Outrage the modesty of a woman
d) Maintenance to the divorced women [AIBE-XI]

Q.71 Outraging the modesty of a woman is punishable under IPC:
a) Section 376(a)
b) Section 376(b)
c) Section 354
d) Section 498 [AIBE-XI]

Q.72 Section 463 of Indian Penal Code deals with the crime of:
a) House breaking
b) Dishonest misappropriation of property
c) Forgery
d) Forgery with cheating [AIBE-XI]

Q.73 Criminal Intimidation is explained in IPC under:
a) Section 503 to 506
b) Section 509 to 516
c) Section 319 to 329
d) None of the above [AIBE-XI]

Q.74 There is either theft or extortion. It is:
a) Robbery
b) Dacoity
c) Criminal breach of trust
d) Receiving stolen property [AIBE-X]

Q.75 This Section was enacted to meet the cases of dowry deaths:
a) Section 366A of IPC
b) Section 477A of IPC
c) Section 498A of IPC
d) Section 489A of IPC [AIBE-X]

Q.76 The rule is that penal statutes must be constructed:
a) Liberally
b) Strictly
c) Golden rule
d) Mischievous [AIBE-X]

Q.77 The various words used to denote *Mens Rea* under the IPC and are defined in the Code itself are:
a) Voluntary, dishonestly, fraudulently & reason to believe
b) Corruptly and want only
c) Malignantly and maliciously
d) Rashly and negligently [AIBE-X]

Q.78 The chief elements necessary to constitute a crime are:
a) A human being
b) An evil intent
c) Injury to another human being or society
d) All of the above [AIBE-X]

Q.79 'A', a surgeon, knowing that a particular operation is likely to cause the death of 'Z', who suffers under a painful complaint, but not intending to cause 'Z''s death & intending in good faith 'Z''s benefit, performs that operation on 'Z' with 'Z''s consent. 'A' has committed no offence. It is contained in:
a) Section 88 of the IPC
b) Section 89 of the IPC
c) Section 90 of the IPC
d) Section 87 of the IPC [AIBE-X]

Q.80 The distinction between sections 299 and 300 was made clear by Melvill J. in:
a) Reg Vs. Gorachand Gope
b) Reg Vs. Govinda
c) Reg Vs. Hayward
d) Govind Vs. Reg [AIBE-X]

Q.81 The provisions relating to compoundable offence are provided under Section:
a) 319
b) 320
c) 265(d)
d) 321 [AIBE-X]

Q.82 In the light of the Criminal Law Amendment Act 2013, which of the following statement is/are correct?
a) The word 'rape' in Section 375 of Indian Penal Code, 1860 has been replaced with sexual assault
b) Rape is now a gender-neutral offence
c) The amendment has fixed the age for consensual sex as 16 years

d) All of the above [AIBE-IX]

Q.83 The offence of stalking upon second or subsequent conviction is:
a) Non-cognizable and Bailable
b) Cognizable and Bailable
c) Cognizable and Non-bailable
d) Non-cognizable and Non-bailable [AIBE-IX]

Q.84 In kidnapping, the consent of minor is:
a) Wholly immaterial
b) Partly immaterial
c) Wholly material
d) Partly material [AIBE-IX]

Q.85 The Committee that led to the passing of the Criminal Law Amendment Act 2013 was headed by:
a) Justice Dalveer Bhandari
b) Justice Altamas Kabir
c) Justice J S Verma
d) Justice J S Anand [AIBE-IX]

Q.86 The *right to private defence* is:
a) Available under all circumstances
b) Available when there is time to have the recourse to the protection of public authorities
c) Available when there is no time to have recourse of public authorities
d) All of the above [AIBE-IX]

Q.87 To establish Section 34:
a) Common intention must be proved but not overt act is required to be proved.
b) Common intention and overt act both are required to be proved
c) Common intention need not be proved but only overt act is required to be proved
d) All of the above [AIBE-IX]

Q.88 The persons taking part in the commission of an offence have been divided into two classes. They are:
a) Principal and abettors
b) Principle and disciples
c) Principal and accessory
d) Debtor and holder [AIBE-VIII]

Q.89 Prosecution for the offence of defamation can be initiated only:
a) On the complaint of the aggrieved party
b) On the basis of an F.I.R.
c) On the basis of a police report
d) If it is a matter related to domestic affairs of a family [AIBE-VIII]

Q.90 'A' issued a warrant to a Police Officer to arrest 'P'. But the officer arrests 'Q' after the due inquiry believing 'Q' to be 'P'. Here:
a) 'P' is liable for criminal negligence
b) 'P' has committed no offence by virtue of S.76 IPC

c) 'P' has committed an offence of wrongful confinement
d) None of these [AIBE-VIII]

Q.91 *Durham doctrine* means:
a) That an accused is not criminally liable if his unlawful act is the product of immature understanding due to immature age
b) That an accused is not criminally liable if his unlawful act is the product of mental disease or mental defect
c) That an accused is criminally liable even if his unlawful act is the product of mental disease or mental defect
d) None of these [AIBE-VIII]

Q.92 *De minimis non curat lex* implies:
a) Every person is liable for his own acts
b) Trifling acts do not constitute an offence
c) Necessity knows no law
d) Nothing is an offence which is done in private defence
[AIBE-VIII]

Q.93 'P' and 'Q' agree to commit theft in 'R''s house, but no theft is actually committed. Here 'P' and 'Q' are guilty of:
a) Abetment of conspiracy
b) Abetment by instigation
c) No offence
d) Criminal conspiracy
[AIBE-VIII]

Q.94 Ramu is suffering from disease of the heart. Rahul, his heir, rushes into his room and shouts in his ear "your house has destroyed by fire" intending thereby to kill Ramu. Ramu dies of the shock. Here, Rahul is liable for the offence of:
a) Attempt to murder
b) Murder
c) Culpable homicide
d) Abetment to murder
[AIBE-VIII]

Q.95 'R' obtained a sum of Rs.50,000 from 'D' by putting 'D' in fear of death. Here 'R' commits:
a) Extortion
b) Cheating
c) Mischief
d) Robbery [AIBE-VII]

Q.96 Whoever causes bodily pain, disease or infirmity to any person is said to have inflicted .... on the victim.
a) Grievous hurt
b) Hurt
c) Assault
d) None of the above [AIBE-VII]

Q.97 Personation at Election is an offence under S....... of the Indian Penal Code.
a) 124A

b) 121A
c) 153B
d) 171D [AIBE-VII]

Q.98 Raman, having found a key of Raju's house which Raju had lost, commits house trespass by entering Raju's house after opening the door with that key. Raman has committed the offence of:
a) House trespass
b) Criminal trespass
c) House breaking
d) None of these [AIBE-VII]

Q.99 Who among the following is not a 'public servant'?
a) Liquidator
b) A Civil Judge
c) Secretary of a co-operative society
d) None of these [AIBE-VII]

Q.100 Putting or attempting to put a person in fear of death or grievous hurt in order to commit extortion is dealt under:
a) Section 385 IPC
b) Section 386 IPC
c) Section 387 IPC
d) Section 388 IPC [AIBE-VI]

Q.101 'F' invited 'C' to have a fix of his heroin. Each filled his own syringe and injected each other several times one night. Next morning 'F' died on the question of causation:
a) 'C' must be convicted of manslaughter
b) 'C' must not be convicted of manslaughter
c) 'C' can be convicted for the possession of heroin only
d) 'C' is neither guilty of possessing heroin nor the death of 'F'
[AIBE-VI]

Q.102 Literally, *Mens Rea* means:
a) Guilty mind
b) Guilty or a wrongful purpose
c) Criminal intent, a guilty knowledge and willfulness
d) All of the above [AIBE-VI]

Q.103 *Mens Rea* is not an essential ingredient for offences under:
a) Revenue Acts
b) Public Nuisance
c) Criminal case which are in summary mode
d) All of these [AIBE-VI]

Q.104 '*Actus non facit reum, nisi mens sit rea*' means:
a) A deed, a material result of human conduct
b) The intent and act must both concur to constitute the crime
c) Putting to death
d) Un commended manner
[AIBE-VI]

Q.105 Cheating and thereby

dishonestly inducing delivery of property, or the making alteration or destruction of a valuable security is dealt under:
a) Section 417 IPC
b) Section 418 IPC
c) Section 419 IPC
d) Section 420 IPC [AIBE-VI]

Q.106 Promoting enmity between different groups on grounds of religion, race, place of birth, residence, language, etc. and doing acts prejudicial to maintenance of harmony is an offence under which provision of Indian Penal Code?
a) S.120A
b) S.120B
c) S.153A
d) S.226 [AIBE-V]

Q.107 The gist of this offence is meeting of minds:
a) S.120A
b) S.133
c) S.221
d) S.340 [AIBE-V]

Q.108 'A' places men with firearms at the outlets of a building and tells 'B' that they will fire at 'B' if 'B' attempts to leave the building. What is the offence committed by 'A' as against 'B'?
a) Wrongful restraint
b) Wrongful confinement
c) Refusal to leave the place
d) None of the above [AIBE-V]

Q.109 Adulteration of food or drink intended for sale is punishable under:
a) S.227
b) S.272
c) S.277
d) S.273 [AIBE-V]

Q.110 Voluntarily causing grievous hurt to deter public servant from his duty is:
a) Cognizable & non-bailable offence
b) Non-cognizable & bailable offence
c) Cognizable and bailable offence
d) None of the above [AIBE-V]

Q.111 'A' obtains property from 'Z' by saying - "Your child is in the hands of my gang and will be put to death unless you send us Rs.10,000." This offence is:
a) Robbery
b) Extortion
c) Dacoity
d) None of the above [AIBE-V]

Q.112 Obstructing public servant in discharge of his public functions is a:
a) Non-bailable offence
b) Bailable offence
c) Civil wrong
d) None of the above [AIBE-V]

Q.113 In the IPC, nothing is an offence which is done by a child under:
a) Eight years
b) Ten years
c) Seven years
d) Twelve years [AIBE-IV]

Q.114 Right of private defence of the body extends to voluntarily causing death if the offence, which occasions the exercise of right:
a) Reasonably causes apprehension that death will be caused
b) Reasonably causes apprehension that simple injury will be caused
c) Is of escaping with stolen property immediately after the theft
d) Is of arresting a person who is running away after having committed an offence of voluntarily causing hurt [AIBE-IV]

Q.115 Under Sec.498 A, the 'cruelty' means and includes:
a) Only demand of dowry
b) Only physical torture
c) Both mental & physical torture
d) None of the above

[AIBE-IV]

Q.116 What is the offence where preparation itself of an offence is punishable?
a) Theft
b) Dacoity
c) Murder
d) Rape [AIBE-IV]

Q.117 In Rex Vs. Govinda, the points of distinction between the two provisions of the IPC were explained:
a) Section 34 and Section 149
b) Section 302 and Section 304
c) Section 299 and Section 300
d) Section 403 and Section 405
[AIBE-IV]

Q.118 'A' has sexual intercourse with his own wife aged about 14 years with her consent. 'A' committed:
a) No offence
b) Offence of Rape
c) Intercourse with own wife is not rape
d) As there was consent hence 'A' cannot be held guilty for the offence rape [AIBE-IV]

TOPIC 5: EVIDENCE ACT

(8 questions are, generally, asked from this subject)

Q.1 Which word is inserted in Section 22 of the BSA that was not present in Section 24 of the Evidence Act ?

(A) Inducement

(B) Coercion

(C) Threat

(D) Promise [AIBE-XIX]

Q.2 Existence of course of business when relevant is discussed in ....

(A) Section 12 of the BSA, 2023

(B) Section 13 of the BSA, 2023

(C) Section 14 of the BSA, 2023

(D) Section 15 of the BSA, 2023 [AIBE-XIX]

Q.3 In a criminal trial, Rajesh is accused of theft. During the investigation, the police recover a stolen laptop from a location known to be frequented by Rajesh. His fingerprints are found on the laptop. According to the Bhartiya Sakshya Adhiniyam, 2023, how should the court interpret this piece of evidence ?

(A) The recovered laptop and fingerprints are automatically considered conclusive proof of Rajesh's guilt.

(B) The recovered laptop and fingerprints are circumstantial evidence that can be considered along with other evidence, but do not by themselves prove guilt beyond reasonable doubt.

(C) The evidence is inadmissible because the police did not obtain a search warrant before recovering the laptop.

(D) The fingerprints must be verified by at least two independent forensic experts before being presented in court. [AIBE-XIX]

Q.4 A Where a document is executed in several parts like printing, lithography or photography, video recording, computer resource as an electronic or digital records, the BSA 2023 classifies each part as a

(A) Primary evidence

(B) Secondary evidence

(C) Circumstantial evidence

(D) Scientific evidence [AIBE-XIX]

Q.5 Which section of BSA provides that no court shall require any communication between the Ministers and the President of India to be produced before it ?

(A) 65

(B) 165

(C) 268

(D) 168 [AIBE-XIX]

Q.6 According to Section 46 of Bhartiya Sakshya Adhiniyam, when character evidence is relevant in civil cases ?

(A) Always relevant to prove conduct

(B) Only when related to other relevant fact

(C) Never relevant

(D) Only in criminal cases

[AIBE-XIX]

Q.7 As per Section 78(2) of the BSA 2023, presumption about the officer signing or certifying a document is:

(A) The officer's signature is assumed to be forgery

(B) The officer did not hold the claimed officer character at the time of signing

(C) The officer held the official character claimed when signing or certifying the document.

(D) The document's authenticity is independent of the official's official character [AIBE-XIX]

Q.8 Under Section 146 of the BSA 2023, when the leading questions are permissible in the court proceedings ?

(A) Leading questions are always allowed during examination-in-chief without restriction.

(B) Leading questions are not allowed during cross-examination

(C) Leading questions can be asked in an examination-in-chief, re-examination, cross-examination without any objection.

(D) Leading questions are permitted during cross-examination and when matters are introductory, undisputed, or sufficiently proved. [AIBE-XIX]

Q.9 A is accused of the murder of B by beating him. Which of the following will not be considered a relevant fact forming part of the same transaction as per the Indian Evidence Act, 1872?

a) Whatever said by A or B at the time of beating

b) Whatever done by A or B at the time of beating

c) Whatever said by bystanders at the time of beating

d) Whatever said by A or B the day before the day of beating

[AIBE-XVIII]

Q.10 Which of the following provisions of the Indian Evidence Act, 1872 says that the confession to a police officer shall not be proved against him?

a) Section 24

b) Section 25

c) Section 26

d) Section 27 [AIBE-XVIII]

Q.11 Under which of the following

provisions of the Indian Evidence Act, 1872 dying declaration may be admitted as evidence?

a) Section 25
b) Section 29
c) Section 32
d) Section 37 [AIBE-XVIII]

Q.12 Which of the following is correct according to the Indian Evidence Act, 1872 pertaining to proof of contents of the documents?

a) Contents of the document shall be provided by primary evidence.
b) Contents of the documents may be proved by secondary evidence.
c) Contents of the documents shall be proved by both primary and secondary evidence.
d) Contents of documents may be proved either by primary or by secondary evidence.
[AIBE-XVIII]

Q.13 Which of the following is the correct statement as per the Indian Evidence Act, 1872?

a) Leading questions may be asked in examination-in-chief.
b) Leading questions may be asked in cross examination.
c) Leading questions may be asked in re-examination.
d) Leading questions cannot be asked in cross examination.
[AIBE-XVIII]

Q.14 In which of the following cases did the Supreme Court of India clarify the admissibility of electronic records as evidence?

a) Anvar P. v P.K. Basheer
b) State of Haryana v Jai Singh
c) State of Maharashtra v Natwarlal Damodardas Soni
d) State of Punjab v Jagir Singh
[AIBE-XVIII]

Q.15 Which of the following is an incorrect statement in the light of Indian Evidence Act, 1872?

a) Confession always goes against a person making it.
b) Admissions are conclusive as to the matters admitted.
c) Admissions may operate as an estoppel.
d) Confession is a statement, written or oral, which is direct admission of suit. [AIBE-XVIII]

Q.16 Which of the following sections of the Indian Evidence Act, 1872 is an exception to the hearsay rule?

a) Section 32(1)
b) Section 32(2)
c) Section 32(3)
d) Section 32(5) [AIBE-XVIII]

Q.17 The doctrine of 'Res Gestae' has been discussed in which section of the Evidence Act?

a) Section 5
b) **Section 6**
c) Section 10
d) Section 11 [AIBE-XVII]

Q.18 When the liability of a person who is one of the parties to the suit depends upon the liability of a stranger to the suit, then an admission by the stranger in respect of his liability shall be an admission on the part of that person who is a party to the suit. It has been so provided under which section of the Indian Evidence Act, 1872?
a) Section 17
b) Section 18
c) **Section 19**
d) Section 2 [AIBE-XVII]

Q.19 Judicial evidence means:
a) **Evidence received by Courts in proof or disproof of facts**
b) Evidence received by a Police Officer
c) Evidence received by the Home Department
d) Evidence received by a Tribunal [AIBE-XVII]

Q.20 Which of the following is not a 'document' according to the Indian Evidence Act, 1872?
a) An inscription on a metal plate or a stone
b) A map or plan
c) A caricature
d) **None of these** [AIBE-XVII]

Q.21 "Presumptions as to dowry deaths" is given under which section?
a) 113A
b) **113B**
c) 114A
d) 114B [AIBE-XVII]

Q.22 Which of the following is not "Secondary evidence" as per Section 63 of Indian Evidence Act, 1872?
a) Copies made from the original by mechanical processes, where in themselves ensure the accuracy of the copy, and copies compared with such copies.
b) Copies made from or compared with the original.
c) Oral accounts of the contents of a document given by some person who has himself seen it.
d) **Copies not certified under section 63**. [AIBE-XVII]

Q.23 A leading question may be asked in:
a) Examination-in-Chief
b) Re-examination
c) **Cross examination**
d) None of these [AIBE-XVII]

Q.24 Extra-judicial confession means:
a) **Confessions made either to**

police or persons other than Judges and Magistrates
b) Confessions made before Magistrates
c) Confessions made before Judges
d) None of these [AIBE-XVII]

Q.25 How many kinds of presumptions are there as classified by the Supreme Court?
a) Permissive presumptions or presumptions of facts
b) Compelling presumptions or presumptions of law (rebuttable presumptions)
c) Irrebuttable presumptions of law or conclusive presumptions
d) **All of them** [AIBE-XVI]

Q.26 Under which section of the Evidence Act, admissions are defined?
a) **17**
b) 16
c) 15
d) 18 [AIBE-XVI]

Q.27 In which of the following cases the Supreme Court has held that the investigating officer should be allowed to refer to the records of investigation:
a) **State of Karnataka Vs Yarappa Reddi**
b) Mohammed Khalid Vs State of West Bengal
c) Baburam Vs State of U.P.
d) State of Rajasthan Vs Om Prakash [AIBE-XVI]

Q.28 The Indian Evidence Act came into force on:
a) 6th October 1860
b) 1st March 1974
c) 15th March 1872
d) **1st September 1872**
[AIBE-XVI]

Q.29 Promissory estoppel against government agencies is decided in:
a) Tweedle Vs Atkinson
b) Dutton Vs Poole
c) **Pournami all Mills Vs State of Kerala**
d) Kedar Nath Vs Gauri Mohamad
[AIBE-XVI]

Q.30 Admission can be broadly categorized into:
a) Judicial
b) Extra-judicial
c) Either A or B
d) **Both A and B** [AIBE-XVI]

Q.31 Section 66, Indian Evidence Act lays down:
a) A notice must be given before secondary evidence can be received under section 65(a), Indian Evidence Act
b) Notice to produce a document must be in writing
c) Order XI, Rule 15 of Civil Procedure Code prescribes the kind

of notice to produce a document
d) **All of them** [AIBE-XVI]

Q.32 When the accused states, "I will produce the share which I have received in such and such robbery", which of the following are not admissible with regard to Section 25, Indian Evidence Act?
I. An admission that there was a robbery
II. An admission that the accused took part in it
III. An admission that he got part of the property
IV. A statement as to where the property is
a) **I, II and III**
b) III and IV
c) II, III and IV
d) All of them [AIBE-XVI]

Q.33 'A' intentionally and falsely leads 'B' to believe that certain land belongs to 'A', and thereby induces 'B' to buy and pay for it. The land afterwards becomes the property of 'A', and 'A' seeks to set aside the sale on the ground that, at the time of the sale, he had no title. He will not be allowed to prove his want of title. Which section of the Evidence Act is applicable?
a) Section 92
b) Section 124
c) Section 115
d) Section 101 [AIBE-XV]

Q.34 The question is, whether 'A' owes 'B' rupees 10,000. Which of the following statements are relevant under Evidence Act?
a) The facts that 'A' asked 'C' to lend him money
b) 'D' said to 'C' in 'A''s presence and hearing - "I advise you not to trust 'A', for he owes 'B' 10,000 rupees"
c) 'A' went away without making any answer
d) All of the above [AIBE-XV]

Q.35 So much of such information, whether it amounts to a confession or not, as relates distinctly to the fact thereby discovered by the Police may be proved under:
a) Section 25 of the Evidence Act
b) Section 26 of the Evidence Act
c) Section 27 of the Evidence Act
d) Section 29 of the Evidence Act [AIBE-XV]

Q.36 When the Court has to form an opinion upon a point of foreign law or of science, or art, or as to identity of handwriting, or finger impressions, the opinions upon that point of persons especially skilled in such foreign law, science or art, or in questions as to identity of handwriting or finger impressions are relevant facts. This is under ……. of the Evidence Act.

a) Section 42
b) Section 45
c) Section 50
d) Section 55 [AIBE-XV]

Q.37 *Res gestae*, relevancy of facts forming part of same transaction is dealt under:
a) Section 6 of the Evidence Act
b) Section 17 of the Evidence Act
c) Section 18 of the Evidence Act
d) Section 20 of the Evidence Act [AIBE-XV]

Q.38 'A' is accused of waging war against the Government of India by taking part in an armed insurrection in which property is destroyed, troops are attacked, and goals are broken open. The occurrence of these facts is relevant, as forming part of the general transaction, though 'A' may not have been present at all of them- under which section of the Indian Evidence Act?
a) Section 12
b) Section 6
c) Section 3
d) Section 5 [AIBE-XV]

Q.39 Section 110 of the Evidence Act deals with:
a) Documentary evidence
b) Exclusion of oral evidence
c) Burden of proof as to ownership
d) Proof of guilt [AIBE-XV]

Q.40 Section 113A of the Evidence Act deals with:
a) Presumption as to abetment of murder
b) Presumption as to rape and abetment of suicide by a woman
c) Presumption as to abetment of kidnap of a girl
d) Presumption as to abetment of suicide by a married woman
[AIBE-XV]

Q.41 One of the following statements is not true, which one is that?
a) A confession by one co-accused implicating other co-accused would be proved.
b) A confession to a Police Officer cannot be proved.
c) A confession by a person in the custody of a Police Officer to any person in the presence of Magistrate can be proved.
d) If the confession of a person leads to recovery of a thing it can be proved. [AIBE-XIV]

Q.42 The Kashmira Singh Vs. State of M. P. is a leading case on:
a) Dying declaration
b) Admission
c) Confession to Police Officer
d) Confession of a co-accused
[AIBE-XIV]

Q.43 Which of the following facts

is not relevant in civil and criminal cases under Section 8 of the Indian Evidence Act?
a) Motive
b) Attempt
c) Conduct
d) Preparation [AIBE-XIV]

Q.44 Under the Indian Evidence Act, the character of a person is not relevant in which of the following cases?
a) Previous good character of an accused in criminal case
b) Previous bad character in reply to good character in criminal case
c) Character to prove conduct imputed in civil case
d) Character affected the amount of damage is civil case [AIBE-XIV]

Q.45 Which one of the following is primary evidence?
a) Document produced for the inspection of the court
b) Copies made from original
c) Certified copies of the document
d) Photostat copies of a document [AIBE-XIV]

Q.46 If it is proved that a man has not been heard of for .... by those who would naturally have heard of him if he were alive, the presumption under Section 108 of the Indian Evidence Act is that he is dead.
a) 5 years
b) 7 years
c) 15 years
d) 20 years [AIBE-XIV]

Q.47 A dumb witness gives his evidence in writing in the open court. Such evidence would be treated as:
a) Oral evidence
b) Documentary evidence
c) Secondary evidence
d) Primary evidence [AIBE-XIV]

Q.48 Which of the following is not a public document?
a) Bank books
b) Post-mortem report
c) Judgment of the High Court
d) Registered Sale Deed
[AIBE-XIV]

Q.49 Under Section 118 of the Indian Evidence Act, a person is a competent witness if he or she:
a) Is a major
b) Is not lunatic
c) Is not of extreme old age
d) Is capable of understanding questions put to him and giving rational answers irrespective of age [AIBE-XIII]

Q.50 Which of the following judgement is irrelevant under Section 43 of Indian Evidence Act?
a) Judgment of an insolvency court

b) Judgment of criminal court
c) Judgment of matrimonial court
d) Judgment of probate court
[AIBE-XIII]

Q.51 Under which section of the Indian Evidence Act, a witness has been given right to refresh his memory?
a) Section 157
b) Section 158
c) Section 159
d) Section 160 [AIBE-XIII]

Q.52 A 'dumb witness' gives his evidence in writing in the open court. Such evidence would be treated as:
a) Oral evidence
b) Documentary evidence
c) Secondary evidence
d) Primary evidence [AIBE-XIII]

Q.53 Under the Indian Evidence Act, which of the following is not a court?
a) Persons legally authorized to take evidence
b) Judges
c) Magistrates
d) Arbitrators [AIBE-XIII]

Q.54 A question suggesting the answers which the person putting it wishes or expects to receive is called:
a) Indecent questions
b) Leading questions
c) Improper questions
d) Proper questions [AIBE-XIII]

Q.55 A communication made to the spouse during marriage, under Section 122 of the Indian Evidence Act:
a) Remains privileged even after dissolution of marriage
b) Does not remain privileged after dissolution of marriage only by divorce
c) Does not remain privileged after dissolution of marriage only by death
d) Does not remain privileged in both the cases (b) and (c)
[AIBE-XIII]

Q.56 Which section of the Indian Evidence Act provides that an accomplice is a competent witness?
a) Section 114, illustration (b)
b) Section 118
c) Section 133
d) Section 134 [AIBE-XIII]

Q.57 Who is prevented from being testified u/s. 118 of Indian Evidence Act?
a) A lunatic who cannot understand the questions put to him
b) Extreme old age person who cannot give rational answer to the questions
c) A tender age person who cannot

give rational answer to the questions

d) All of the above [AIBE-XII]

Q.58 Any confessional statement by the accused given to the Magistrate is:

a) Admissible

b) Not admissible

c) Challengeable

d) None of the above

[AIBE-XII]

Q.59 Kashmira Singh Vs. State of Punjab is a leading case on:

a) Dying declaration

b) Admission

c) Confession

d) None of the above

[AIBE-XII]

Q.60 In civil cases, Indian Evidence Act bestows burden of proof on:

a) The petitioner

b) The respondents

c) The State Government

d) The Court [AIBE-XII]

Q.61 Dying declaration must be made by:

a) The dying person in hospital

b) The doctor who is treating the deceased in hospital

c) The deceased before death

d) Nearest relative of the deceased

[AIBE-XII]

Q.62 Any question suggesting the answer which the person putting it expects to receive is called:

a) Coercive question

b) Confusing question

c) Misleading question

d) Rhetoric question

[AIBE-XII]

Q.63 Indian Evidence Act was enacted in:

a) 1972

b) 1872

c) 1955

d) 1986 [AIBE-XII]

Q.64 Proving of hand writing is provided in Indian Evidence Act:

a) By the opinion of experts

b) By the evidence of a person who is acquainted with the handwriting

c) After police verification

d) (a) and (b) [AIBE-XI]

Q.65 Section 26 of Indian Evidence Act provides:

a) No confession made by a person in police custody is admissible

b) Confession made by a person in police custody is admissible

c) Confession made in the immediate presence of a Magistrate is admissible

d) (a) and (c) [AIBE-XI]

Q.66 The term 'Evidence' means and includes:

a) Oral evidence
b) Documentary evidence
c) Electronic records produced for the inspection of the court
d) All of the above [AIBE-XI]

Q.67 Under Sections 59 to 60 of Indian Evidence Act, the oral statement means:
a) All statements made before the court by the witness
b) All statement made before the Police by the accused
c) All statement of facts which a witness heard to say
d) All of the above [AIBE-XI]

Q.68 Under the Evidence Act, 'Court' includes:
a) All Judges
b) All Magistrates
c) All Arbitrators
d) (a) and (b) [AIBE-XI]

Q.69 Admissibility of contents of electronic records may be proved in accordance with the provisions of:
a) Under Section 61 of Indian Evidence Act
b) Under Section 65 of Indian Evidence Act
c) Under Section 65B of Indian Evidence Act
d) None of the above [AIBE-XI]

Q.70 Which is not a public record as per the provisions of Indian Evidence Act?
a) Documents forming the acts or records of the sovereign authority
b) Documents forming the acts or records of official bodies, tribunals
c) Documents and correspondence from Advocate and Notary office
d) Documents and circulars from University of Delhi [AIBE-XI]

Q.71 Under Section 18 of the Indian Evidence Act, the admission of which of the following person is not admissible against the other:
a) One of the plaintiffs
b) One of the defendants
c) Agents of the parties
d) Statement of the third party
[AIBE-X]

Q.72 Which of the following statement is correct?
a) A confession made by an accused to the Police Officer is relevant
b) A confession made by an accused in police custody to a Magistrate is not relevant
c) A confession made by an accused in the police custody and discovery made from the information received from confession, both confession and discovery are relevant
d) None of the above is correct
[AIBE-X]

Q.73 What is the maximum number

of witness which can be produced in a case?
a) 5
b) 10
c) 15
d) No limit [AIBE-X]

Q.74 Which section of Indian Evidence Act is based on English doctrine of *res gestae*?
a) 5
b) 6
c) 7
d) 8 [AIBE-X]

Q.75 In relation to Relevancy of Character in civil cases, which of the following is not correct?
a) It is not at all relevant
b) It is relevant when it affects award of damage
c) When character is itself an issue
d) When it appears from the fact otherwise relevant [AIBE-X]

Q.76 Pakala Narayana Swami Vs. Emperor is a leading case on:
a) Dying Declaration
b) Confession
c) Accomplice
d) Expert witness [AIBE-X]

Q.77 Section 112 of Indian Evidence Act provides that a child would be treated as legitimate if after dissolution of marriage, he/she has been born within:
a) 180 days
b) 270 days
c) 280 days
d) 300 days [AIBE-X]

Q.78 In joint trial, the evidentiary value of confession of a co-accused affecting himself and others has been discussed by the Supreme Court in:
a) Kashmira Singh Vs. State of M. P.
b) State of U. P. Vs. Deoman Upadhyaya
c) Ram Bharose Vs. State of U. P.
d) Rameshwar Vs. State of Rajasthan [AIBE-X]

Q.79 Indian Evidence Act applies to:
a) Proceedings before tribunals
b) Proceedings before the arbitrator
c) Judicial proceedings in court
d) All of the above [AIBE-IX]

Q.80 *Fact in issue* means:
a) Fact, existence or non-existence of which is admitted by the parties
b) Fact, existence or non-existence of which is disputed by the parties
c) Fact, existence or non-existence of which is not disputed by the parties
d) All of the above [AIBE-IX]

Q.81 The question whether a

statement was recorded in the course of investigation is a:

a) Question of law

b) Question of fact

c) Mixed question of law and fact

d) Question of law or of fact depends on facts and circumstances [AIBE-IX]

Q.82 Necessity rule as to admissibility of evidence is applicable when the maker of a statement:

a) Is dead or has become incapable of giving evidence

b) Is a person who can be found but his attendance cannot be procured without unreasonable delay or expenses

c) Is a person who cannot be found

d) All of the above [AIBE-IX]

Q.83 Secondary evidence of a document means:

a) Copies of the document

b) Oral account of the contents of the documents

c) Both (a) and (b)

d) None of the above [AIBE-IX]

Q.84 A *will* is required to be proved by calling at least one attesting witness:

a) When it is registered

b) When it is unregistered

c) When it is admitted

d) All of the above [AIBE-IX]

Q.85 Any person in Section 106 of Evidence Act refers to:

a) A party to the suit

b) A stranger to the suit

c) A person who is not a party to the suit but interested in the outcome of the suit

d) All of the above [AIBE-IX]

Q.86 A retracted confession:

a) Can be solely made the basis of conviction

b) Cannot be solely made the basis of conviction

c) Cannot be solely made the basis of conviction unless the same is corroborated

d) Both (a) and (c) are correct [AIBE-IX]

Q.87 A confession to be inadmissible under Section 25 of the Act:

a) Must relate to the same crime for which offender is charged

b) May relate to the same crime for which offender is charged

c) Must relate to another crime

d) None of the above [AIBE-IX]

Q.88 An unjustified and unexplained long delay on the part of the investigating officer in recording the statement of a material witness would render the evidence of such witness:

a) Unreliable
b) Inadmissible
c) Inadmissible and unreliable
d) None of the above [AIBE-IX]

Q.89 The presumption of continuance of life is contained in Sec _____ of the Evidence Act.
a) 107
b) 108
c) 207
d) 115 [AIBE-VIII]

Q.90 Testimony of a witness to the existence or non-existence of the fact or facts in issue is:
a) Oral evidence
b) Original evidence
c) Direct evidence
d) Both (a) and (b) [AIBE-VIII]

Q.91 'A' sees 'B' running away from a room and afterwards sees 'C' lying down in a pool of blood in the same room. 'A''s evidence in as far as seeing 'B' running away is direct but as far as the murder is concerned, it is a:
a) Primary evidence
b) Circumstantial evidence
c) Real evidence
d) Substantial evidence [AIBE-VIII]

Q.92 A statement made by an accused person before the trial begins by which he admits to have committed the offence but which he repudiates at the trial is known as:
a) Extra-judicial confession
b) Judicial confession
c) Retracted confession
d) Voluntary confession
[AIBE-VIII]

Q.93 Expert opinion under Sec.45 is:
a) A conclusive proof
b) Not a conclusive proof
c) Supportive and corroborative in nature
d) None of these [AIBE-VIII]

Q.94 Leading questions can be asked during:
a) Re-examination
b) Examination-in-Chief
c) Cross examination
d) None of these [AIBE-VIII]

Q.95 *Estoppel* is a rule by which a party to litigation is:
a) Stopped from asserting or denying a fact
b) Prevented from appearing in person
c) Prevented from hiding an evidence
d) Both (a) and (b) [AIBE-VIII]

Q.96 Under Sec.122 of the Evidence Act, a communication made to the spouse during marriage:

a) Remains privileged after the dissolution of marriage by divorce but not so on after death
b) Does not remain privileged after the dissolution of marriage by divorce, but remains privileged even after death
c) Does not remain privileged after dissolution of marriage by divorce or death
d) Remains privileged communication after the dissolution of marriage by divorce or death [AIBE-VIII]

Q.97 Evidences to document unmeaning in reference to existing facts is called as:
a) Patent ambiguity
b) Latent ambiguity
c) Both of them
d) None of the above [AIBE-VII]

Q.98 Original document is the best evidence. Exception to this rule is contained in:
a) Indian Evidence Act
b) Criminal Procedure Code
c) Bankers Book Evidence Act
d) None of these [AIBE-VII]

Q.99 S.82 IPC is an illustration for:
a) Presumption of fact
b) Presumption of law
c) Presumption of fact and presumption of law
d) None of the above [AIBE-VII]

Q.100 Meaning of *'nemo moriturus praesumitur mentire'* is:
a) A dying man can never speak truth
b) A dying man can never speak falsehood
c) A dying man can speak truth
d) A dying man may not speak falsehood [AIBE-VII]

Q.101 Rabindra Kumar Pal @ Dara Singh Vs. Republic of India, a famous case coming under S.30 of Evidence Act, is also well known as:
a) Graham Staines' murder case
b) Graham Bell's murder case
c) Graham Street's murder case
d) Graham Stout's murder case [AIBE-VII]

Q.102 Statement by a person who is dead is a relevant fact under ……. of the Indian Evidence Act:
a) S.32(3)
b) S.32(4)
c) S.32(5)
d) S.32(6) [AIBE-VII]

Q.103 A charge sheet filed under S.173 of CrPC is an example of:
a) Public document
b) Private document
c) Patent document
d) Latent document [AIBE-VII]

Q.104 Presumption of law is:

a) Discretionary and rebuttable
b) Mandatory and rebuttable
c) Mandatory and irrebuttable
d) All of the above [AIBE-VI]

Q.105 In Selvi's case, the Supreme Court of India examined the constitutionality of tests like Narco Analysis, Polygraph and Brain Mapping on the touchstones of:
a) Art.20(3) and Art.21
b) Art.21 and Art.23(2)
c) Art.23 and Art.21
d) Art.20(2) and Art.20(1)
[AIBE-VI]

Q.106 According to the Law Commission of India 69th Report, S.27 of the Indian Evidence Act is based on the:
a) Doctrine of introspection
b) Doctrine of testimonial incrimination
c) Doctrine of confirmation
d) None of the above [AIBE-VI]

Q.107 S.99 of the Indian Evidence Act says persons who are not parties to a document or their representatives in interest may give evidence of any facts tending to show a contemporaneous agreement varying the terms of the document. This is based on the principle:
a) Pacta tertis nec nocent nec prosunt
b) Pacta sunt servanda
c) Actio personalis moritur cum persona
d) None of the above [AIBE-VI]

Q.108 Burden of proving that person is alive who has not been heard of for seven years is on whom:
a) One who denies it
b) One who affirms it
c) Any third person / stranger
d) None of the above [AIBE-VI]

Q.109 The Court's discretion to permit leading questions is confined only to matters which are:
a) Introductory facts
b) Undisputed facts
c) Facts already sufficiently proved to the satisfaction of the Court
d) All of the above [AIBE-VI]

Q.110 The question is whether 'A' murdered 'B'. Marks on the ground, produced by a struggle at or near the place where the murder was committed, are relevant facts under:
a) S.7
b) S.6
c) S.8
d) S.11 [AIBE-VI]

Q.111 S.93 of the Indian Evidence Act treats the patent ambiguity as:
a) Curable
b) Incurable

c) Proper
d) None of the above [AIBE-VI]

Q.112 Which are the provisions under Indian Evidence Act 1872 that deal with relevancy of opinion of experts?
a) Ss.49 & 50
b) Ss.23 & 24
c) Ss.45 & 46
d) Ss. 81 & 82 [AIBE-V]

Q.113 The contents of documents may be proved either by:
a) Primary evidence or by secondary evidence
b) Direct evidence or circumstantial evidence
c) Primary evidence or documentary evidence
d) Primary evidence or direct evidence [AIBE-V]

Q.114 An oral account of the contents of a document given by some person, who has himself seen it, is:
a) Direct evidence
b) Circumstantial evidence
c) Best evidence
d) Secondary evidence [AIBE-V]

Q.115 "The DNA test cannot rebut the conclusive presumption envisaged under S.12 of the Indian Evidence Act. The parties can avoid the rigour of such conclusive presumption only by proving non-access which is a negative proof." It was so held in which case?
a) Shaik Fakruddin Vs. Shaik Mohammed Hasan AIR 2006 AP 48
b) Siddaramesh Vs. State of Karnataka (2010) 3 SCC 152
c) Kailash Vs. State of Madhya Pradesh AIR 2007 SC 107
d) Somvanti Vs. State of Punjab AIR 1963 SC 151 [AIBE-V]

Q.116 The statements of dead persons are relevant under which provision?
a) S.48
b) S.49
c) S.32(4)
d) S.13(a) [AIBE-V]

Q.117 "Witnesses are the eyes and ears of Justice." Whose statement is this?
a) Lord Atkin
b) Bentham
c) Lord Denning
d) Phipson [AIBE-V]

Q.118 An accomplice is unworthy of credit unless he is corroborated in material particulars is a:
a) Presumption of fact
b) Presumption of law
c) Conclusive proof
d) None of the above [AIBE-V]

Q.119 Patent ambiguity in interpreting documents renders it:
a) Curable
b) Incurable
c) Curable and incurable
d) None of the above [AIBE-V]

Q.120 Which of the following is irrelevant fact under Evidence Act 1872?
a) Facts regarding motive
b) Facts regarding statements without related conduct
c) Facts regarding statements clubbed with conduct
d) Facts which make other relevant fact as highly probable
[AIBE-IV]

Q.121 Test of competency of witness is:
a) Her being intelligent
b) Must be major
c) Understanding the nature of question
d) Capable of understanding the nature of question and giving rational answer [AIBE-IV]

Q.122 Which one is exception to 'rule of hearsay' evidence?
a) Dying declaration
b) Facts forming part of same transaction
c) Facts forming plea of alibi
d) Facts regarding character of accused [AIBE-IV]

Q.123 Communication between husband and wife is treated as privileged if communication:
a) Was made during marriage with promise of confidentiality
b) Was made during marriage, even without promise of confidentiality
c) Was made before marriage with promise of confidentiality
d) Is made after marriage
[AIBE-IV]

Q.124 Leading questions can be asked even without permission of Court during:
a) Examination-in-Chief
b) Cross Examination
c) Re-examination
d) All of the above [AIBE-IV]

Q.125 What do you mean by word 'evidence'?
a) Every fact connected with case
b) Facts introduced in court of law
c) Both
d) None [AIBE-IV]

Q.126 What is *fact in issue*?
a) Facts involved indirectly
b) Necessary facts to arrive or determine rights, liability or immunity
c) Both
d) None [AIBE-IV]

Q.127 *Relevant fact* is:
a) Facts logically relevant to any fact in issue
b) Facts legally relevant to any fact in issue
c) Both
d) None [AIBE-IV]

TOPIC 6: FAMILY LAW

(8 questions are, generally, asked from this subject)

Q.1 Which sections discusses with regard to "sapinda relationships" under the Hindu Marriage Act, 1955 ?

(A) Sections 3 (f) (i), 5 (v)

(B) Sections 3 (f) (i), 5 (iv)

(C) Sections 3(f) (i) & (ii), Explanation to section 3 (g), 5(iv)

(D) Sections 3(f) (i) & (ii), Explanation to section 3 (g), 5(v)

[AIBE-XIX]

Q.2 Under Section 15 of Hindu Marriage Act, 1955 the divorced person, to marry again ....

(A) have to wait for a period of one year from the date of the decree.

(B) have to wait for a period of six month from the date of the decree.

(C) may marry immediately thereafter without the leave of the court as a matter of right.

(D) None of these [AIBE-XIX]

Q.3 Aarti and Rajesh have been married for five years. Over time, Aarti has been subjected to continuous cruelty by Rajesh, which has led to emotional and mental distress. Aarti decides to file for divorce on the grounds of cruelty under Section 13(1)(ia) of the Hindu Marriage Act, 1955.

Which of the following statements is true regarding the grounds for divorce under the Hind Marriage Act ?

(A) Aarti can only seek divorce on the grounds of adultery.

(B) Aarti can seek divorce on the grounds of cruelty, as long as she proves mental physical cruelty.

(C) Aarti cannot seek divorce on the grounds of cruelty as it is not recognized under the Hindu Marriage Act.

(D) Aarti must prove Rajesh's cruelty was intentional to succeed in the divorce petition. [AIBE-XIX]

Q.4 On matters where Dayabhaga is silent, what prevails ?

(A) The local customs

(B) The Smritis

(C) The Shruti

(D) Mitakshara [AIBE-XIX]

Q.5 Nisha and Aakash are separated, and they both seek custody of their minor child, Aarav. Nisha has been the primary caregiver, while Aakash claims that he can provide better financial stability for Aarav. They both approach the court under the Guardian and Wards Act, 1890.

Which of the following factors will the court primarily consider in determining the custody of Aarav ?

(A) The financial stability of both parents.

(B) The gender of the child.

(C) The welfare and best interests of the child.

(D) The parent who is financially more stable is granted custody automatically. [AIBE-XIX]

Q.6 Match the following:

a. Spoken words	(i) Sunnat-ul-Qaul
b. Deepika vs. CAT	(ii) Customary Law
c. Silence	(iii) Sunnat-ul-Taqrir
d. Aas Kaur	(iv) Atypical Relationships
e. Shayara Bano	(v) Triple Talaq
	(vi) Maintenance

Choose the correct option:

(A) a-iii, b-ii, c-i, d-v, e-vi

(B) a-i, b-iv, c-iii, d-ii, e-v

(C) a-iii, b-iv, c-i, d-ii, e-vi

(D) a-i, b-ii, c-iii, d-iv, e-vi

[AIBE-XIX]

Q.7 Fatima, a Muslim woman, has been divorced by her husband, Imran, through Talaq. Fatima is now seeking maintenance from Imran for herself and her two minor children. Imran argues that Fatima has remarried and, therefore, is not entitled to any maintenance. Under Muslim law, which of the following statements is true regarding Fatima's claim for maintenance ?

(A) Fatima is not entitled to maintenance because she has remarried.

(B) Fatima is entitled to maintenance only for a period of three months after the divorce.

(C) Fatima entitled to maintenance for herself during her iddat period and for her children until they are self-supporting.

(D) Fatima can claim maintenance for herself and her children indefinitely, irrespective of her remarriage or the children's age.

[AIBE-XIX]

Q.8 The remedy of restitution of conjugal rights is given in Section ...... of Hindu Marriage Act, 1955.

(A) 13

(B) 11

(C) 6

(D) 9 [AIBE-XIX]

Q.9 When may two persons be said to be related to each other by half-blood in accordance with the Hindu Marriage Act, 1955?

a) When they are descended from a common ancestor by the same wife

b) When they are descended from a common ancestor by different wives

c) When they are descended from a common ancestor by different husbands

d) When they are not descended

from a common ancestor at all
[AIBE-XVIII]

Q.10 Which of the following is generally not considered as a valid condition for a Hindu marriage as per the Hindu Marriage Act, 1955?
a) The parties should not have a spouse living at the time of the marriage.
b) The parties should be within the degrees of prohibited relationship.
c) The parties should not be sapindas of each other.
d) The parties should not be suffering from epilepsy.
[AIBE-XVIII]

Q.11 Section 13(1) of the Hindu Marriage Act, 1955 provides for the following:
i. Grounds for restitution of conjugal rights
ii. Grounds for judicial separation
iii. Grounds for divorce
a) i & ii
b) ii & iii
c) iii & i
d) Only iii [AIBE-XVIII]

Q.12 What is the meaning of *batil* marriage in Muslim law?
a) Valid marriage
b) Void marriage
c) Voidable marriage
d) Irregular marriage [AIBE-XVIII]

Q.13 What is 'a contract of marriage which may be dissolved by the wife under a power delegated to her' called under the Muslim law?
a) Talaq-us-sunnat
b) Talaq-ul-biddat
c) Talaq-i-tafweez
d) Talat-a-hasan [AIBE-XVIII]

Q.14 A Hindu boy and a Hindu girl may be married under the following law:
i. The Hindu Marriage Act, 1955
ii. The Special Marriage Act, 1954
a) Only i is correct.
b) Only ii is correct.
c) Both i and ii are correct.
d) Neither i nor ii is correct.
[AIBE-XVIII]

Q.15 Through which of the following amendment acts the rights in the coparcenary property is made available to a girl child as well?
a) The Hindu Succession (Amendment) Act, 2002
b) The Hindu Succession (Amendment) Act, 2004
c) The Hindu Succession (Amendment) Act, 2005
d) The Hindu Succession (Amendment) Act, 2006
[AIBE-XVIII]

Q.16 What should be the age

difference between the adoptive father and his adopted daughter for a valid adoption?
a) 15 years
b) 18 years
c) 21 years
d) No specific age difference required [AIBE-XVIII]

Q.17 The provision for 'maintenance pendente lite' in Hindu Marriage Act, 1955 is given in:
a) Section 22
b) Section 23
c) **Section 24**
d) Section 25 [AIBE-XVII]

Q.18 A Muslim wife may sue for divorce under the Dissolution of Muslim Marriage Act, 1939, Section 2, if the husband has been insane for a period of:
a) 1 year
b) **2 years**
c) 5 years
d) 7 years [AIBE-XVII]

Q.19 A Muslim woman has the option to be governed by the provisions of Section 125 to 128 of Criminal Procedure Code, 1973. Which section of the Muslim Women (Protection of Rights on Divorce) Act, 1986 deals with it?
a) **Section 5**
b) Section 6
c) Section 7
d) None of these [AIBE-XVII]

Q.20 Which of the following is not a ground of void marriage under Section 11 of the Hindu Marriage Act?
a) Bigamy
b) Degrees of prohibited relationship
c) Sapinda relationship
d) **Child marriage** [AIBE-XVII]

Q.21 Sapinda relationship means:
a) 3rd generation (mother), 7th generation (father)
b) **3rd generation (mother), 5th generation (father)**
c) 3rd generation (mother), 4th generation (father)
d) 2nd generation (mother), 5th generation (father) [AIBE-XVII]

Q.22 Which one of the following is not a ground of divorce in the Hindu Marriage Act?
a) Mental disorder
b) Venereal Disease in communicable form
c) Incurable Unsound Mind
d) **Living separately for less than three months** [AIBE-XVII]

Q.23 Indian Christians can obtain divorce under which of the following enactments?
a) Special Marriage Act, 1954

b) Christian Marriage Act, 1872
c) **Indian Divorce Act, 1869**
d) Special Marriage Act, 1872
[AIBE-XVII]

Q.24 The Section 12 of Hindu Maintenance and Adoption Act, 1956 deals with:
a) Rights of adoptive parents to dispose of their properties
b) **Effects of adoption**
c) Presumption as to the document relating to adoption
d) Cancellation of adoption
[AIBE-XVII]

Q.25 The Hindu Marriage Act, 1955 _____ petition in which a decree of restitution of conjugal rights has been passed to apply to the court for a decree for divorce by showing that there has been no restitution of conjugal rights as between parties of marriage for a period of one year or upwards words after passing of the decree.
a) does not permit any party to that
b) does not permit the party against whom the
c) **does not permit any party to that**
d) does permit any party related to either party to that [AIBE-XVI]

Q.26 The offences under the Prohibition of Child Marriage Act, 2006 are:
a) Cognizable and bailable
b) Non-cognizable and non-bailable
c) **Cognizable and non-bailable**
d) Non-cognizable and bailable
[AIBE-XVI]

Q.27 Which of the following sections of the Hindu Adoption and Maintenance Act, 1956 deals with "amount of maintenance"?
a) Section 21
b) Section 22
c) **Section 23**
d) Section 24 [AIBE-XVI]

Q.28 Which of the following statement/statements is/are false for the purpose of the Hindu Marriage Act, 1955?
I. It is assumed that a person who is not Muslim, Santhal, Christian, Jew or Parsi by religion is Hindu
II. A person who belongs to Lingayat sub sect is assumed to be Hindu
III. A person who converted to another religion needs to follow local ritual/custom for converting back to Hinduism
a) I only
b) I and II
c) **III only**
d) I and III [AIBE-XVI]

Q.29 In which of the following cases was it held that, "the rights conferred under Section 25 of the

Hindu Adoption and Maintenance Act, 1956 supersedes any contact to the contrary. The fact that the date of decree makes no difference"?

a) Surenderabal Vs Suppiah

b) Mukesh Teli Vs Bharti Teli

c) **Sesi Ammal versus Thaiyu Ammal**

d) Laxmi Vs Krishna [AIBE-XVI]

Q.30 On which of the following dates did Hindu Marriage Act, 1955 come into operation?

a) **18th May 1955**

b) 17th June 1955

c) 22nd May 1955

d) 18th June 1955 [AIBE-XVI]

Q.31 Which of the following properties will section 30 of the Hindu Succession Act, 1956 govern?

I. Tarwad

II. Tavazhi

III. Kutumba

IV. Kavaru

V. Illom

a) I, III and V

b) II, IV and V

c) **I and II**

d) All of the above [AIBE-XVI]

Q.32 Which of the following sections of the Muslim Personal Law (Shariat) Application Act, 1937 have been repealed/ amended by section 6 of the Dissolution of Muslim Marriage Act, 1939?

a) Section 4

b) **Section 5**

c) Section 6

d) Section 7 [AIBE-XVI]

Q.33 Requisites of a valid adoption: no adoption shall be valid unless- (i) the person adopting has the capacity, and also the right, to take in adoption; (ii) the person giving in adoption has the capacity to do so; (iii) the person adopted is capable of being taken in adoption; and (iv) the adoption is made in compliance with the other conditions mentioned in this Chapter. - mentioned under:

a) Section 6 of Hindu Adoptions and Maintenance Act

b) Section 8 of Hindu Adoptions and Maintenance Act

c) Section 12 of Hindu Adoptions and Maintenance Act

d) Section 10 of Hindu Adoptions and Maintenance Act [AIBE-XV]

Q.34 According to the Muslim women (Protection of Rights on Marriage) Act 2019 any pronouncement of *talaq* as defined under the Act by a Muslim husband upon his wife, by words, either spoken or written or in electronic form or in any other manner whatsoever, shall be:

a) Void

b) Cognizable
c) Compoundable
d) All of the above [AIBE-XV]

Q.35 The Hindu Succession (Amendment) Act 2005 provides for women:
a) Coparcenary rights at par with men
b) Inheritance rights in agricultural land from her parents at par with her brothers
c) Inheritance of the self-acquired agricultural land of her deceased husband
d) All of the above [AIBE-XV]

Q.36 Section 25 of the Hindu Marriage Act provides for:
a) Custody of the children
b) Permanent alimony and maintenance
c) Maintenance *pendente lite*
d) Division of matrimonial property [AIBE-XV]

Q.37 A Hindu wife had been living with her children and all the children had been brought up by her without any assistance and help from the husband many years. The wife was entitled to separate residence and maintenance under:
a) Section 18(2)(f) of Hindu Adoptions and Maintenance Act
b) Section 18(2)(d) of Hindu Adoptions and Maintenance Act
c) Section 18(2)(a) of Hindu Adoptions and Maintenance Act
d) Section 18(2)(g) of Hindu Adoptions and Maintenance Act [AIBE-XV]

Q.38 On and from the commencement of the Hindu Succession (Amendment) Act 2005, in a Joint Hindu family governed by the Mitakshara law, conferring on daughter coparcenary status by substituting new section for:
a) Section 6
b) Section 10
c) Section 11
d) Section 13 [AIBE-XV]

Q.39 Section 5 of Hindu Marriage Act relates to:
a) Void marriages
b) Voidable marriages
c) Ceremonies of Hindu marriage
d) Conditions of Hindu marriage [AIBE-XV]

Q.40 A girl of 22 years marries her maternal uncle's son of 23 years in accordance with the Special Marriage Act. Such marriage is:
a) Valid
b) Voidable
c) Void
d) Valid only in North India [AIBE-XV]

Q.41 Under the Dissolution of Muslim Marriage Act 1939 a

Muslim wife can seek dissolution of marriage if the husband fails to perform marital obligations for:

a) 2 years

b) 3 years

c) 4 years

d) 5 years [AIBE-XIV]

Q.42 The case of Muhammad Allahdad Khan Vs. Muhammad Ismail Khan is related to:

a) Pre-emption

b) Gift

c) Mahr

d) Acknowledgement of paternity [AIBE-XIV]

Q.43 In which of the following cases, the Supreme Court in 2017 declared pronouncements of 'talaq' three times at a time by a Muslim husband as unconstitutional?

a) Shayara Bano Vs. Union of India

b) Shamim Ara Vs. State of U. P.

c) Bai Tahira Vs. Ali Hussain

d) Danial Latifi Vs. Union of India [AIBE-XIV]

Q.44 Which of the following provisions of the Hindu Marriage Act 1955 incorporates the fault theory of divorce?

a) Section 13(1)

b) Section 11

c) Section 13B

d) Section 13(2) [AIBE-XIV]

Q.45 Under the Hindu Maintenance and Adoption Act 1956, in which of the following circumstances can a dependent enforce his right to maintenance against a transferee of an estate out of which he has a right to receive maintenance?

a) Only when the Transferee has notice of such right

b) Only when the transfer is gratuitous

c) Both (a) & (b)

d) None of the above [AIBE-XIV]

Q.46 Which of the following provisions of the Hindu Succession Act 1956 lays down for the escheat?

a) Section 25

b) Section 26

c) Section 27

d) Section 29 [AIBE-XIV]

Q.47 If a man marries a girl who is within his prohibited relationship and his custom does not permit such marriage, such a man would be punished under:

a) Section 17 of the Hindu Marriage Act 1955

b) Section 18(a) of the Hindu Marriage Act 1955

c) Section 18(b) of the Hindu Marriage Act 1955

d) No punishment for such marriages [AIBE-XIV]

Q.48 Which section of the Hindu Marriage Act 1955 provides that a child from a void marriage would be legitimate?
a) Section 11
b) Section 13A
c) Section 12
d) Section 16 [AIBE-XIV]

Q.49 Section 19 of the Hindu Adoption and Maintenance Act 1956 provides for the maintenance of:
a) Wife
b) Parents
c) Widowed Daughter-in-law
d) Children [AIBE-XIII]

Q.50 Section 30 of the Hindu Successions Act 1956 deals with:
a) Woman Estate
b) Testamentary Successions
c) Male Successions
d) Female Succession [AIBE-XIII]

Q.51 Option of puberty is a ground of divorce under Hindu Marriage Act 1955 for:
a) Only Husband
4) Only Wife
c) Both Husband and Wife
d) None of the above [AIBE-XIII]

Q.52 Which section of The Hindu Marriage Act 1955 provides that a child from a void marriage would be legitimate?
a) Section 11
b) Section 13(a)
c) Section 12
d) Section 16 [AIBE-XIII]

Q.53 Which of the following is essential for a valid adoption under the Hindu Marriage Act 1955?
a) Datta homam
b) Actual giving and taking of child
c) Both (a) and (b)
d) None of the above [AIBE-XIII]

Q.54 A Hindu male can adopt a female child if the difference of age between the two is of more than:
a) 15 years
b) 18 years
c) 20 years
d) 21 years [AIBE-XIII]

Q.55 Which of the following relations is not dependent under Section 21 of the Hindu Adoption and Maintenance Act 1956?
a) Grandmother
b) Mother
c) Widow
d) Daughter [AIBE-XIII]

Q.56 'Hadees' is one of the sources of Muslim law. It comprises:
a) Very words of god
b) Words and actions of the prophet

c) Unanimous decision of jurists
d) Analogical decisions [AIBE-XIII]

Q.57 Shah Bano case was related to:
a) Dowry demand
b) Harassment at work place
c) Maintenance of divorced Muslim women
d) Triple divorce of Muslim Women [AIBE-XII]

Q.58 Which of the following is not a legal guardian of the property of Muslim minor?
a) Father
b) Brother
c) The executor appointed by father
d) Grandfather [AIBE-XII]

Q.59 A marriage with a woman before completion of her *iddat* is:
a) Irregular
b) Void
c) Voidable
d) None of these [AIBE-XII]

Q.60 The family courts have concurrent jurisdiction to pass a decree for dissolution of marriage under the Indian Divorce Act - in which case, the order was passed?
a) Handa Vs. Handa AIR 1955
b) Dr. Mary Vs. Dr. Vincent AIR 1991
c) Peter Vs. Anglina AIR 1992
d) None of the above [AIBE-XII]

Q.61 Who of the following Muslim is not entitled to maintenance?
a) Son who is a minor
b) Daughter who is not married
c) Grandparents
d) An illegitimate son [AIBE-XII]

Q.62 Dayabhaga School presumes that a family, because it is joint, possesses joint property.
a) This statement is correct
b) This presumption is under Mitakshara School
c) This statement is incorrect
d) None of these [AIBE-XII]

Q.63 Deferred *mahr* is payable at the time of divorce or at the time of death of spouse.
a) This statement is true under Sunni law
b) This statement is not true
c) Deferred *mahr* is payable only at the time of divorce
d) Deferred *mahr* is payable only at the time of death of the spouse
[AIBE-XII]

Q.64 The last amendment to the Indian Succession Act was made in:
a) 2000
b) 2001
c) 2002
d) 2004 [AIBE-XI]

Q.65 Which is the correct

statement?

a) There can be a will without a codicil

b) There can be a codicil without a will

c) Every will has a codicil

d) A codicil precedes a will [AIBE-XI]

Q.66 As per Section 63 of Indian Succession Act, a Will should be attested by:

a) By two witnesses

b) By two or more witnesses

c) Only one witness who is not a relative of testator

d) None of the above [AIBE-XI]

Q.67 *'Iddat'* under Mohammaden law refers to:

a) A gift made on the occasion of marriage

b) The right of the husband to divorce his wife

c) Attaining of puberty

d) None of the above [AIBE-XI]

Q.68 Under the Christian Marriage Act, the Marriage Registrar for any district is appointed by:

a) State Government

b) The Central Government

c) The Clergyman of the Church

d) High Court Judges [AIBE-XI]

Q.69 Under the Hindu Adoptions and Maintenance Act, the person who is taken in adoption:

a) Must be a Hindu only

b) A Hindu or Jew

c) May be Hindu or Christian

d) None of the above [AIBE-XI]

Q.70 Polygamy was permitted for Hindus before the year:

a) 1956

b) 1954

c) 1955

d) 1978 [AIBE-XI]

Q.71 Mohan gets married to his sister's daughter Kriti.

a) The marriage is valid if the custom allows it

b) The marriage is void

c) The marriage is valid only if the Court approves it

d) The marriage is valid only if the Panchayat permits [AIBE-XI]

Q.72 Which of the following heirs is not Class I heir under the Hindu Succession Act 1956?

a) Son

b) Widow

c) Father

d) Mother [AIBE-X]

Q.73 Natural guardian of an adopted son under the Hindu Minority & Guardianship Act 1956 is:

a) Original father

b) In the absence of (a), original

mother

c) Adoptive father

d) None of the above [AIBE-X]

Q.74 In respect of family relations, the law applicable in India is:

a) Secular law in India

b) Statutory law

c) Religious law

d) Personal law of the parties

[AIBE-X]

Q.75 What should be the difference of age under the Hindu Adoption and Maintenance Act 1956 if a female adopts male?

a) 21 years

b) 25 years

c) 18 years

d) 16 years [AIBE-X]

Q.76 A person cannot be a next friend, a guardian of a person if:

a) He is a minor

b) He is an opposite party in the suit

c) He has not given consent in writing

d) All of the above [AIBE-X]

Q.77 In which section of the Hindu Succession Act 1956, the Law of Mitakshara has been incorporated?

a) Section 8

b) Section 7

c) Section 9

d) Section 6 [AIBE-X]

Q.78 A Hindu's widow, if there are more than one, shall take:

a) One share each

b) One share for all the widows

c) One share each to the maximum of two shares, if there are more than two widows

d) None of the above [AIBE-X]

Q.79 Maintenance application under Section 18(2) of HAMA is filed in:

a) Matrimonial court

b) District Court

c) High Court

d) Any of the above [AIBE-X]

Q.80 Onus to prove reasonable excuse for withdrawal from the society of the other is on:

a) Petitioner

b) Respondent

c) Both (a) and (b)

d) Either (a) or (b) [AIBE-IX]

Q.81 A disqualified person/heir:

a) Transmits an interest to his or her own heir

b) Transmits no interest to his or her own heir

c) May or may not transmit an interest to his or her own heir as per the discretion of the court

d) May only transmit an interest to his or her own heir with the consent of the other heirs. [AIBE-IX]

Q.82 '*Talak-e-tafwiz*' is:
a) Talak by delegation
b) Triple talak
c) Talak by agreement
d) Improper talak [AIBE-VIII]

Q.83 Any immovable property possessed by a female Hindu, acquired before or after the commencement of Hindu Succession Act, shall be held by her after the commencement of the Act as:
a) A limited owner
b) A full owner
c) No ownership
d) Not as absolute owner
[AIBE-VIII]

Q.84 Conditions of Hindu Marriage have been laid down under .... of Hindu Marriage Act:
a) Sec.9
b) Sec.10
c) Sec.5
d) Sec.13 [AIBE-VII]

Q.85 The Hindu Succession (Amendment) Act 2005:
a) Allows daughters of the deceased equal rights with daughter
b) Allows sons of the deceased equal rights with widows
c) Allows daughters of the deceased equal rights with wife
d) Allows daughters of the deceased equal rights with sons
[AIBE-VII]

Q.86 'A' is the mother of 'B'. She becomes a widow and re-marries. 'B' dies. Can 'A' succeed to him as mother? (Both are Hindus)
a) No
b) Yes
c) Depends on their School
d) Only when B has no sons
[AIBE-VI]

Q.87 Referring to Section 6 of Hindu Minority and Guardianship Act, the Supreme Court observed that the words 'after him' does not mean 'after the life time of the father'. Indeed, it means in the absence of. If the father is non-functional as guardian for various reasons like indifference, physical or mental incapacity, away from the place where the child lives with the mother, by mutual understanding, it may be treated as the 'absence' of the father. In which case?
a) Lily Thomas case
b) Sarla Mudgal case
c) Githa Hariharan case
d) Goverdhan Lal case [AIBE-VI]

Q.88 By a recent amendment, the daughter of a coparcener by birth becomes a coparcener in her own right in the same manner as the son - which Amendment?

a) The Hindu Succession (Amendment) Act 2004
b) The Hindu Succession (Amendment) Act 2005
c) The Hindu Succession (Amendment) Act 2006
d) The Hindu Succession (Amendment) Act 2012 [AIBE-VI]

Q.89 Shamim Ara Vs. State of U. P. relates to:
a) The condition precedent for a Muslim husband for rendering divorce is the pronouncement of divorce which has to be proved on evidence
b) Option of puberty
c) Guardianship in marriage
d) Dower [AIBE-VI]

Q.90 Section 9 of the Hindu Marriage Act 1955 deals with:
a) Restitution of Conjugal Rights
b) Void Marriages
c) Judicial Separation
d) Grounds of Divorce [AIBE-V]

Q.91 Daughter is equated with the son with reference to joint family property under:
a) Hindu Succession Amendment Act 2002
b) Hindu Succession Amendment Act 1976
c) Hindu Succession Amendment Act 1978
d) Hindu Succession Amendment Act 2005 [AIBE-V]

Q.92 *Mubarat* under Muslim law refers to:
a) Divorce at the instance of wife
b) Cruelty
c) Dissolution of marriage with mutual consent
d) Ila [AIBE-V]

Q.93 The discriminatory aspects of S.10 of Indian Divorce Act (now Divorce Act) were removed by substituting new section by the:
a) Indian Divorce Amendment Act of 2001
b) Divorce Amendment Act of 2002
c) Indian Divorce Amendment Act of 2006
d) Indian Divorce Amendment Act of 2012 [AIBE-V]

Q.94 A *Sunni* Muslim marries with *Kitabiya* girl. The marriage is:
a) Valid
b) Void
c) Irregular
d) None of these [AIBE-IV]

Q.95 The Dissolution of Muslim Marriage Act 1939 is based on which School of Muslim law:
a) Hanafi School
b) Shafi School
c) Maliki School
d) Zaidi School [AIBE-IV]

Q.96 Under the Hindu Adoption and Maintenance Act 1956, a female Hindu has the capacity to take a son or daughter in adoption if:

a) She is not married

b) She is married

c) She is widow and has no son or daughter, but has a widowed daughter- in-law

d) She cannot adopt at all

[AIBE-IV]

Q.97 A child born of void and voidable marriage under Hindu law is:

a) Legitimate

b) Illegitimate

c) Illegal

d) None of these [AIBE-IV]

TOPIC 7: LAW OF CONTRACT, SPECIFIC RELIEF, PROPERTY LAWS, NEGOTIABLE INSTRUMENTS ACT

(8 questions are, generally, asked from this subject)

Q.1 An agreement not enforceable by law is stated to be void under ……

(A) Section 2(d)
(B) Section 2(e)
(C) Section 2(f)
(D) Section 2(g) [AIBE-XIX]

Q.2 The concept of invalid guarantee is covered under Sections …….

(A) 142-146
(B) 142-144
(C) 143-147
(D) 140-143 [AIBE-XIX]

Q.3 "A", a real estate developer, entered into a contract with "B", the owner of a piece of prime land, for the purchase of her property. The contract stipulated that "A" would' pay ₹50 lakhs in advance and the remaining ₹1 crore within six months. In return, "B" agreed to transfer the title to the land.
However, after receiving the advance payment, "B" refused to execute the sale deed, claiming that she received a better offer from another buyer. "A" demanded the enforcement of the contract under the Specific Relief Act, 1963, but "B" denied his claim. "A" has to file a suit in a court of law.
On the basis of the above problem, select the correct answer.

(A) "A" may file a suit in the criminal court having the powers under the Bhartiya Nagarik Suraksha Sanhita, 2023.
(B) "A" may file a suit in the special court constituted under the Specific Relief Act, 1963.
(C) "A" may file a suit in the civil court having the powers under the Civil Procedure Code, 1908.
(D) No suit can be brought against "A" as there in no breach of contract. [AIBE-XIX]

Q.4 "A" transfers a piece of land to "B" on the condition that "B" shall not transfer the land to anyone else for the next 10 years. In this case , "B" has no right to transfer the land to someone else for the next 10 years.
On the basis of the above problem, select the correct option:

(A) It amounts to Conditional Transfer of Property.
(B) It amounts to Conditional Limitations on Transfer of

Property.

(C) It amounts to Subsequent Transfer of Property.

(D) It amounts to conditions precedent in the Transfer of Property. [AIBE-XIX]

Q.5 Mr. Rajesh issued a cheque of ₹50,000 to his supplier, Mr. Sharma, for the payment of goods purchased. When Mr. Sharma deposited the cheque, it was returned by the bank with the remark "Insufficient Funds".

On the basis of the above problem, select the correct option.

(A) A complaint in writing is to be made by Mr. Sharma in the court within three months for the dishonour of the cheque.

(B) A complaint in writing is to be made by Mr. Sharma in the court within one month for the dishonour of the cheque.

(C) A complaint in writing is to be made by Mr. Sharma in the court within five months for the dishonour of the cheque.

(D) A complaint in writing is to be made by Mr. Sharma in the court within two months for the dishonour of the cheque.

[AIBE-XIX]

Q.6 Section 31 of the Specific Relief Act, 1963 is related to ……….

(A) Rescission of contracts

(B) Cancellation of instruments

(C) Declaratory decrees

(D) Perpetual injunction

[AIBE-XIX]

Q.7 How the recovery of specific immovable property may be enforced ?

(A) A person entitled to the possession of specific immovable property may recover it in the manner provided by The Specific Relief Act, 1963.

(B) A person entitled to the possession of specific immovable property may recover it in the manner provided by the Transfer of Property Act, 1882.

(C) A person entitled to the possession of specific immovable property may recover it in the manner provided by the Code of Criminal Procedure, 1973.

(D) A person entitled to the possession of specific immovable property may recover it in the manner provided by the Code of Civil Procedure, 1908.

[AIBE-XIX]

Q.8 Which section of Law of Contract defines, "A proposal may be revoked at any time before, but not after, communication of its acceptance is complete as against the proposer."

(A) Section 5
(B) Section 4
(C) Section 6
(D) Section 7 [AIBE-XIX]

Q.9 Which of the following is not a fraud as per the Indian Contract Act, 1872?
a) A promise made without intention of performing it.
b) An active concealment of fact by one having knowledge of the fact.
c) Mere silence if not duty bound to speak.
d) Any act or omission law specifically declares to be fraudulent. [AIBE-XVIII]

Q.10 Which of the following statements is correct if A, intending to deceive B, falsely represents that five hundred maunds of Indigo are made annually at A's factory, and thereby induces B to buy the factory?
a) Contract is void ab initio.
b) Contract is voidable at the option of A.
c) Contract is voidable at the option of B.
d) Contract is voidable at the option of A and B. [AIBE-XVIII]

Q.11 Which of the following injunction can be granted only by the decree made at hearing and upon the merit of the suit?
a) Temporary injunction
b) Perpetual injunction
c) Mandatory injunction
d) Prohibitory injunction [AIBE-XVIII]

Q.12 A stipulation in a bond for payment of compound interest on failure to pay simple interest at the same rate as was payable upon the principle is not a penalty within the meaning of which of the following provisions of the Indian Contract Act, 1872?
a) Section 73
b) Section 74
c) Section 75
d) Section 76 [AIBE-XVIII]

Q.13 What is the default interest payable under section 63A of the Transfer of Property Act, 1882?
a) 6% per annum
b) 8% per annum
c) 9% per annum
d) No default rate prescribed [AIBE-XVIII]

Q.14 Which of the following is the time limit given under Section 17 of the Transfer of Property Act, 1882?
a) Life of the transferee
b) A period of 18 years from the date of transfer
c) Either (A) or (B) whichever is longer

d) Neither (A) nor (B) [AIBE-XVIII]

Q.15 Which of the following is not a negotiable instrument as per the Negotiable Instruments Act, 1881?
a) Promissory note
b) Hundi
c) Bill of exchange
d) Cheque [AIBE-XVIII]

Q.16 In the light of the Negotiable Instruments Act, 1881 at what rate interest will be charged if the rate of interest is not mentioned on the negotiable instruments?
a) 6% per annum
b) 10% per annum
c) 18% per annum
d) 20% per annum [AIBE-XVIII]

Q.17 'B', the proprietor of a newspaper publishes at A's request a libel upon 'C' in the paper, and 'A' agrees to indemnify 'B' against the consequences of the publication, and all costs and damages of any action in respect thereof. 'B' is sued by 'C' and has to pay damages, and also incurs expenses. Decide in the light of the Section 224 of the Indian Contract Act, 1872.
a) **'A' is not liable to 'B' upon indemnity**.
b) 'A' is liable to 'B' upon indemnity.
c) 'A' is not liable to 'C' upon indemnity.
d) None of these [AIBE-XVII]

Q.18 A person whom the agent names to act for the principle in the business of the agency under the express or implied authority to name, is called _____.
a) Sub-agent
b) **Substituted agent**
c) Agent
d) Procured agent [AIBE-XVII]

Q.19 A _____ injunction can only be granted by the decree made at the hearing and upon the merits of the suit; the defendant is thereby perpetually enjoined from the assertion of a right, or from the commission of an act which could be contrary to the rights of the plaintiff.
a) Temporary
b) **Perpetual**
c) Both Temporary and Perpetual
d) None of these [AIBE-XVII]

Q.20 According to Section 5 of Specific Relief Act 1963, a person entitled to the possession of specific immovable property may recover it in the manner provided in _____.
a) The Specific Relief Act, 1963
b) **The Code of Civil Procedure, 1908**
c) The Code of Criminal Procedure, 1973
d) The Transfer of Property Act,

1882 [AIBE-XVII]

Q.21 Where the mortgagor delivers possession of the mortgaged property to the mortgagee and authorizes him to retain such possession until payment of the mortgage-money, and to receive the rents and profits occurring from the property in lieu of interest, or in payment of the mortgage-money, the transaction is called an _____ mortgage.

a) Conditional
b) English
c) Sample
d) **Usufructuary** [AIBE-XVII]

Q.22 In which of the following cases, it was decided that the contract with a minor is void?

a) Carlill Vs Carbolic Smoke Ball Co
b) Chinnaiah Vs Ramaiah
c) **Mohori Bibee Vs Dharmodas Ghose**
d) Harvey Vs Facey [AIBE-XVII]

Q.23 Which of the following is/are CORRECT with respect to "declaratory decrees" under the Specific Relief Act, 1963?

a) Section 34 of the said Act deals with it.
b) It is discretionary in nature.
c) **Both (Section 34 of the said Act deals with it) and (It is discretionary in nature)**
d) None of these [AIBE-XVII]

Q.24 Which of the following is not a Negotiable Instrument as defined under the Negotiable Instrument Act 1881?

a) Promissory Note
b) Bill of Exchange
c) Cheque
d) **Billing Receipt** [AIBE-XVII]

Q.25 What is the Period of Limitation for expeditious disposal of Suit under Specific Relief Act 1963?

a) 6 months
b) 10 months
c) **12 months**
d) 18 months [AIBE-XVI]

Q.26 Law laid down under Section 73 of the Indian Contract Act 1872 is related to which of the following cases:

a) Hothester Vs De-la-tur
b) Rabinson Vs Devison
c) **Hedley Vs Baxendal**
d) Dikinson Vs Dads [AIBE-XVI]

Q.27 Contractual Liability arises, where:

a) There is offer and acceptance only
b) **There is intention to create**

legal relation
c) There is loss to one party
d) The loss of one party is the gain of other party [AIBE-XVI]

Q.28 Frustration of contract is provided by which section of the Indian Contract Act?
a) Sec. 73
b) Sec. 70
c) Sec. 2(d)
d) **Sec. 56** [AIBE-XVI]

Q.29 Specific Relief Act, 1963 contains:
a) 6 chapters and 40 sections
b) 7 chapters and 42 sections
c) 8 chapters and 43 sections
d) **8 chapters and 44 sections** [AIBE-XVI]

Q.30 When Perpetual Injunction may be granted-
a) Where the defendant is trustee of the property for the plaintiff.
b) Where there is no standard for ascertaining the actual damage.
c) Compensation in money would not afford adequate relief.
d) **All of the above**. [AIBE-XVI]

Q.31 'X', 'Y', and 'Z' jointly promise to pay 'A' an amount of Rs.50,000. Subsequently 'X', 'Y' became untraceable. Can 'A' compel 'Z' to pay?
a) 'A' can, under Section 43 para 1
b) 'A' can under Section 49 para 1
c) 'A' cannot and will have to wait till X and Y become traceable
d) 'Z' can be compelled only for one third [AIBE-XV]

Q.32 Delivery of goods by one person to another for some purpose upon a contract that they shall, when the purpose is accomplished, be returned or disposed of according to the directions of the person delivering them. This process is termed as:
a) Agency
b) Bailment
c) Guarantee
d) Contingency [AIBE-XV]

Q.33 Section 14A inserted by The Specific Relief (Amendment) Act 2018 relates to:
a) Power of the Courts to engage experts
b) Establishment of Special Court
c) Expeditious disposal of case
d) Specific performance with regard to contracts [AIBE-XV]

Q.34 Indemnity contract is defined under:
a) Section 124 of the Indian Contract Act
b) Section 67 of the Indian Contract Act
c) Section 127 of the Indian

Contract Act
d) Section 128 of the Indian Contract Act [AIBE-XV]

Q.35 Peek Vs. Gurney is a famous case related to:
a) Coercion
b) Fraud
c) Mistake of fact
d) Mistake of law [AIBE-XV]

Q.36 The definition of Contract is defined under:
a) Section 2(a) of the Indian Contract Act
b) Section 2(h) of the Indian Contract Act
c) Section 2(d) of the Indian Contract Act
d) Section 2(g) of the Indian Contract Act [AIBE-XV]

Q.37 Under Section 70 of the Indian Contract Act, where a person lawfully does anything for another person, or delivers anything to him, not intending to do so gratuitously, and such other person enjoys the benefit thereof, the latter is bound to make compensation to the former in respect of, or to restore, the thing so done or delivered. This principle is known as:
a) A Contract of *Uberrimae fidei*
b) Implied Agency
c) *Quantum meruit*
d) *De novo* contract [AIBE-XV]

Q.38 Agreement is:
a) A promise or set of promises forming consideration to each other
b) Enforceable by law
c) Enforceable contract
d) Un-enforceable by law
[AIBE-XV]

Q.39 Which one of the following sentence is correctly matched?
a) In India; consideration must follow from promisee only.
b) In India, consideration must follow from only promisor or only promisee.
c) In India, consideration must follow from promisor or any other person.
d) In India, consideration must follow from promisee or any other person. [AIBE-XIV]

Q.40 Assertion (A): Collateral transactions to wagering are valid.
Reason (R): Only wagering agreements are declared void under Section 30 of the Indian contract Act.
Codes:
a) (A) is true, but (R) is false.
b) (A) is false, but (R) is true.
c) Both (A) and (R) are true, but (R) is not correct explanation of (A)
d) Both (A) and (R) are true, and (R) is correct explanation of (A)

[AIBE-XIV]

Q.41 Term 'holder' includes:
a) The payee
b) The bearer
c) The endorsed
d) All of the above [AIBE-XIV]

Q.42 'Mesne Profits' of property means:
a) Those profits by which the person in wrongful possession of such property actually received or might have received there from, together with interest on such profits
b) The profits due to improvements made by person in wrongful possession
c) Both (a) & (b)
d) None of the above [AIBE-XIV]

Q.43 Which of the following statements are true?
i. Minor's contract can be ratified on attaining majority.
ii. Minor's contact be ratified on attaining majority.
iii. Minor's contract can be ratified jointly by both the parties to the contract.
iv. Minor is not liable under minor's contract.
a) (i) and (iii)
b) (ii) and (iv)
c) (i) and (ii)
d) (ii) and (iii) [AIBE-XIV]

Q.44 Which of the following is not a vested interest?
a) 'A' stipulates that title in a property shall pass to 'C' on his death.
b) 'A' stipulates' that title in a property shall pass to 'C' on the death of 'B'.
c) 'A' stipulates that title in a property shall pass to 'C' if he marries 'B'.
d) 'A' stipulates that title in a property shall pass to 'C' after ten years. [AIBE-XIV]

Q.45 Effect of 'not negotiable' crossing is mentioned under:
a) Section 125
b) Section 130
c) Section 131
d) Section 128 [AIBE-XIV]

Q.46 Section 16 of Negotiable Instruments Act 1881 defines:
a) Restrictive endorsement
b) Conditional endorsement
c) Endorsement 'in full' and Endorsement 'in blank'
d) All of the above [AIBE-XIV]

Q.47 The liability under Section 138 of the Negotiable Instruments Act 1881 is:
a) Strict liability
b) Vicarious liability
c) Both (a) and (b)
d) None of the above [AIBE-XIV]

Q.48 Who among the following cannot transfer an immovable property?

a) Hindu widow

b) Muslim widow

c) Natural guardian of a minor

d) Karta or manager of joint Hindu family [AIBE-XIII]

Q.49 The doctrine of *'Lis pendens'* was explained in the leading case of:

a) Bellamy Vs. Sabine

b) Cooper Vs. Cooper

c) Streatfeild Vs. Streatfeild

d) Tulk Vs. Moxhay [AIBE-XIII]

Q.50 The parties which cannot be compelled to perform specific performances of contract are provided in which section of Specific Relief Act?

a) 27

b) 28

c) 29

d) 30 [AIBE-XIII]

Q.51 What kind of property is transferable?

a) Pension

b) Public office

c) Right to re-entry

d) Any kind of property if not prohibited by law [AIBE-XIII]

Q.52 Which of the following does not come under the 'immovable property' as per the T. P. Act?

a) Sales of a ceiling fan

b) Right to claim maintenance

c) Right relating to lease

d) Easementary right [AIBE-XIII]

Q.53 A person entitled to the possession of specific immovable property may recover in the manner provided by:

a) The Code of Civil Procedure, 1908

b) The Indian Registration Act 1908

c) The Indian Contract Act 1872

d) The Transfer of Property Act 1882 [AIBE-XIII]

Q.54 Section 39 of Specific Relief Act deals with:

a) Registration of Instrument

b) Cancellation of Instruments

c) Correctness of Instruments

d) None of the above

[AIBE-XIII]

Q.55 Specific relief _____ where the agreement is made with minor. Fill in the blank:

a) Can get

b) Cannot be given

c) Can release

d) Implemented with law

[AIBE-XIII]

Q.56 For Specific Performance of a contract, suit is to be instituted in:

a) 3 years

b) 3 months
c) 6 months
d) No specific time limit unless mentioned in the contract
[AIBE-XII]

Q.57 Recovery of specific immovable property is defined:
a) Section 5 of Specific Relief Act
b) Section 120B of IPC
c) Under Section 10 of Sale of Goods Act
d) None of the above [AIBE-XII]

Q.58 What is main objective of Section 138 of Negotiable Instruments Act?
a) Recovery of stolen property
b) Recovery of seized vehicles from RTO
c) Recovery of the cheque amount in case cheque issued by the payer is bounced
d) None of the above [AIBE-XII]

Q.59 Which of the following is not an essential for a valid sale?
a) The parties must be competent to contract
b) There must be mental consent
c) There must be a transfer of property
d) There must be an agreement to sell [AIBE-XII]

Q.60 Which section of Sale of Goods Act 1930 deal with anticipatory breach of contract?
a) Section 50
b) Section 65
c) Section 60
d) Section 70 [AIBE-XII]

Q.61 Which section of Indian Registration Act 1908 provides with compulsory registration of Instrument of Gifts and Immovable Properties?
a) Section 11
b) Section 13
c) Section 17
d) None of the above [AIBE-XII]

Q.62 Doctrine of '*lis pendens*' is given under which section of the Transfer of Property Act?
a) 41
b) 52
c) 53
d) 53A [AIBE-XII]

Q.63 Cancellation of instrument is mentioned in:
a) Sections 8-25 of Specific Relief Act
b) Sections of 26 of Specific Relief Act
c) Sections 31-33 of Specific Relief Act
d) Sections 36-42 of Specific Relief Act [AIBE-XII]

Q.64 Which section of Specific Relief Act prohibits filing a case

against the government?
a) Section 5
b) Section 6
c) Section 7
d) Section 8 [AIBE-XI]

Q.65 Cheque bouncing cases charged u/s. 138 of Negotiable Instruments Act is trialed by:
a) Bank Tribunal
b) Consumer Forum
c) Magistrate Court
d) Sessions court [AIBE-XI]

Q.66 Court's power to award compensation is provided in Specific Relief Act:
a) Under Section 20
b) Under Section 21
c) (a) and (b)
d) None of the above [AIBE-XI]

Q.67 Which of the following is not an essential of a contract of guarantee?
a) Concurrence of three parties
b) Surety's distinct promise to be answerable
c) Liabilities to be legally enforceable
d) Existence of only one contract [AIBE-XI]

Q.68 The term 'Agent' is defined in Indian Contract Act under Section:
a) 180
b) 181
c) 182
d) 183 [AIBE-XI]

Q.69 A person who gives the guarantee is called:
a) Bailee
b) Creditor
c) Debtor
d) Surety [AIBE-XI]

Q.70 Which is not a right of an unpaid seller against the goods?
a) Lien
b) Stoppage in transit
c) Right of resale
d) To ascertain price [AIBE-XI]

Q.71 Sections 36 to 42 of Specific Relief Act provides:
a) Injunctions
b) Court's discretion on specific performance
c) Cancellation of instruments
d) None of the above [AIBE-XI]

Q.72 'A' sells a field to 'B'. There is a right of way over the field of which 'A' has direct personal knowledge but which he conceals from 'B'.
a) 'B' has the right to rescind the contract
b) 'B' cannot rescind the contract
c) 'A' has the right to rescind the contract
d) 'A' is not legally liable [AIBE-X]

Q.73 Pre-emption on the ground of *Shafi-i-Jar* was declared unconstitutional in:
a) Bhau Ram Vs. Baijnath
b) Gobind Dayal Vs. Inayatullah
c) Bhagawan Das Vs. Chet Ram
d) Ram Saran Lall Vs. Mst. Domini Kuer [AIBE-X]

Q.74 A contract can be specifically enforced:
a) Where compensation is adequate relief for the non-performance of the contract
b) Where the contract by its nature is determinable
c) Where it involves the performance of continuous duty which the court cannot supervise
d) None of the above [AIBE-X]

Q.75 A contract of 'indemnity', under the Indian Contract Act 1872, has been defined in Section:
a) 124
b) 123
c) 125
d) 126(a) [AIBE-X]

Q.76 Liability of drawer to compensate the drawee in case of dishonour is primarily provided under:
a) Section 29(a)
b) Section 29
c) Section 30
d) Section 31 [AIBE-X]

Q.77 The parties which cannot be compelled to perform specific performances of contract are provided in which section of Specific Relief Act?
a) 27
b) 28
c) 29
d) 30 [AIBE-X]

Q.78 The undertaking contained in a promissory note to pay a certain sum of money is:
a) Conditional
b) Unconditional
c) May be conditional or unconditional depending upon the circumstances
d) All of the above [AIBE-X]

Q.79 Who are the partners in a bill of exchange?
a) Drawer & Drawee
b) Payee
c) Both (a) and (b)
d) None of the above [AIBE-X]

Q.80 A perpetual injunction can only be granted by the decree at the hearing and upon the:
a) Demand of the party
b) Discretion of the Court
c) Merit of the suit
d) None of the above [AIBE-X]

Q.81 What is true of *Perpetual*

Injunction?
a) It is a judicial process
b) Preventive in nature
c) The thing prevented is a wrongful act
d) All of the above [AIBE-IX]

Q.82 If an instrument may be construed either as promissory note or bill of exchange, it is:
a) A valid instrument
b) An ambiguous instrument
c) A returnable instrument
d) None of the above [AIBE-IX]

Q.83 A contingent contract based on the specified uncertain events not happening within a fixed time under Section 35:
a) Remains valid even if the event does not happen within that fixed time
b) Becomes void at the expiration of the time fixed
c) Becomes void if the happening of that event becomes impossible before the expiry of time fixed
d) Both (b) and (c) [AIBE-IX]

Q.84 Which is correct?
a) Proposal + Acceptance = Promise
b) Promise + Consideration = Agreement
c) Agreement + Enforceability = Contract
d) All of the above [AIBE-IX]

Q.85 Communication of acceptance is complete as against the proposer:
a) When it comes to the knowledge of the proposer
b) When it is put in course of transmission to him so as to be out of power of the acceptor
c) When the acceptance is communicated to the proposer
d) All of the above [AIBE-IX]

Q.86 In cases of general offer, for a valid contract:
a) The acceptor need not have the knowledge of the offer
b) The acceptor must have the knowledge of the offer before acceptance by performance
c) The acceptor may acquire the knowledge of the offer after the performance or the condition for acceptance
d) Knowledge does not matter so long as the condition is performed with or without knowledge
[AIBE-IX]

Q.87 Under the provision of the Transfer of Property Act 1882, the unborn person acquires vested interest on transfer for his benefit:
a) Upon his birth
b) 7 days after his birth
c) 12 days after his birth
d) No such provision is made
[AIBE-IX]

Q.88 Every transfer of immovable property made with intent to defeat or delay the creditors of the transferor shall be voidable:
a) At the option of creditor so defeated or delayed
b) At the option of debtor
c) At the option of Court
d) None of the above [AIBE-IX]

Q.89 Where co-judgement debtors are in the position of joint promisors, each is:
a) Not jointly and severally liable to the decree holder
b) Jointly and severally liable to the decree holder
c) Jointly liable to the decree holder only
d) Severally liable to the decree holder only [AIBE-IX]

Q.90 '*At sight*' under Section 21 of the Negotiable Instruments Act 1881 means:
a) On presentation
b) On demand
c) On coming into vision
d) None of the above [AIBE-IX]

Q.91 Contract without consideration made in writing and registered and made on account of natural love and affection is:
a) Void
b) Reasonable
c) Valid
d) Unenforceable [AIBE-IX]

Q.92 Under the Transfer of Property Act 1882:
a) The salary of a public officer can be transferred
b) The salary of a public officer cannot be transferred
c) Public office can be transferred
d) None of the above [AIBE-IX]

Q.93 Where a debt is transferred for the purpose of securing an existing or future debt, the debt so transferred if received by the transferor or recovered by the transferee is applicable first, in payment of cost of such recovery. This is the provision of:
a) Mortgaged debt
b) Gift
c) Actionable claim
d) Lease [AIBE-IX]

Q.94 A suit under Section 6 of the Specific Relief Act can be brought by:
a) Trespasser
b) A tenant holding over
c) Servant
d) Manager [AIBE-IX]

Q.95 Injunction cannot be granted in a suit:
a) In which the specific performance cannot enforced

b) For breach of negative contract to enforce specific contract
c) For declaration where the plaintiff is in possession
d) Neither (a) nor (b) nor (c)
[AIBE-IX]

Q.96 Peek Vs. Gurney is a famous case relating to:
a) Mistake
b) Misrepresentation
c) Fraud
d) Frustration of contract
[AIBE-VIII]

Q.97 There was a contract to supply oil-seeds but the Government rendered the sale and purchase of oil-seed illegal under the Defence of India Rules. Identify the effect:
a) Party at default is held liable
b) Both parties are discharged from the performance of such contract
c) Both parties are directed specific performance of the contract
d) None of the above [AIBE-VIII]

Q.98 Principles evolved in Hadley Vs. Baxendale are the basis of Section …. of the Indian Contract Act.
b) 74
b) 55
c) 87
d) 73 [AIBE-VIII]

Q.99 Section 6 of the Specific Relief Act 1963 states thus: If any person is dispossessed without his consent of immovable property otherwise than in due course of law, he or any person claiming through him may, by .... recover possession thereof, notwithstanding any other title that may be set up in such suit:
a) Application
b) Restitution application
c) Suit
d) Reference [AIBE-VIII]

Q.100 As per the Specific Relief Act 1963, identify the situation wherein any person interested in a contract may sue to have it rescinded, and such rescission may be adjudged by the Court:
a) Where the contract is voidable or terminable by the plaintiff
b) Where the contract is unlawful for causes not apparent on its face and the defendant is more to blame than the plaintiff
c) Both (a) and (b)
d) None of the above [AIBE-VIII]

Q.101 A/An .... is one which is drawn by one person and accepted by another, without consideration, merely to enable the drawer to raise money on the bill by discounting it.
a) Bills in sets

b) Documentary bill
c) Bearer instrument
d) Accommodation bill
[AIBE-VIII]

Q.102 Which provision of the Negotiable Instruments Act discusses about material alteration of an instrument and its effects?
a) Section 77
b) Section 88
c) Section 87
d) Section 78 [AIBE-VIII]

Q.103 'A' transfers property to 'B' for life, and after his death to 'C' and 'D', equally to be divided between them, or to the survivor of them. 'C' dies during the lifetime of 'B'. 'D' survives 'B'. At 'B"s death:
a) The property passes to 'D'
b) The property reverts back to 'A"s heirs.
c) The property is declared as having no owner
d) None of the above [AIBE-VIII]

Q.104 'A' will transfer Rs.500 to his niece 'C' if she will desert her husband. The transfer is:
a) Void
b) Voidable
c) Valid
d) None of the above [AIBE-VIII]

Q.105 Which section under the Transfer of Property Act 1882 discusses about the rights and liabilities of buyer and the seller of immovable property?
a) 45
b) 54
c) 55
d) 44 [AIBE-VIII]

Q.106 Identify the wrong statement from the following:
a) An indemnity is for reimbursement of a loss, while a guarantee is for security of the creditor.
b) In a contract of indemnity, the liability of the indemnifier is secondary and arises when the contingent event occurs. In case of contract of guarantee the liability of surety is primary and arises when the principal debtor defaults.
c) The indemnifier after performing his part of the promise has no rights against the third party and he can sue the third party only if there is an assignment in his favor. Whereas in a contract of guarantee, the surety steps into the shoes of the creditor on discharge of his liability, and may sue the principal debtor.
d) In a contract of indemnity, the liability of the indemnifier is primary and arises when the contingent event occurs. In case of contract of guarantee the liability of surety is secondary and arises when

the principal debtor defaults. [AIBE-VIII]

Q.107 Which is true of contracts of agency?
a) The relation between the agent and the principal is of a trust.
b) It is only when a person acts as a representative of the other in the creation, modification or termination of: contractual obligations; between that order and third persons that he is an agent.
c) The only essence of a contract of agency is the agent's representative capacity.
d) None of the above [AIBE-VIII]

Q.108 Point out an example not related to a contract of bailment:
a) Delivering a watch or radio for repair
b) Leaving a car or scooter at a parking stand
c) Leaving luggage in a cloak room
d) A shareholder executes an agreement / bond favoring the company thereby agreeing to satisfy the company for any loss caused as a consequence of his own act [AIBE-VIII]

Q.109 A corporate resolution is not an offer unless efforts are made to communicate it. Which case held so?
a) Blair Vs. Western Mutual Benefit Association
b) R. Vs. Dawood
c) Harvela Investments Ltd. Vs. Royal Trust Co. of Canada
d) None of the above [AIBE-VIII]

Q.110 Doctrine of election is based on the foundation that a person taking the benefit of an instrument must:
a) Not bear the burden
b) Burden is not the subject of election
c) Burden is the subject of election
d) Bear the burden [AIBE-VII]

Q.111 In bailment, if the goods are lent free of cost to the bailee for his use, it is known as bailment by:
a) Deposition
b) Pledge
c) Commodation
d) None of the above [AIBE-VII]

Q.112 Where the proposal and acceptance is through letters, the contract is made at the place where:
a) The acceptance is received
b) The letter of acceptance is posted
c) Both the above answers
d) None of the above [AIBE-VII]

Q.113 The surety stands discharged by:
a) Death

b) Revocation
c) Variance in the terms of the contract without his consent
d) None of the above [AIBE-VII]

Q.114 All contracts which are unlawful and void are known as:
a) Illegal contracts
b) Nugatory contracts
c) Voidable contracts
d) None of the above [AIBE-VII]

Q.115 S........ of the Negotiable Instruments Act deals with 'noting'.
a) 100
b) 101
c) 102
d) 99 [AIBE-VII]

Q.116 Cancellation of crossing is also called:
a) Marking
b) Opening of crossing
c) Cancellation
d) None of the above [AIBE-VII]

Q.117 Negotiable claim issued by a bank in return for a term deposit is called:
a) Share certificate
b) Certificate of incorporation
c) Certificate of deposit
d) Term deposit [AIBE-VII]

Q.118 Wager relate with:
a) Present event
b) Past event
c) Future event
d) Any of the above [AIBE-VII]

Q.119 The concept of 'privity of contract' was rejected in:
a) Winterbottom Vs. Wright
b) Donoghue Vs. Stevenson
c) Longmeid Vs. Holliday
d) Heaven Vs. Pender [AIBE-VII]

Q.120 What are the remedies open to the party aggrieved in a suit on contracts?
a) Specific performance and injunction
b) Specific performance and damages
c) Specific performance only
d) All of the above [AIBE-VII]

Q.121 Frost Vs. Knight is a leading case on:
a) S.32
b) S.33
c) S.34
d) S.35 [AIBE-VII]

Q.122 Which among the following is a law based on equity?
a) Indian Contract Act 1872
b) Indian Penal Code 1863
c) Indian Partnership Act 1932
d) Specific Relief Act 1963
[AIBE-VII]

Q.123 Which section of the Specific Relief Act describes temporary

Injunction?
a) 45
b) 41
c) 37
d) 36 [AIBE-VII]

Q.124 The maintenance amount which can be transferred is:
a) Future maintenance
b) Right to future maintenance
c) Arrears of maintenance up to a certain date
d) None of the above [AIBE-VII]

Q.125 The maximum period during which property can be tied up is:
a) Only 15 years
b) One or more life or lives in being at the date of transfer and the minority of an unborn person
c) During the lifetime of the transferor and the minority period of an unborn person
d) None of the above [AIBE-VII]

Q.126 A promise or set of promises forming consideration to each other - is known as:
a) Proposal
b) Consideration
c) Agreement
d) Contract [AIBE-VI]

Q.127 A past consideration under Indian Law:
a) Invalid
b) Valid
c) Void
d) Voidable [AIBE-VI]

Q.128 'Caveat emptor' means:
a) Purchaser beware
b) Seller beware
c) Things outside commerce
d) A warning letter [AIBE-VI]

Q.129 *Consensus ad idem* means:
a) Good faith
b) Opinion of third parties
c) Opinion of the offeree
d) Meeting of the minds
[AIBE-VI]

Q.130 Agreement in restraint of marriage is:
a) Contingent contract
b) Wager
c) Void
d) Valid [AIBE-VI]

Q.131 'A' tells 'B', the shopkeeper, "Give 'Z' the Goods, I will see you paid." - this contract is:
a) Bailment
b) Agency
c) Guarantee
d) Indemnity [AIBE-VI]

Q.132 A contract to perform the promise or discharge the liability of a third person in case of his default - is a contract of:
a) Guarantee
b) Default

c) Indemnity
d) Partnership [AIBE-VI]

Q.133 "He who does an act through another, does it himself" - is a contract of:
a) Sale
b) Purchase
c) Agency
d) Partnership [AIBE-VI]

Q.134 When at the desire of the promisor, the promisee or any other person has done or abstained from doing something or does or abstains from doing something or promises to do or abstain from doing something, such act or abstinence or promise is called a:
a) Proposal
b) Consideration
c) Acceptance
d) Agreement [AIBE-VI]

Q.135 'X' owes 'Y' Rs.20,000 but this debt is barred by Limitation Act. 'X' executes a written promise to pay 'Y' Rs.15,000 on account of debt. This is
a) Invalid
b) Void
c) Valid
d) Voidable [AIBE-VI]

Q.136 When a negotiable instrument is delivered conditionally or for a special purpose as a collateral security or for safe custody only, and not for the purpose of transferring absolutely property therein, it is called:
a) Fictitious Bill
b) Inchoate instrument
c) Escrow
d) Clean Bill [AIBE-VI]

Q.137 Which one of the following is a promissory note when 'A' signs the instrument?
a) I promise to pay 'B' or order Rs.10,000 on demand
b) Mr. 'B'! I owe you Rs.10,000
c) I promise to pay 'B' Rs.10,000 and such other sums which shall be due to him
d) I promise to pay 'B' on his request Rs.10,000 on the death of 'X' [AIBE-VI]

Q.138 Transfer of Property Act applies to transfers:
a) By partition in a joint family
b) Inter vivos
c) Both between animate and inanimate objects
d) Between living and non-living persons [AIBE-VI]

Q.139 'A' transfers property of which he is the owner to 'B' in trust for 'A' and his intended wife successively for their lives and, after the death of the survivor, for the eldest son of the intended marriage for life, and after his death for 'A"s second son. The interest so created for the benefit of the eldest son:

a) Does not take effect
b) Takes effect
c) Partially takes effect
d) None of the above [AIBE-VI]

Q.140 A transfer of an interest in specific immoveable property for the purpose of securing the payment of money advanced or to be advanced by way of loan, an existing or future debt, or the performance of an engagement which may give rise to a pecuniary liability - is called:

a) Sale
b) Gift
c) Mortgage
d) Lease [AIBE-VI]

Q.141 A lease of immovable property from year to year, or for any term exceeding one year or reserving a yearly rent, can be made only by a:

a) Oral agreement
b) Written agreement
c) Partition
d) Registered instrument
[AIBE-VI]

Q.142 Specific performance of contract can be ordered, at discretion of Court:

a) When the act agreed to be done is such that compensation in money for non-performance will not give sufficient relief
b) When the act agreed to be done is such that compensation in money for non-performance will give sufficient relief
c) Contract, performance of which involves a continuous duly, which Court cannot supervise
d) Specific performance of contract of personal nature cannot be ordered [AIBE-VI]

Q.143 Under Section 9 of Specific Relief Act, the person against whom the relief is claimed may plead by way of defense any ground which is available to him:

a) Under law of torts
b) Under any law relating to contracts
c) Under IPC
d) Under CrPC [AIBE-VI]

Q.144 The following contract cannot be specifically enforced:

a) A contract the performance of which involves the performance of a continuous duty which the court cannot supervise
b) A contract the performance of which involves the performance of a continuous duty which the court can supervise
c) A Tort the discharge of which involves the performance of a

continuous obligation
d) A contract for the non-performance of which compensation is not adequate relief [AIBE-VI]

Q.145 'A' sells a TV to a minor, who pays for it by means of a cheque. 'A' endorses that cheque to 'X'. 'X' takes it in good faith and for value. This cheque was dishonoured on presentation. 'X' can enforce payment of the cheque:
a) Against Minor
b) Against Minor and 'A'
c) Against 'A' only
d) Cannot enforce against anybody [AIBE-VI]

Q.146 A contract made by a trustee in excess of his powers or in breach of trust cannot be specifically enforced as per:
a) S.12
b) S.11(2)
c) S.12(2)
d) S.13 [AIBE-V]

Q.147 Under S.41 of the Specific Relief Act, an injunction cannot be granted:
a) To restrain any person from instituting or prosecuting any proceeding in a court not subordinate to that from which the injunction is sought
b) To restrain any person from applying to any legislative body
c) To restrain any person from instituting or prosecuting any proceeding in a criminal matter
d) All of the above [AIBE-V]

Q.148 Specific relief can be granted only for the purpose of enforcing individual civil rights and not for the mere purpose of enforcing a penal law. Which provision brings in such prohibition?
a) S.4
b) S.5
c) S.7
d) S.10 [AIBE-V]

Q.149 Delivery of goods by one person to another for some purpose upon a contract that they shall, when the purpose is accomplished, be returned or disposed of according to the directions of the person delivering them. What is this type of contract called as?
a) Indemnity
b) Guarantee
c) Bailment
d) Pledge [AIBE-V]

Q.150 The essence of a contract of agency is the agent's:
a) Representative capacity coupled with a power to affect the legal relations of the principal with third persons
b) Power and title to the property

that is being dealt with
c) Authority and status of dealing with the trade
d) None of the above [AIBE-V]

Q.151 "A Contract is an agreement between two or more persons which is intended to be enforceable at law and is contracted by the acceptance by one party of an offer made to him by the other party to do or abstain from doing some act." - Whose statement is this?
a) Halsbury
b) Salmond
c) Phipson
d) Pollock [AIBE-V]

Q.152 'A''s nephew has absconded from his home. He sent his servant to trace his missing nephew. When the servant had left, 'A' then announced that anybody who discovered the missing boy, would be given the reward of Rs.500. The servant discovered the missing boy without knowing the reward. When the servant came to know about the reward, he brought an action against 'A' to recover the same. But his action failed. It was held that the servant was not entitled to the reward because he did not know about the offer when he discovered the missing boy. Name the case on reading the facts:
a) Lalman Shukla Vs. Gauri Dutt
b) Donoghue Vs. Stevenson
c) Tweddle Vs. Atkinson
d) Dutton Vs. Poole [AIBE-V]

Q.153 A debtor owes several distinct debts to the same creditor and he makes a payment which is insufficient to satisfy all the debts. In such a case, a question arises as to which particular debt the payment is to be appropriated. Which sections of the Contract Act provide an answer to this question?
a) Section 59 to 61
b) Section 22 of 31
c) Section 10 to 12
d) Section 55 to 60 [AIBE-V]

Q.154 What property cannot be transferred under S.6 of Transfer of Property Act 1882?
a) An easement apart from the dominant heritage
b) An interest in property restricted in its enjoyment to the owner personally
c) A right to future maintenance, in whatsoever manner arising, secured or determined
d) All of the above [AIBE-V]

Q.155 'A' transfers property of which he is the owner, to 'B' in trust for 'A' and his intended wife successively for their lives, and, after the death of the survivor, for the eldest son of the intended marriage for life, and after his death for 'A"s second son. Can the interest so created for the benefit of the eldest son take effect?

a) Yes

b) No

c) It is a valid transfer

d) None of the above [AIBE-V]

Q.156 Accepting any other satisfaction than the performance originally agreed is known as:

a) Reciprocal agreement

b) Reciprocal acceptance

c) Reciprocal accord and satisfaction

d) Accord and satisfaction

[AIBE-V]

Q.157 "Where two parties have made a contract which one of them has broken, the damage which the other party ought to receive in respect of such breach of contract should be either such as may fairly and reasonably be considered arising naturally i.e. according to the usual course of things from such breach of contract itself or such as may reasonably be supposed to have been in the contemplation of the parties at the time they made the contract as the probable result of breach of it." - In which case the principle was laid down so?

a) Clegg Vs. Hands

b) Kapur Chand Vs. Himayat Ali Khan

c) Frost Vs. Knight

d) Hadley Vs. Baxendale

[AIBE-V]

Q.158 When a misrepresentation has been made, what are the alternative courses open to an aggrieved?

a) He can avoid or rescind the contract

b) He can affirm the contract and insist on the misrepresentation being made

c) He can rely on upon the misrepresentation, as a defence to an action on the contract

d) All of the above [AIBE-V]

Q.159 A solicitor sold certain property to one of his clients. The client subsequently alleged that the property was considerably overvalued and his consent was caused by _____. Court considered the relationship between the parties to reach the decision.

a) Coercion

b) Misrepresentation

c) Undue influence

d) Estoppel [AIBE-V]

Q.160 The law of contract is intended to ensure that what a man has been led to expect shall come to pass, that what has been promised shall be performed. Whose

statement is this?
a) Lord Black
b) Henderson
c) Anson
d) Salmond [AIBE-V]

Q.161 Intention not to create a legal obligation was clear from the conduct of parties. Which among the popular cases deals on the topic?
a) Balfour Vs. Balfour
b) Donoghue Vs. Stevenson
c) Derry Vs. Peek
d) Birch Vs. Birch [AIBE-V]

Q.162 According to the Indian law, in a lawful contract, consideration:
a) Must move from promisee only
b) May move from promisee or any other person
c) Is not necessary at all
d) None of the above [AIBE-V]

Q.163 Raghav owes Murli Rs.10,000. This debt is time barred by the Limitation Act. Even then, Murli promises in writing to pay Raghav Rs.4,500 on account of debt and signs the document. This contract is:
a) Enforceable
b) Unenforceable
c) Void
d) None of the above [AIBE-V]

Q.164 An agency can be terminated by:
a) Agreement between parties
b) By renunciation by the agent
c) By completion of business of agency
d) All of the above [AIBE-V]

Q.165 Which types of loss are not covered by a contract of indemnity?
a) Loss arising from accidents, like fire or perils of the sea
b) Loss caused by the promisor himself or by a third person
c) Loss arising by human agency
d) None of the above [AIBE-V]

Q.166 Which of the following is correct of a standard form contract?
a) It is a valid contract
b) One party has no choice but to accept and sign the contract
c) Both (i) and (ii)
d) The consent is not a free consent [AIBE-IV]

Q.167 As a general rule, an agreement made without consideration is:
a) Void
b) Voidable
c) Valid
d) Unlawful [AIBE-IV]

Q.168 A contingent agreement based on an impossible event under Section 36 is:
a) Void
b) Void till impossible is known

c) Void when even becomes impossible
d) Voidable [AIBE-IV]

Q.169 The *consensus ad idem* means:
a) General consensus
b) Reaching an agreement
c) Meeting of minds upon the same thing in the same sense
d) All of the above [AIBE-IV]

Q.170 In famous Carlill Vs. Carbolic Smoke Ball Co. (1893) 1 QBD 256, the Hon'ble Court held that the contract was accepted on being:
a) Communicated
b) Acted upon
c) Refused
d) Advertised [AIBE-IV]

Q.171 Inadequacy of consideration does not make the contract:
a) Void
b) Voidable
c) Unenforceable
d) Neither void nor voidable
[AIBE-IV]

Q.172 *Jus in personam* means a right against:
a) A specific person
b) The public at large
c) A specific thing
d) None of these [AIBE-IV]

Q.173 Exposure of goods by a shopkeeper is:
a) Offer for Sale
b) Invitation to Offer
c) Offer
d) Acceptance [AIBE-IV]

Q.174 An agreement to remain unmarried is:
a) Valid
b) Void
c) Voidable
d) Unenforceable [AIBE-IV]

Q.175 An agreement enforceable at law is:
a) Enforceable acceptance
b) Accepted offer
c) Approved promise
d) Contract [AIBE-IV]

Q.176 An agreement shall be void for:
a) Mistake of fact by one party
b) Mistake of fact by both the parties
c) Mistake of foreign law
d) All of the above [AIBE-IV]

Q.177 *Void agreement* signifies:
a) Agreement illegal in nature
b) Agreement not enforceable by law
c) Agreement violating legal procedure
d) Agreement against public policy
[AIBE-IV]

Q.178 A *proposal* when accepted becomes:

a) Promise under Section 2(b)

b) Agreement under Section 2(e)

c) Contract under Section 2(h)

d) None of the above [AIBE-IV]

Q.179 '*Offer*' under Section 2(a) is:

a) Communication from one person to another

b) Suggestion by one person to another

c) Willingness to do or abstain from doing an act in order to obtain the assent of other thereto

d) None of the above [AIBE-IV]

Q.180 Which of the following statement is incorrect?

a) Specific relief Act 1963 extends to the whole of India except State of Jammu and Kashmir

b) Specific performance is granted where there exists no standard for ascertaining damage

c) Where the aggrieved party can be adequately compensated in money, he will get only a decree for damages and not the recourse to

d) None of the above [AIBE-IV]

Q.181 Which the following is the correct statement?

a) Under Sec.7, the suit may be for recovery of special movable property or, in the alternative, for compensation

b) Under Sec.8, pecuniary compensation is not an adequate relief to the plaintiff for the loss of the article and the relief prayed is for injunction restraining the defendant from disposing of the article or otherwise injuring or concealing it, or for return of the same

c) Both (a) and (b) are correct

d) All are incorrect [AIBE-IV]

Q.182 Unborn person acquires vested interest on transfer for his benefit under Transfer of property Act 1882:

a) Upon his birth

b) 7 days after his birth

c) 12 days after his birth

d) None of all [AIBE-IV]

Q.183 Which Section of the Transfer of Property Act deals with onerous gift?

a) Section 127

b) Section 126

c) Section 125

d) Section 124 [AIBE-IV]

Q.184 The Negotiable Instruments Act 1881 came into force on:

a) 9th December, 1881

b) 19th December, 1881

c) 1st March, 1882

d) None of the above [AIBE-IV]

Q.185 The term 'Negotiable

Instrument' is defined in the Negotiable Instruments Act 1881, under Section:
a) Section 12
b) Section 13
c) Section 13A
d) Section 13B [AIBE-IV]

TOPIC 8: LAW OF TORT INCLUDING MOTOR VEHICLES ACT AND CONSUMER PROTECTION ACT

(5 questions are, generally, asked from this subject)

Q.1 Ms. J, a banker refuses to honour cheque of Ms. F. Though she was having sufficient balance yet it does not suffer any loss to Ms. F. Ms. F can file the case under which scenario ?

(A) Volenti-non-fit-injuria
(B) Injuria-sine-damnum
(C) Damnum-sine-injuria
(D) Res-ipsa-loquitur [AIBE-XIX]

Q.2 Mr. B told Mr. A to leave the premises in occupation of Mr. A. When Mr. A refused then Mr. B collected some of his workmen who mustered round Mr. A. They tucking up their sleeves and aprons and threatened to break the plaintiff's neck, he did not leave. Under which tortious act, Mr. A can file the case ?

(A) False Imprisonment
(B) Assault
(C) Battery
(D) Hurt [AIBE-XIX]

Q.3 Ms. J knowing while taking the lift that driver Mr. T was under the influence of alcohol. Consequently, car met with an accident and Ms. J got injuries and she has filed the case for compensation. Which defence could be claimed by Mr. T ?

(A) Volenti-non-fit-injuria
(B) Act of God
(C) Inevitable Accident
(D) Act of Necessity [AIBE-XIX]

Q.4 Mr. K is owner of a building containing a large number of rooms and had derived a considerable income by letting them. Mr. Y is owner of an adjacent cotton mill which erected after the occupation by Mr. K. Owing to noise and smoke of the mill several rooms remain vacated that results into loss for Mr. K. Examine relevant tort for the case.

(A) Damnum-sine-injuria
(B) Trespass to land
(C) Nuisance
(D) Negligence [AIBE-XIX]

Q.5 There was a collision between two buses, one owned by the government and another was a private bus. Wherein private bus was coming from wrong side and government bus was coming rashly, neither slowing down his bus after seeing the other bus. Determine the tortious act.

(A) Private bus owner is negligent.
(B) Government bus owner is negligent.
(C) Inevitable accident.
(D) Contributory negligence
[AIBE-XIX]

Q.6 Who has defined tort as 'tortious liability arises from the breach of duty primarily fixed by law; this duty is towards persons generally and its breach is redressable by an action for unliquidated damages'?
a) Lindsell
b) Pollock
c) Salmond
d) Winfield [AIBE-XVIII]

Q.7 Gloucester Grammar School case relates to which of the following important maxims?
a) Damnum sine injuria
b) Injuria sine damno
c) Ubi jus ibi remedium
d) Volenti non-fit injuria
[AIBE-XVIII]

Q.8 Which of the following provisions of the Motor Vehicles Act, 1988 relates to no fault liability?
a) Section 140
b) Section 151
c) Section 162
d) Section 128 [AIBE-XVIII]

Q.9 How many consumer rights are identified under the Consumer Protection Act, 2019?
a) 2
b) 4
c) 6
d) 8 [AIBE-XVIII]

Q.10 Which of the following body constituted under the Consumer Protection Act, 2019 is authorised to render advice on promotion and protection of consumers' right under the Act?
a) Central Consumer Protection Authority
b) Central Consumer Protection Council
c) State Consumer Protection Authority
d) State Consumer Protection Council [AIBE-XVIII]

Q.11 Suppose a road accident occurs, then being an advocate, what is the correct way of approaching the situation?
a) **FIR > Petition > Summon to Insurance Company**
b) Petition > FIR > Summon to Insurance Company
c) Summon to Insurance Company > Petition > FIR
d) FIR > Summon to Insurance Company > Petition [AIBE-XVII]

Q.12 The principle of "Ubi jus ibi

idem remedium" was recognized in:
a) Winterbottom Vs Wright
b) Chapman Vs Pickersgill
c) **Ashby Vs White**
d) Rylands Vs Fletcher
[AIBE-XVII]

Q.13 Gloucester Grammar School case is a landmark case based on which of the following maxim?
a) **Damnum sine injuria**
b) Injuria sine damnum
c) Volenti non-fit injuria
d) Audi alteram partem
[AIBE-XVII]

Q.14 The National Consumer Disputes Redressal Commission under Consumer Protection Act, 2019 shall have the jurisdiction to complaints where the value of goods or services paid as consideration exceeds rupees:
a) 1 Crore
b) **10 Crores**
c) 50 Crores
d) 100 Crores [AIBE-XVII]

Q.15 Under section 41 of Consumer Protection Act, 2019 an appeal from the order of District Commission lies to _____.
a) **State Commission**
b) Consumer Tribunal
c) National Commission
d) High Court [AIBE-XVII]

Q.16 According to section 2 of Motor Vehicles Act 1988, the term 'motor cab' means any motor vehicle constructed or adapted to carry not more than:
a) 5 passengers including the driver
b) 6 passengers including the driver
c) 5 passengers excluding the driver
d) **6 passengers excluding the driver** [AIBE-XVI]

Q.17 The National Commission of Consumer Protection is composed of:
a) 7 members
b) **5 members**
c) 8 members
d) 6 members [AIBE-XVI]

Q.18 Maxim "Res Ipsa Loquitur" means:
a) **The thing speaks for itself**
b) Where there is right there is remedy
c) Where there is remedy there is right
d) Where there is no fault, there is no remedy [AIBE-XVI]

Q.19 The rule of Strict Liability is based on the decision in:
a) Donoghue Vs Stevenson
b) Homes Vs Ashford
c) **Rylands Vs Fletcher**
d) None of the above [AIBE-XVI]

Q.20 The Rule of Last opportunity

was laid down in:
a) **Davies Vs Manh**
b) State of A.P. Vs Ranganna
c) Nugent Vs Smith
d) Kalavati Vs State of H.P. [AIBE-XVI]

Q.21 In M. C. Mehta Vs. Union of India AIR 1987 SC 1086 (Sri Ram Fertilizers case), the Court held that:
a) In escape of toxic gas, the enterprise is strictly and absolutely liable to compensate all those who are affected by the accident and such liability is not subject to any of the exceptions which operate vis-a-vis the tortious principle of strict liability.
b) In escape of a dangerous animal, the owner is strictly and absolutely liable to compensate all those who are affected by the accident and such liability is not subject to any of the exceptions which operate vis-a-vis the tortious principle of strict liability.
c) In escape of toxic gas, the enterprise is strictly liable to compensate all those who are affected by the accident and such liability is subject to any of the exceptions which operate vis-a-vis the tortious principle of strict liability
d) A company or a corporation is not a state and hence, not liable for leak of toxic gas affecting the health of the people. [AIBE-XV]

Q.22 *Vis major* means:
a) Act of God
b) Act of individual
c) Act of other party
d) Act of plaintiff [AIBE-XV]

Q.23 Classical doctrine of 'Act of State' in law of Torts means:
a) An act of the sovereign power of a country that cannot be challenged, controlled or interfered with by municipal courts
b) An act of the Judiciary of a country that cannot be challenged, controlled or interfered with by municipal courts
c) An act of the sovereign power of a country that can be challenged, controlled or interfered with by municipal courts
d) None of the above [AIBE-XV]

Q.24 In Torts, all persons who aid, or counsel, or direct or join in the committal of a wrongful act, are known as:
a) Abettors
b) Joint tortfeasors
c) Tort holders
d) Tort holders in common
[AIBE-XV]

Q.25 The National Consumer

Dispute Redressal Commission was constituted in the year:

a) 1988

b) 1998

c) 1999

d) 1997 [AIBE-XV]

Q.26 What is the limitation period applicable to the three forums in entertaining a complaint under The Consumer Protection Act 1986?

a) 3 years from the date on which the cause of action has arisen

b) 5 years from the date on which the cause of action has arisen

c) 4 years from the date on which the cause of action has arisen

d) 2 years from the date on which the cause of action has arisen [AIBE-XV]

Q.27 Which one of the following is true about Latin maxim '*Ubi Jus Ibi remedium*'?

a) Where there is right, there is remedy.

b) Where there is remedy, there is right.

c) Both (a) & (b)

d) None of the above [AIBE-XIV]

Q.28 The Latin word '*Injuria Sine Damnum*' literally means:

a) Infringement of legal right without damages

b) Damages without Infringement of legal right

c) Both (a) & (b)

d) None of the above [AIBE-XIV]

Q.29 The Provision relating to Claims Tribunal is given under ………… of Motor Vehicles Act.

a) Section 165-175

b) Section 175-180

c) Section 170-175

d) Section 171-177 [AIBE-XIV]

Q.30 The Consumer Protection Act 1986 came into effect on:

a) 24th August 1986

b) 15th April 1986

c) 24th May 1986

d) 24th December 1986 [AIBE-XIV]

Q.31 Which one of the following sections of Consumer Protection Act 1986 defines the term 'Consumer'?

a) Section 2(1)(a)

b) Section 2(1)(b)

c) Section 2(1)(c)

d) Section 2(1)(d) [AIBE-XIV]

Q.32 Which one of the following is a leading case on '*Injuria Sine Damnum*'?

a) Rylands Vs. Fletcher

b) Ashby Vs. White

c) Donoghue Vs. Stevenson

d) All of the above [AIBE-XIII]

Q.33 Which one is leading case on

Strict Liability?
a) Allen Vs. Flood
b) Rylands Vs. Fletcher
c) Bourhill Vs. Young
d) Donoghue Vs. Stevenson
[AIBE-XIII]

Q.34 Which of the following section of the Motor Vehicle Act 1988 defines the term 'Owner'?
a) Section 2(30)
b) Section 2(31)
c) Section 2(25)
d) Section 2(32) [AIBE-XIII]

Q.35 The Latin word '*Res Ipsa Laquitur*' means:
a) Things speak its story itself.
b) Where there is consent, there is no injury.
c) Both (a) and (b)
d) None of the above [AIBE-XIII]

Q.36 In which of the following cases, the 'Principal of common Employment' evolved for the first time?
a) Rylands Vs. Fletcher
b) Priestley Vs. Fowler
c) Ashby Vs. White
d) Wagon Mound [AIBE-XIII]

Q.37 Definition of 'complainant' is described in Consumer Protection Act under:
a) Section 2(1)(b)
b) Section 20
c) Section 21
d) None of the above [AIBE-XII]

Q.38 English case Rylands Vs. Fletcher laid down a very important rule:
a) Absolute liability
b) Vicarious liability
c) Indirect liability
d) Financial liability [AIBE-XII]

Q.39 An Appeal against order passed under Section 27 of the Consumer Protection Act 1986 by the National Commission lies in:
a) The High Court
b) The Supreme Court
c) The Central Government
d) Not appealable [AIBE-XII]

Q.40 State Government's power to control the road transport is provided in the Motor Vehicle Act 1988 under Section:
a) 67
b) 68
c) 69
d) None of the above [AIBE-XII]

Q.41 In the tort of conspiracy, the purpose of combination must be to:
a) Violate legal right of the victim
b) Cause damage to the victim
c) Obtain benefit for the combiners
d) Perfect the interest of combiners
[AIBE-XII]

Q.42 Definition of complainant is described in Consumer Protection Act under Section:
a) Section 29
b) Section 35
c) Section 37
d) All of the above [AIBE-XI]

Q.43 Section 67 of Motor Vehicle Act 1988 provides:
a) Possession of Driving License while driving
b) Possession of Insurance Certificate and PUC certificate in the vehicle
c) Revoking Driving License if drunk driving is detected
d) State Government's power to control the road transport
[AIBE-XI]

Q.44 The term 'Tort' is a:
a) Latin Word
b) French Word
c) English word
d) Italian word [AIBE-XI]

Q.45 In Tort, what is 'vicarious liability'?
a) A person is generally liable for his own wrongful act
b) A person is liable for the wrongful act done by other person
c) A person is liable for the wrongful act in his absence
d) None of the above [AIBE-XI]

Q.46 Under Section 2(1)(f) of Consumer Protection Act 1986, 'defect' is meant by any fault, imperfection or shortcomings in _____ in relation to the goods.
a) Quality and Quantity
b) Potency
c) Purity or standard
d) All of the above [AIBE-XI]

Q.47 Which of the following falls under the categories of Act of God?
a) Storm and cyclone
b) Extra ordinary rainfall or flood
c) Lightning and thunder
d) All of the above [AIBE-XI]

Q.48 Complaint means allegation in writing made by a complainant that:
a) An unfair trade practice or restrictive trade practice has been adapted by any traders or service provider
b) The goods bought by him or agreed to be bought by him suffer from one or more defect
c) A traders or the service provider as the case may be has charged for the goods or for the services mentioned in the complaint a price in excess of the price
d) All of the above [AIBE-X]

Q.49 The maxim *'audi alteram partem'* denotes:

a) No one shall be judge of his own cause
b) No one shall be condemned unheard
c) Rights are better than duties
d) None of the above [AIBE-X]

Q.50 Which one of the following is known as Consumer Disputes Redressal Agency?
a) District Forum
b) State Commission
c) National Commission
d) All of the above [AIBE-X]

Q.51 Where the complaint alleges a defect in the goods which cannot be determined without proper analysis or test of the goods, the sample of goods are forwarded to appropriate laboratory for laboratory test. In such types of case, finding report within:
a) 30 days
b) 40 days
c) 45 days
d) 60 days [AIBE-X]

Q.52 Motor Vehicles Act 1939 came into force in:
a) 1939
b) 1940
c) 1941
d) 1942 [AIBE-X]

Q.53 'Dealer' includes a person who is engaged:
a) In building bodies for attachment to chassis
b) In the repair of motor vehicles
c) In the business of hypothecation, leasing or hire purchase of motor vehicle
d) All of the above [AIBE-X]

Q.54 Spurious goods under the provisions of the Consumer Protection Act 1986 imply:
a) Such goods and services which are of poor quality
b) Such goods and services which are claimed to be genuine but they are actually not so
c) Such goods and services which might be stolen in nature
d) Such goods and services which are not usable in nature [AIBE-IX]

Q.55 Who is liable to pay compensation in case of death or permanent disablement?
a) Owner of the vehicle
b) State Government
c) Driver
d) Insurance Company [AIBE-IX]

Q.56 The essential ingredients of the tort of negligence are:
1. When one owes a duty of care towards the other
2. When one commits a breach or that duty, and
3. The other person suffers damage as a consequence thereof

Choose correct response for below-

a) None of them are essential ingredients.

b) Only the first is an essential ingredient.

c) All of them are essential ingredients.

d) Even if the first is absent, the tort of negligence is committed [AIBE-IX]

Q.57 *Vicarious Liability* includes:

a) Liability of the principal for the tort of his agent

b) Liability of the master for the tort of his servant

c) Liability of the partners for each other's tort

d) All of the above [AIBE-IX]

Q.58 Under the provisions of the Consumer Protection Act 1986, the period of limitation for filing complaint before the National Commission is:

a) 1 year from the date on which cause of action has arisen

b) 2 years from the date on which cause of action has arisen

c) 3 years from the date on which cause or action has arisen

d) 4 years from the date on which cause of action has arisen [AIBE-IX]

Q.59 'Grievous hurt' under the Motor vehicles Act 1988 means:

a) Grievous hurt as defined in IPC

b) Grievous hurt as defined in medical laws

c) Grievous hurt as detected by medical practitioner

d) None of the above [AIBE-IX]

Q.60 In tort, there are two broad categories of activities for which a plaintiff may be held strictly liable:

a) Possession of certain animals and abnormally dangerous activities

b) Assault and battery

c) Battery and negligence

d) None of the above [AIBE-VIII]

Q.61 The Supreme Court observed - where an enterprise is engaged in a hazardous or inherently dangerous activity and harm results to anyone on account of an accident in the operation of such hazardous or inherently dangerous activity resulting, for example, in escape of toxic gas the enterprise is strictly and absolutely liable to compensate all those who are affected by the accident and such liability is not subject to any of the exceptions which operate vis-a-vis the tortious principle of strict liability. In such a case, the measure of compensation must be correlated to the magnitude and capacity of the enterprise because such compensation must have a deterrent effect. The larger and more prosperous the enterprise, the greater must be the amount of compensation payable by it for the harm caused on account of an accident in the carrying on of the hazardous or inherently dangerous activity by the enterprise. Name the case.

a) Subhash Kumar Vs. State of Bihar 1991

b) Rural Litigation and Entitlement Kendra Vs. State of U. P. 1985

c) M C Mehta Vs. Union of India 1986

d) Union Carbide Vs. Union of India 1984 [AIBE-VIII]

Q.62 Sec.47(3) Motor Vehicles Act empowers the Regional Transport Authority to limit the number of stage carriage permits. Explain the nature of the function exercised:

a) This is a judicial function, as the Authority's decision is based on an official policy.

b) This is a quasi-judicial function, as the Authority's decision is based on an official policy.

c) This is an administrative function, as the Authority's decision is based on an official policy.

d) None of the above [AIBE-VIII]

Q.63 *Pigeon Hole theory* was proposed by:

a) Winfield

b) Salmond

c) Blackstone

d) Lord Knight [AIBE-VIII]

Q.64 According to Motor Vehicles Act 1988, no person under the age of ……. years shall drive a motor vehicle in any public place.

a) 20

b) 16

c) 18

d) 21 [AIBE-VIII]

Q.65 According to the Consumer Protection Act 1986, what is the limitation period applicable to the three forums in entertaining a complaint?

a) 2 years from the date on which the cause of action has arisen

b) 2 years from which the article was purchased

c) 3 years

d) None of the above [AIBE-VIII]

Q.66 Any person aggrieved by an order made by the District Forum may prefer an appeal against such order to the ………… within a period of …. days from the date of the order.

a) State Commission, 30

b) State Tribunal, 30

c) State Forum, 30

d) State Commission, 60

[AIBE-VIII]

Q.67 The National Consumer Dispute Redressal Commission was constituted in the year:
a) 1998
b) 1988
c) 1999
d) 2000 [AIBE-VIII]

Q.68 The *doctrine of civil conspiracy* was enunciated by the House of Lords in:
a) Walsby Vs. Anley
b) Moghul Steamship Company Vs. McGregor, Gow and Company
c) Allen Vs. Flood
d) Quinn Vs. Leathern
[AIBE-VIII]

Q.69 Gloucester Grammar School case is a leading case to explain the:
a) Volenti non-fit injuria
b) Injuria non-fit volenti
c) Damnum sine injuria
d) Injuria sine damnum [AIBE-VII]

Q.70 '*Ex dolo malo non oritur actio*' is:
a) Infringes
b) An action could not prevent a legal right
c) No action on an immoral act
d) None of the above [AIBE-VII]

Q.71 '*Qui facit per alium facit per se*' means:
a) act of an agent is the act of principal
b) act of an agent is not an act of principal
c) principal and agent are liable jointly
d) agent must not act in contravention of the act of principal
[AIBE-VII]

Q.72 .... is observed as the World Consumer Rights Day.
a) 15th of March
b) 16th of March
c) 12th of March
d) 11th of March [AIBE-VII]

Q.73 Accountability of medical professional and the need for qualitative change in the attitude of the medical service provided by the hospitals was emphasized by the Supreme Court in which of the following cases?
a) Bhatia International Vs. Bulk Trading S A
b) Indian Medical Association Vs. V P Shantha and Ors.
c) Maneka Gandhi Vs. Union of India
d) Lucknow Development Authority Vs. M K Gupta
[AIBE-VII]

Q.74 Renewal of driving licenses is envisaged under S...... of the Motor Vehicles Act 1988:
a) 20
b) 21
c) 22

d) 15 [AIBE-VII]

Q.75 The type of damages awarded in the law of torts:
a) Liquidated Damages
b) Unliquidated damages
c) Penal damages
d) Exemplary damages [AIBE-VI]

Q.76 Ashby Vs. White is an example of:
a) Damnum sine injuria
b) Uberrimae fidei
c) Injuria sine damnum
d) Usufruct [AIBE-VI]

Q.77 The Supreme Court of India invoked the principle of absolute liability on an enterprise carrying on business with hazardous and inherently dangerous toxic chemicals in:
a) Ganga Pollution case
b) Fletcher case
c) Sri Ram Fertilizers case
d) Prabhu Dayal case [AIBE-VI]

Q.78 '*Res ipsa loquitur*' means:
a) Things speak for themselves
b) Tithes imperiled
c) Vicarious liability
d) Dangerous animals [AIBE-VI]

Q.79 A motor cycle with engine capacity not exceeding 50cc may be driven in a public place by a person:
a) After attaining the age of sixteen years
b) After attaining the age of eighteen years
c) After attaining the age of fifteen years
d) After attaining the age of twenty-one years [AIBE-VI]

Q.80 According to Consumer protection Act, the National Commission shall have jurisdiction over complaints where the value of the goods or services and compensation, if any, claimed exceeds rupees:
a) 2 lakhs
b) 10 lakhs
c) 20 lakhs
d) 50 lakhs [AIBE-VI]

Q.81 Contributory negligence means:
a) The failure by a person to use reasonable care for the safety of either of himself or his property
b) Volunteer to pay for the negligence of others
c) Contributing the money or money's worth for others wrongs
d) Inciting others to commit civil wrong [AIBE-V]

Q.82 "Where an enterprise is engaged in a hazardous or inherently dangerous activity and harm results to anyone on account of an accident in the operation of

such hazardous or inherently dangerous activity resulting, for example, in escape of toxic gas the enterprise is strictly and absolutely liable to compensate all those who are affected by the accident and such liability is not subject to any of the exceptions which operate vis-a-vis the tortious principle of strict liability." - Held in the case of:
a) Francis Coralie Vs. UT of Delhi
b) Shri Ram Food and Fertilisers case
c) PUCL Vs. Union or India
d) State of Punjab Vs. Mohinder Singh Chawla [AIBE-V]

Q.83 "A tort is a civil wrong for which the remedy is an action for unliquidated damages and which is not exclusively the breach of a contract, or the breach of a trust, or the breach of other merely equitable obligation". - Whose Statement is this?
a) Winfield
b) Salmond
c) Pollock
d) Griffith [AIBE-V]

Q.84 Under Section 20 of the M. V. Act, if a person is convicted of an offence punishable under Section 189 of the Motor Vehicles Act, the Court shall ordinarily order for:
a) Imposing penalty only
b) Punishment only
c) Both punishment and penalty
d) Disqualification under the Act
[AIBE-V]

Q.85 Consumer Protection Act was brought into operation in the year:
a) 1987
b) 1986
c) 1985
d) 1984 [AIBE-V]

Q.86 Under Consumer Protection Act, the jurisdiction of the District Forum should not exceed rupees:
a) Fifty Thousands
b) Twenty-Five Thousands
c) One lakh
d) Twenty lakhs [AIBE-V]

Q.87 The Consumer Protection Act was enacted in:
a) 1985
b) 1986
c) 2005
d) 2008 [AIBE-IV]

Q.88 Appeal against the award of Claims Tribunals under the Motor Vehicles Act 1988 can be made under:
a) Section 171
b) Section 172
c) Section 173
d) Section 174 [AIBE-IV]

Q.89 After the amendment in Motor Vehicles Act in 1994, the

compensation in case of death of the person is:
a) Rs.25,000
b) Rs.50,000
c) Rs.70,000
d) Rs.90,000 [AIBE-IV]

Q.90 Under the *vicarious liability*, the liability is:
a) Joint
b) Several
c) Both (i) and (ii)
d) Either of the above depending upon facts and circumstances of the case [AIBE-IV]

Q.91 In Torts, in case of *defamation*:
a) Intention to defame is not necessary
b) Intention to defame is necessary
c) Both (a) and (b)
d) Either (a) or (b) [AIBE-IV]

Q.92 Consumer Protection Act 1986 is predominantly based on UN General Assembly resolution with due negotiations in the:
a) UNCITRAL
b) UNCTAD
c) UN ECOSOC
d) None of the above [AIBE-IV]

TOPIC 9: LABOUR AND INDUSTRIAL LAWS

(4 questions are, generally, asked from this subject)

Q.1 Which of the following is/are included under the definition of employer given under The Industrial Relations Code, 2020 ?

(1) Occupier of the factory
(2) Contractor
(3) Manager of the factory
(4) Managing director of the factory

(A) (4) Only
(B) (1), (3) and (4)
(C) (1), (2) and (4)
(D) (1), (2) and (3) [AIBE-XIX]

Q.2 Which of the following legislations has been included under the Social Security Code, 2020 ?

(1) The Maternity Benefit Act, 1961
(2) The Payment of Gratuity Act, 1972
(3) The Payment of Bonus Act, 1965
(4) The Employment Exchanges (Compulsory Notification of Vacancies) Act, 1959

(A) Only (3)
(B) (3) and (4)
(C) (1), (2) and (4)
(D) (1), (2), (3) and (4) [AIBE-XIX]

Q.3 .... have not been set up under the provisions of the Industrial Disputes Act, 1947 for adjudication of industrial disputes in an organization.

(A) Industrial Tribunals
(B) Environmental Tribunals
(C) Labour Courts
(D) National Tribunal [AIBE-XIX]

Q.4 XYZ Textiles Ltd., a manufacturing company, recently terminated 04 workers without providing any compensation. The termination was because of the misconduct on the part of the workers. The company issued a show cause notice and the disciplinary enquiry conducted against them. On the basis of the recommendations of the committee the services which was rejected by the management. Aggrieved by the rejection the workers have filed a of these employees were terminated. The workers claimed the retrenchment compensation complaint in the Labour Court under the provisions of the Industrial Disputes Act, 1947.

Based on the above problem, select the correct answer.

(A) The termination does not amount to retrenchment, hence no compensation.

(B) The termination amounts to lay-off, hence compensation will be awarded.

(C) The termination amounts to retrenchment; hence compensation will be awarded.

(D) The termination violated the provisions under the Industrial Disputes Act, 1947, hence the compensation will be awarded.

[AIBE-XIX]

Q.5 For what duration is a woman entitled to leave with wages for tubectomy operation as per the Maternity Benefit Act, 1961?

a) 2 weeks

b) 4 weeks

c) 6 weeks

d) 8 weeks [AIBE-XVIII]

Q.6 What should be the minimum number of workers originally employed in any factory for having at least one canteen in the factory as per the Factories Act, 1948?

a) 100 workers

b) 150 workers

c) 200 workers

d) 250 workers [AIBE-XVIII]

Q.7 Who among the following is not included in the definition of a workman as per the Industrial Disputes Act, 1947?

a) A supervisor drawing a monthly salary of ₹6,000.

b) A supervisor drawing a monthly salary of ₹8,000.

c) A supervisor drawing a monthly salary of ₹10,000.

d) A supervisor drawing a monthly salary of ₹12,000. [AIBE-XVIII]

Q.8 What is the maximum period for which any woman shall be entitled to maternity benefit under the Maternity Benefit Act, 1961?

a) 6 weeks

b) 8 weeks

c) 12 weeks

d) 26 weeks [AIBE-XVIII]

Q.9 The minimum number of members required for registration of a trade union is:

a) 2

b) 3

c) 5

d) **7** [AIBE-XVII]

Q.10 The text of the certified standing order shall be prominently posted by the employer in _____ and in the language understood by majority of his workmen.

a) Hindi

b) **English**

c) Devanagari script

d) Language specified in 8th Schedule of the Constitution

[AIBE-XVII]

Q.11 A person who has the ultimate control over the affairs of the factory under Factories Act, 1948 is

called as _____.
a) **Occupier**
b) Managing Director
c) Chairman
d) Manager [AIBE-XVII]

Q.12 If the factory employs more than 1000 workers, they should appoint qualified _____ to carry out the prescribed duties.
a) **Safety officer**
b) Welfare officer
c) Development officer
d) None of these [AIBE-XVII]

Q.13 The payment of compensation to railway employees by the railway Administration for injury by accident is governed by:
a) **The Employees Compensation Act, 1923**
b) The Payment of Wages Act, 1936
c) Rights of Persons with Disabilities Act, 2016
d) The Workmen Compensation Act, 1986 [AIBE-XVI]

Q.14 A railway servant was killed in a bus accident during the course of employment. His family members may claim compensation under:
a) The Motor Vehicle Act
b) The Employees Compensation Act 1923
c) Both (a) and (b)
d) **Either under (a) or under (b)** [AIBE-XVI]

Q.15 The minimum amount of compensation payable under Employees Compensation Act, 1923 in case of total permanent disablement of a railway servant due to accident is _____.
a) Rs. 80,000
b) Rs. 90,000
c) **Rs. 1,40,000**
d) Rs. 1,20,000 [AIBE-XVI]

Q.16 Schedule II of the Employees Compensation Act 1923 deals with:
a) Age factor for calculating the amount of compensation
b) **List of persons who are included in the definition of 'Employee'**
c) List of occupational diseases
d) List of injuries deemed to result in Permanent Total Disablement [AIBE-XVI]

Q.17 A *teacher* is not a workman within the purview of Industrial Disputes Act - held in the case of:
a) The Workmen Vs. Greaves Cotton & Co. Ltd. & Ors.
b) John Joseph Khokar Vs. Bhadange B S & Ors.
c) A Sundarambal Vs. Government of Goa
d) Dinesh Sharma and Ors. Vs. State of Bihar [AIBE-XV]

Q.18 According to Factories Act:

a) 'Child' means a person who has not completed his fifteenth year of age
b) 'Child' means a person who has not completed his fourteenth year of age
c) 'Child' means a person who has not completed his eighteenth year of age
d) 'Child' means a person who has not completed his sixteenth year of age [AIBE-XV]

Q.19 "Mere illegality of the strike does not per se spell unjustifiability"- Justice Krishna Iyer. Name the case.
a) Chandramalai Estate Vs. Its workmen
b) Associated Cement Ltd. Vs. Their workmen
c) Gujarat Steel Tubes Vs. Gujarat Steel Tubes Mazdoor Sabha
d) Indian General Navigation of Railway Co. Ltd. Vs. Their workmen [AIBE-XV]

Q.20 Workman aggrieved by the order of .... may directly make an application to the labour court or tribunal for adjudication of the dispute and the court/tribunal is empowered to adjudicate such dispute as it had been referred to it by the appropriate government:
a) Dismissal, discharge and retrenchment
b) Dismissal, discharge, retrenchment or otherwise termination of service
c) Discharge simpliciter exclusively
d) Dismissal and retrenchment exclusively [AIBE-XV]

Q.21 Section 2(j) of the Industrial Disputes Act 1947 defines 'Industry' as any:
i. Business trade, undertaking
ii. Manufacture or calling of employers
iii. Included any calling, service, employment, handicraft
iv. Industrial occupation of workmen
a) (i) and (ii)
b) (i), (ii) and (iii)
c) (iii) and (iv)
d) All of the above [AIBE-XIV]

Q.22 Ensuring the safety, health and welfare of the employees is the primary purpose of the:
a) Payment of wages Act 1936
b) Industrial Disputes Act 1947
c) Factories Act 1948
d) Equal Remuneration Act 1976 [AIBE-XIV]

Q.23 In which case Supreme Court held that teachers are not workmen?
a) Dharangadhara Chemical Works Ltd. Vs. State of Saurashtra AIR

1957 SC 264
b) University of Delhi Vs. Ram Nath AIR 1963 SC 1873
c) J K Cotton Spinning and Weaving Mills Co. Ltd. Vs. L.T AIR 1964 SC 737
d) Sunderambal Vs. Government of Goa AIR 1988 SC 1700
[AIBE-XIV]

Q.24 Under Section 2(cc) of the Industrial Disputes Act 1947, 'closure' means:
a) The permanent closing down of a place of employment or part thereof
b) The partly closing down of a place of employment or part thereof
c) The temporary closing down of a place of employment or part thereof
d) The short-term closing down of a place of employment or part of thereof [AIBE-XIV]

Q.25 'Industrial dispute' means any dispute or difference between:
i. Employers and employers
ii. Employers and workmen
iii. Workmen and workmen
iv. Master and worker
a) (i) and (ii)
b) (iv)
c) (i), (ii) , (iii) and (iv)
d) (i), (ii) and (iii) [AIBE-XIII]

Q.26 'industrial establishment' means:
(i) A factory
(ii) A mine
(iii) A plantation
(iv) An industry
a) (i), (ii), (iii), (iv)
b) (i), (ii), (iii)
c) (i) and (ii)
d) Only (i) [AIBE-XIII]

Q.27 Strike should be called only if at least _____ percent of workers are in support of strike. (Fill in the blank).
a) 10
b) 15
c) 20
d) 25 [AIBE-XIII]

Q.28 Industrial relations cover the following area(s):
(i) Collective bargaining
(ii) Labour legislation
(iii) Industrial relations training
(iv) Trade unions
a) (i)
b) (i) and (ii)
c) (i), (ii) and (iii)
d) (i), (ii), (ii) and (iv) [AIBE-XIII]

Q.29 Who is a protected workman?
a) Workman given police protection during labour strike
b) Workman protected by insurance coverage
c) Workman who is an executive

or office bearer of a registered trade union in the establishment
d) Workman protected from being arrested by a court order
[AIBE-XII]

Q.30 Meaning of 'Industrial Dispute' according to the Industrial Disputes Act 1947 is:
a) Dispute between employers and employers
b) Dispute between employers and workman
c) Dispute between workmen and workmen in connection with employment and non-employment
d) All of the above [AIBE-XII]

Q.31 Section 49 of Factories Act 1947 explains about:
a) Canteen
b) Crèche
c) Welfare officer
d) Rest room [AIBE-XII]

Q.32 Unfair labour practice by the employers includes:
a) Victimization
b) False implication in criminal case
c) Untrue allegations of absence without leave
d) All of the above [AIBE-XII]

Q.33 Under the Workmen's Compensation Act, which is helpful in deciding the extent of injury for compensation?
a) Insurance certificate
b) Medical examination
c) Medical certificate
d) (b) and(c) [AIBE-XI]

Q.34 Section 23 of Workmen Compensation Act 1923 says that the Commissioner shall have the power of:
a) A court
b) A Tribunal
c) A quasi-judicial forum
d) All of the above [AIBE-XI]

Q.35 The objective of the Industrial Disputes Act 1947 is:
a) Industrial peace and economic justice
b) To create harmonious relation between employer and employee
c) To prevent illegal strike or lockout etc.
d) All of the above [AIBE-XI]

Q.36 Section 2(q) of Industrial Disputes Act 1947 provides the definition of:
a) Lock out
b) Lay off
c) Strike
d) Hartal [AIBE-XI]

Q.37 Government employees may refer their unresolved grievances and labour dispute to:
a) Internal Labour Department
b) Bureau of Labour Relations

c) Public Sector Labour-Management Council
d) Department of Labour [AIBE-X]

Q.38 Who is an adolescent as per Factories Act 1948?
a) Who has completed 17 years of age
b) Who is less than 18 years of age
c) Who is more than 15 years but less than 18 years of age
d) None of these [AIBE-X]

Q.39 Who is responsible for payment to a person employed by him in a factory under the Payment of Wages Act 1936?
a) Accounts Manager
b) HR Manager
c) Floor Manager
d) Owner [AIBE-X]

Q.40 To close down a factory the occupier has to give how many days' notice to the authorities:
a) 30 days
b) 60 days
c) 90 days
d) 14 days [AIBE-X]

Q.41 Under the provisions of the Trade Unions Act 1926, any person who has attained the age of _____ may be a member of a registered trade union subject to any rules of the trade union to the contrary:
a) 14 years
b) 15 years
c) 18 years
d) 21 years [AIBE-IX]

Q.42 The provisions of _____ do not apply to trade unions registered under the provisions of Trade Union Act 1926.
a) The Co-operative Societies Act 1912
b) The Companies Act 1956
c) Both (a) and (b)
d) Neither (a) nor (b) [AIBE-IX]

Q.43 Which of the following can be considered retrenchment under the provisions of the Industrial Disputes Act 1947?
a) Termination due to ill-health
b) Abandonment of job by an employee
c) Termination on account of reaching the age of superannuation
d) None of these [AIBE-IX]

Q.44 Which of the following statements holds true regarding imprisonment under the provisions of Section 14(3) of the Child Labour (Prohibition and Regulation) Act 1986?
a) It may extend to one year
b) It may extend to two years
c) It may extend to six months
d) It may extend to one month
[AIBE-IX]

Q.45 Under the provisions of the Industrial Disputes Act 1947, the appropriate government can by order in writing:
a) Refer the dispute to a Board for promoting a settlement of the dispute
b) Refer any matter appearing to be relevant to the dispute to a Court for inquiry
c) Both (a) and (b)
d) Neither (a) nor (b) [AIBE-IX]

Q.46 Which of the following statement is true for loss of confidence by management in the workman?
a) Even when dismissal or discharge is held to be wrongful, the Court may not yet order reinstatement if the employer is able to establish that the workman held a position of trust and there was loss of confidence.
b) Loss of confidence may also be a ground for discharge simpliciter of the workman
c) Both (a) and (b)
d) Neither (a) nor (b) [AIBE-IX]

Q.47 "Mere illegality of the strike does not per se spell unjustifiability" - J. Krishna Iyer in which case declared so?
a) Chandramalai Estate Vs. Its workmen
b) Associated Cement Companies Vs. Their workmen
c) Gujarat Steel Tubes Vs. Gujarat Steel Tubes Mazdoor Sabha
d) Indian General Navigation of Railway Co. Ltd. Vs. Their workmen [AIBE-VIII]

Q.48 Pick out the case that is popularly called as the *Solicitor's case.*
a) Ahmadabad Textile Industry's Research Association Vs. State of Bombay
b) National Union of Commercial Employees Vs. Industrial Tribunal, Bombay
c) Salem Advocates Bar Association Vs. Union of India
d) Central Machine Tools Institute Vs. Dy. Registrar of Trade Unions [AIBE-VIII]

Q.49 Identify the case that is related to the need for promotion and preservation of internal democracy within trade unions:
a) Jay Engineering Works Ltd. Vs. State of West Bengal
b) Railway Union Vs. Registrar of Trade Unions
c) ONGC Workmen's Association Vs. State of West Bengal
d) Hanumantha Rao Vs. Dy. Registrar of Trade Unions [AIBE-VIII]

Q.50 Rashtriya Swasthya Bima

Yojana is mainly meant to serve the needs of:

a) Organized workers

b) Unorganized workers

c) Unorganized sector workers belonging to BPL category and their family members

d) Organized sector workers belonging to BPL category and their family members [AIBE-VII]

Q.51 Equal pay for equal work for both men and women is proclaimed under …………… of the Constitution of India.

a) Art.39(a)

b) Art.39(d)

c) Art.39(b)

d) Art.39(c) [AIBE-VII]

Q.52 Where any workman is suspended by the employer pending investigation or inquiry into complaints or charges of misconduct against him, the employer shall pay to such workman subsistence allowance. This provision was inserted in the Industrial Employment (Standing Orders) Act 1946 in which year?

a) 1992

b) 1982

c) 2009

d) 2010 [AIBE-VII]

Q.53 ………………………… was a leading case on the point as to whether an employer has a right to deduct wages unilaterally and without holding an enquiry for the period the employees go on strike or resort to go slow.

a) Bank of India Vs. T S Kelawala and Ors.

b) Randhir Singh Vs. Union of India

c) Kamani Metals and Alloys Ltd. Vs. Their workmen

d) Workmen Vs. Reptakos Brett and Co. Ltd. [AIBE-VII]

Q.54 Under the Industrial disputes Act, if the employer terminates the services of an individual workman, any dispute / difference arising out of such termination shall be deemed to be:

a) Industrial dispute

b) Individual dispute

c) Both individual and industrial dispute

d) None of these [AIBE-VII]

Q.55 The Sampoorna Grameen Rozgar Yojana (Universal Rural Employment Programme) was launched in 2001 and was implemented through:

a) Labour offices

b) Government

c) Panchayati Raj Institutions

d) All of the above [AIBE-VII]

Q.56 The provision under the

Industrial Disputes Act 1947, which guarantees the right of workmen laid off to claim for compensation:
a) S.25C
b) S.26
c) S.25O
d) S.25A [AIBE-VI]

Q.57 The number of persons required to form trade union:
a) 6
b) 7
c) 8
d) 9 [AIBE-VI]

Q.58 The temporary closing of the work place or suspension of the work at work place by the employer is known as:
a) Lay off
b) Lock out
c) Retrenchment
d) None of the above [AIBE-VI]

Q.59 Which of the following acts has a direct relevance for grievance handling practices?
a) The Industrial Disputes Act
b) Factories Act
c) The Industrial Employment (Standing Order) Act
d) All of the above [AIBE-VI]

Q.60 Section 10A of the Industrial disputes Act refers to:
a) Voluntary reference of disputes to arbitration
b) Definition of workman
c) Definition of industry
d) Appeals [AIBE-VI]

Q.61 'Wages' under Workmen's Compensation Act:
a) Includes any privilege or benefit which is capable of being estimated in money
b) Does not include any privilege or benefit which is capable of being estimated in money
c) Includes any privilege or benefit which is not capable of being estimated in money
d) None of the above [AIBE-VI]

Q.62 "Contravention of Contract Labour Act would not create employment relationship between contract labour and principal establishment." It was so held in which case?
a) SAIL Vs. National Union Waterfront Workers
b) Air India Statutory Corporation Vs. United Labour Union & Ors.
c) Bangalore Water Supply and Sewerage Board Vs. R Rajappa
d) State of U. P. Vs. Jai Bir Singh [AIBE-V]

Q.63 The Principal regulator envisaged under the Trade Unions Act 1926:
a) Regulator of trade unions
b) Inspector of trade unions

c) Registrar of trade unions
d) Industrial relations committee
[AIBE-V]

Q.64 A teacher is not a workman falling under the category of workman under Industrial Disputes Act 1947. This was upheld in which case?
a) Miss A Sundarambal Vs. Government of Goa, Daman & Diu & Ors.
b) Ahmedabad Pvt. Primary Teachers' Assn. Vs. Administrative Officer
c) University of Delhi Vs. Ram Nath
d) Secretary, Madras Gymkhana Club Employees Union Vs. Management [AIBE-V]

Q.65 The type of disablement envisaged under the Employees Compensation Act that reduces the capacity to work in any employment similar to that the worker was performing at the time of the accident is referred to as:
a) Permanent partial disablement
b) Permanent total disablement
c) Temporary disablement
d) Temporary total disablement
[AIBE-V]

Q.66 The contribution payable under the ESI Act in respect of an employee shall comprise of:
a) Contribution payable by the employer only
b) Contribution payable by the employee only
c) Contribution payable by government only
d) Contribution payable by employer and employee
[AIBE-V]

Q.67 Which provision under the Industrial Disputes Act 1947 guarantees the right of workmen laid off to claim for compensation?
a) S.25O
b) S.26
c) S.25C
d) S.25M [AIBE-V]

Q.68 The term '*Lock-out*' under the Industrial Disputes Act defined in:
a) Section 2(i)
b) Section 2(o)
c) Section 3(1)
d) Section 2(m) [AIBE-IV]

Q.69 The term '*Lay-off*' has been defined under the Industrial Disputes Act:
a) Sec 2(kkk)
b) Sec 2(o)
c) Sec 2(i)
d) Sec 3(1) [AIBE-IV]

Q.70 The Trade Union Act was enacted:

a) 1926
b) 1946
c) 1947
d) 1988 [AIBE-IV]

Q.71 The term *'Minimum Wage'* has been described in:
a) The Trade Union Act
b) The Industrial Disputes Act
c) The Minimum Wage Act
d) None of the above [AIBE-IV]

Q.72 The Minimum Wages Act was enacted:
a) 1921
b) 1923
c) 1947
d) 2007 [AIBE-IV]

Q.73 The Trade Union Act provides for:
a) Registration of trade union
b) Registration of trade union for workers
c) Recognition of registration of trade union as Juristic Persons
d) All of the above [AIBE-IV]

TOPIC 10: LAW RELATED TO TAXATION

(4 questions are, generally, asked from this subject)

Q.1 The term "Income" is described in the Income Tax Act, 1961 under.......

(A) Section 2 (24)

(B) Section 2 (40)

(C) Section 3

(D) Section 10E [AIBE-XIX]

Q.2 Mr. X deposits ₹65,000 in the term deposit of 5 years with the Post Office to avail tax deduction under section 80C. Assuming Mr. X does not opt for concessional tax regime u/s 115BAC of the Income Tax Act, 1961.

On the basis of the above problem, select the correct option:

(A) Mr. X is guilty of tax evasion / tax avoidance.

(B) Mr. X is not guilty of either tax evasion / tax avoidance.

(C) No tax deduction can be availed under Section 80 C.

(D) It is an unlawful act to treat a personal expenditure. [AIBE-XIX]

Q.3 Read the given statements and choose the correct option:

Statement 1: Agricultural income is exempt from tax under Section 10(1) of Income Tax Act, 1961.

Statement 2: Tax on Non-Agricultural in case of Non-Agricultural Income exceeds Basic Exemption limit and Agricultural Income exceeds ₹5,000 is determined by Scheme of Partial Integration of Non-Agricultural Income with Agricultural Income.

(A) Both the Statements are incorrect.

(B) Only Statement 1 is true.

(C) Only Statement 2 is true.

(D) Both the Statements are correct. [AIBE-XIX]

Q.4 Rent-Free Accommodation provided by an employer to employee is

(A) Perquisite as per Section 17 (2) of the Income Tax Act

(B) Perquisite as per Section 16 (2) of the Income Tax Act

(C) Allowance under Section 10 (13A) of the Income Tax Act

(D) Allowance under Section 10 (1) of the Income Tax Act [AIBE-XIX]

Q.5 Which of the following provisions of the Constitution of India states that no tax can be levied or collected except by authority of law?

a) Article 246

b) Article 256

c) Article 260

d) Article 265 [AIBE-XVIII]

Q.6 Which of the following would be the first previous year in case of a business of profession newly set up on 31st March, 2020 as per the Income Tax Act, 1961?

a) Start from 1st April, 2019 and will end on 31st March, 2020

b) Start from 31st March, 2020 and will end on 31st March, 2020

c) Start from 1st April, 2020 and will end on 31st December, 2020

d) Start from 1st January, 2020 and will end on 31st March, 2020

[AIBE-XVIII]

Q.7 As per the Income Tax Act, 1961 a person is said to be resident of India in any previous year if he had been in India for a period of the following number of days in the previous year:

a) 180 days

b) 182 days

c) 184 days

d) 186 days [AIBE-XVIII]

Q.8 Income is defined under which of the following provisions of the Income Tax Act, 1961?

a) Section 2(31)

b) Section 2(24)

c) Section 2(9)

d) Section 3 [AIBE-XVIII]

Q.9 For an individual to be deemed to be resident in India in any previous year, one of the conditions is:

a) **If he is in India for a period of 182 days or more during the previous year.**

b) If he is in India for a period of 180 days or more during the previous year.

c) If he is in India for a period of 181 days or more during the previous year.

d) If he is in India for a period of 360 days or more during the previous year. [AIBE-XVII]

Q.10 Mr. Kapoor purchased a residential house in January 2021 for ₹80,00,000. He sold the house in April 2022 for ₹94,00,000. In this case, the gain of ₹14,00,000 arising on account of the sale of residential house will be charged to tax under which of the following head?

a) **Income from capital gains**

b) Income from house property

c) Income from profits and gains from business or profession

d) Income from other sources

[AIBE-XVII]

Q.11 Mr. Manjot is a trader supplying goods from his M/s Singh Traders. The office of the firm is located in Delhi, whereas its godowns are located in the state of Uttar Pradesh, Punjab and Jammu & Kashmir respectively. M/s Singh

Traders made following intra-state supplies from different states during the current financial year:
Delhi - Taxable supplies ₹21,00,000
Punjab - Exempted supplies ₹6,00,000
Uttar Pradesh - Taxable and Exempted supplies ₹3,00,000 each respectively
J&K - Taxable and exempted supplies ₹8,00,000 and ₹3,00,000 respectively

Ascertain the States in which Mr. Manjot is required to take registration under GST:
a) Delhi, Punjab, Uttar Pradesh and J&K
b) **Delhi, Uttar Pradesh and J&K**
c) Delhi and Uttar Pradesh
d) Delhi [AIBE-XVII]

Q.12 The primary GST slabs for any regular taxpayers are presently pegged at:
a) 0%, 5%, 12%, 18%, 26%
b) 0%, 6%, 12%, 18%, 28%
c) **0%, 5%, 12%, 18%, 28%**
d) 0%, 5%, 12%, 16%, 28%
[AIBE-XVII]

Q.13 Health and Education Cess is applicable to:
a) **All assesses**
b) All assesses except company
c) Individual/HUF
d) Company only [AIBE-XVI]

Q.14 Rate of additional depreciation will be _____ under section 32 of Indian Income Tax Act.
a) 10 %
b) **20 %**
c) 15 %
d) 30 % [AIBE-XVI]

Q.15 Amount of deduction under section 24 of the Income Tax Act from annual value is:
a) ½ of annual value
b) 1/3 of annual value
c) **3/10 of annual value**
d) 17/10 of annual value
[AIBE-XVI]

Q.16 A company which is not a domestic company will pay income tax at the rate of:
a) 25%
b) 30%
c) **40%**
d) 20% [AIBE-XVI]

Q.17 The definition of 'money' under GST law does not include:
a) Letter of Credit
b) Currency held for numismatic value
c) Pay order
d) Traveler cheque [AIBE-XV]

Q.18 Under Article 279A, GST Council is constituted by:
a) Prime Minister and his Council of Ministers

b) Respective Governors of the State

c) The President

d) A collective body of Union and States [AIBE-XV]

Q.19 According to Income Tax Act 'zero coupon bond' means a bond:

a) Issued by any infrastructure capital company or infrastructure capital fund or public sector company or scheduled bank on or after the 1st day of June, 2005

b) In respect of which no payment and benefit is received or receivable before maturity or redemption from infrastructure capital company or infrastructure capital fund or public sector company or scheduled bank

c) Which the Central Government may, by notification in the Official Gazette, specify in this behalf

d) All of the above [AIBE-XV]

Q.20 Provisions relating to GST are inserted in the Constitution by:

a) The Constitution (One Hundred and First Amendment) Act 2016

b) The Constitution (One Hundred and Second Amendment) Act 2016

c) The Constitution (Eighty Fourth Amendment) Act 2016

d) The Constitution (Seventy Seventh Amendment) Act 2016

[AIBE-XV]

Q.21 For the first time in India, Income Tax was introduced by Sir James Wilson in the year:

a) 1886

b) 1868

c) 1860

d) None of the above [AIBE-XIV]

Q.22 In which case Justice J C Shah of SC observed "Since by the exercise of the power a serious invasion is made upon the rights, privacy and freedom of the tax payer, the power must be exercised strictly in accordance with law and only for the purpose for which law authorizes it to be exercised."?

a) Director of Inspection Vs. Pooran Mal

b) ITO Vs. Seth Brothers

c) P R Metrani Vs. CIT

d) None of the above [AIBE-XIV]

Q.23 The principle of Law of Taxation that "No tax shall be levied or collected except by authority of law" - is contained under:

a) Article 265 of the Constitution

b) Article 300 of the Constitution

c) Article 19(1)(g) of the Constitution

d) Article 285 of the Constitution

[AIBE-XIV]

Q.24 Under which section of Income Tax Act, income of other

persons is included in assessee's total income?
a) Sections 56-58
b) Sections 139-147
c) Section 246-262
d) Section 60-65 [AIBE-XIV]

Q.25 Under which section of Income tax Act 1961 'Income of other persons' included in Assessee's total income?
a) 56-58
b) 60-65
c) 45-54
d) All of the above [AIBE-XIII]

Q.26 A period of 12 months commencing on the 1st day of April of every year is known as:
a) Assessment year
b) Leap year
c) Previous year
d) None [AIBE-XIII]

Q.27 Adam Smith has enumerated cannons of taxation which are accepted universally. They are:
a) Equality and Certainty
b) Equality, Convenience and Economy
c) Equality and Economy
d) Equality, Certainty, Convenience and Economy
[AIBE-XIII]

Q.28 For the first time in India, Income Tax law was introduced by Sir James Wilson in the year:
a) 1886
b) 1868
c) 1860
d) None of the above [AIBE-XIII]

Q.29 Permanent Account Number (PAN) is defined under:
a) Wealth Tax
b) GST
c) Income Tax Act 1961
d) Finance Act 1992 [AIBE-XII]

Q.30 Section 29 of the Wealth Tax Act deals with:
a) Revision petition in division bench of High Court
b) Appeal in Supreme Court
c) Return of wealth tax
d) None of the above [AIBE-XII]

Q.31 GST came into force from:
a) 1st January 2017
b) 1st April 2017
c) 1st July 2017
d) 1st August 2017 [AIBE-XII]

Q.32 Section 154 under IT Act is:
a) For filing return of income
b) For filing return with late fee
c) Rectification of mistakes
d) Appeal against the order passed by the ITO [AIBE-XI]

Q.33 Which of the following is not included in the Capital Asset under Section 2(14) of Income Tax Act?

a) Any stock in Trade
b) Special Bearer Bonds 1991 issued by Central Government
c) (a) and (b)
d) None of the above [AIBE-XI]

Q.34 Income Tax Act was enacted in:
a) 1951
b) 1961
c) 1971
d) None of the above [AIBE-XI]

Q.35 'Income' is defined under Section 24 of the Income Tax Act as:
a) Profits and gains
b) Dividend
c) Voluntary contribution received by a Trust for charitable purpose
d) All of the above [AIBE-XI]

Q.36 In case of a cooperative society, the maximum amount on which income tax is not chargeable is:
a) 50,000
b) 30,000
c) 20,000
d) Nil [AIBE-X]

Q.37 An appeal to the High Court against the order of ITAT should be filed within:
a) 45 days when the order is communicated
b) 60 days when the order is communicated
c) 90 days when the order is communicated
d) 120 days when the order is communicated [AIBE-X]

Q.38 Indian Computer Emergency Response Team to serve as National Agency for incident response is constituted under Section:
a) 71 of IT Act
b) 70 of IT Act
c) 70(a) of IT Act
d) 70(b) of IT Act [AIBE-X]

Q.39 Incomes which accrue or arise outside India but are directly received into India are taxable in case of:
a) Residents only
b) Both ordinarily residents and non-resident
c) Non-resident
d) All the assessee [AIBE-X]

Q.40 Which of the following belong to the category of direct tax?
a) Goods and Services Tax
b) Excise Duty and Customs Duty
c) Income Tax and Gift Tax
d) All of the above [AIBE-X]

TOPIC 11: PROFESSIONAL ETHICS AND CASES OF PROFESSIONAL MISCONDUCT UNDER BCI RULES

(4 questions are, generally, asked from this subject)

Q.1 What does "conflict of interest " refer to in professional ethics ?
(A) A situation involving legal disputes
(B) A situation where two professionals disagree
(C) A conflict between ethics and laws
(D) A situation where personal interests conflict with professional duties [AIBE-XIX]

Q.2 Advocate Mr. X was representing a client, Mr. Y, in a property dispute case. During the proceedings, Advocate Mr. X accepted a bribe from the opposing party to delay the case, causing significant harm to Mr. Y's interests. Moreover, Mr. X failed to inform his client about critical hearing dates, leading to adverse judgments. On the basis of the above problem, select the correct option:
(A) It is a violation of Rules made by the Bar Council of India for the professional ethics
(B) It is only an offence under the Prevention of Corruption Act, 2018
(C) It amounts to criminal conspiracy under the Bhartiya Nyaya Sanhita, 2023 (D) It amounts to the Contempt of Court under the Contempt of Courts Act, 1971
[AIBE-XIX]

Q.3 The nature of proceedings in the cases of professional misconduct:
(1) Criminal in nature (2) Neither civil nor criminal
(3) Quasi-criminal in nature (4) Civil in nature

(A) Both (1) and (4)
(B) Only (2)
(C) Only (3)
(D) (1), (3) and (4) [AIBE-XIX]

Q.4 Appropriate procedural safeguards help reduce threats to objectivity and counter any perception of possible bias, which of the following is/are not procedural safeguard/s ?
(1) Act in a fraudulent manner
(2) Providing peer-review of valuation, if necessary
(3) Non-Disclosure of any prior association with the client
(4) Non-Disclosure of any possible source of conflict of interest

(A) (3) and (4)
(B) Only (2)

(C) Only (4)
(D) (2) and (4) [AIBE-XIX]

Q.5 What penalty is prescribed for persons illegally practicing in court under the Advocate Act, 1961?
a) Imprisonment up to 3 months
b) Imprisonment up to 6 months
c) Imprisonment up to 9 months
d) Imprisonment up to 12 months [AIBE-XVIII]

Q.6 Which provision of the Advocate Act, 1961 empowers the Bar Council of India to prescribe the standard of professional conduct and etiquette to be observed by advocates?
a) Section 42
b) Section 42A
c) Section 48A
d) Section 49 [AIBE-XVIII]

Q.7 Which of the following is incorrect according to the Bar Council of India rules?
a) An advocate can plead in any matter in which he himself is pecuniarily interested.
b) An advocate shall appear in court at all times only in the prescribed dress.
c) An advocate shall not stand as a surety for his client.
d) An advocate shall not influence the decision of a court by any improper means. [AIBE-XVIII]

Q.8 Which of the following authority acts as an appellate authority against the order made by the Disciplinary Committee of the Bar Council of India?
a) Chairman of the Bar Council of India
b) Vice-chairman of the Bar Council of India
c) High courts
d) Supreme Court of India [AIBE-XVIII]

Q.9 Rules are made by the Bar Council of India in exercising its rule making power under:
a) The Advocates Act, 1951
b) The Advocates Act, 1954
c) **The Advocates Act, 1961**
d) The Advocates Act, 1964 [AIBE-XVII]

Q.10 An advocate may, while practicing, take up teaching of Law in any educational institution which is affiliated to a university, so long as the hours during which he is so engaged in the teaching of Law do not exceed ____ hours in a day.
a) 5
b) **3**
c) 2
d) 4 [AIBE-XVII]

Q.11 In which of the following landmark cases, the Advocate was held guilty of professional

misconduct as he had forged the court order?
a) **Pratap Narain Vs Y.P. Raheja**
b) Vikramaditya Vs Jamila Khatoon
c) Babulal Jain Vs Subhash Jain
d) P. Pankajam Vs B.H. Chandrashekhar [AIBE-XVII]

Q.12 If any advocate is aggrieved by an order of the Disciplinary Committee of the State Bar Council made under section 35 of the Advocate Act or Advocate General of the State, may prefer an appeal to the Bar Council of India within ___ days of the date of communication of order.
a) 30
b) 45
c) **60**
d) 90 [AIBE-XVII]

Q.13 Advocates Act, 1961 came into force on:
a) **19th May 1961**
b) 19th April 1961
c) 1st May 1961
d) 19th January 1961 [AIBE-XVI]

Q.14 Punishment of advocates for misconduct has been given under section ___ of the Advocates Act, 1961:
a) 30
b) 32
c) **35**
d) None [AIBE-XVI]

Q.15 An advocate is under an obligation to uphold the rule of law and ensure that the public justice system is enabled to function at its full potential. Any violation of the principle of professional ethics by an advocate is unfortunate and unacceptable. Ignoring even minor violation/ misconduct militates against the fundamental foundation of the public justice system. It was said in:
a) Hikmant Ali Khan Vs Ishwar Prasad Arya, 1997 3 SCC 131
b) **O. P. Sharma Vs High Court of Punjab and Haryana (2011) 6 SCC 86**
c) L. D. Jaikwal Vs State of Uttar Pradesh, (1984) 3 SCC 405
d) Shamsher Singh Bedi Vs High Court of Punjab and Haryana, (1996) 7 SCC 99 [AIBE-XVI]

Q.16 The maximum limit of the members of the State Bar Council is:
a) 15
b) 20
c) **25**
d) None [AIBE-XVI]

Q.17 The Bar Council of India has to lay down the standards of professional conduct and etiquette for the Advocates under:
a) Section 3 of the Advocates Act

1961
b) Section 7(1)(b) of the Advocates Act 1961
c) Section 17 of the Advocates Act 1961
d) Section 18 of the Advocates Act 1961 [AIBE-XV]

Q.18 According to Section 49 of the Advocates Act of 1961, the Bar Council of India has power to make rules:
a) Qualifications for membership of a Bar Council and the disqualifications for such membership
b) The class or category of persons entitled to be enrolled as advocates
c) The standards of legal education to be observed by universities in India and the inspection of universities for that purpose.
d) All of the above [AIBE-XV]

Q.19 Among other things, the function of Bar Council of India includes laying down standards of professional conduct and etiquette for advocates -under which section of the Advocates Act?
a) Section 7
b) Section 8
c) Section 9
d) Section 6 [AIBE-XV]

Q.20 According to Justice 'Abbot Parry', what are the 'Seven Lamps of Advocacy'?
a) (i)Honesty (ii)Courage (iii)Professionalism (iv)Wit (v)Eloquence (vi)Judgment and (vii)Fellowship
b) (i)Honesty (ii)Courage (iii)Industry (iv)Wit (v)Eloquence (vi)Judgment and (vii)Fellowship
c) (i)Influence (ii)Courage (iii)Industry (iv)Wit (v)Eloquence (vi)Judgment and (vii)Fellowship
d) (i)Honesty (ii)Courage (iii)Industry (iv)Seriousness (v)Eloquence (vi)Judgment and (vii)Fellowship [AIBE-XV]

Q.21 Which of the following can be done by a Senior Advocate in accordance with the Rules of Bar Council of India?
a) Make concessions on behalf of client on instructions from junior advocate
b) Accept instructions to draft a pleading
c) Accept brief directly from a client
d) None of the above [AIBE-XIV]

Q.22 Which of the following is not a duty of an Advocate to Court?
a) To not commit breach of Section 126 of Evidence Act
b) To not to appear on behalf of any organization of whose Executive
Committee he is a member

c) To not appear before a Court, Tribunal or Authority in which his near relation is a member
d) To conduct himself with dignity and self-respect during presentation of a case before a Court and otherwise acting before a Court [AIBE-XIV]

Q.23 Which of the following rules of Chapter II of Part VI of the Bar Council Rules deal with the duty of an Advocate in respect of any moneys received by him from Client?
a) Rule 25
b) Rule 33
c) Rule 24
d) None of the above [AIBE-XIV]

Q.24 Which of the following provisions of the Advocates Act 1961 provides for the power of Bar Council of India to withdraw to itself, any proceedings for disciplinary action pending before any State Bar Council?
a) Section 35
b) Section 37
c) Section 36(2)
d) None of the above [AIBE-XIV]

Q.25 Disciplinary Committee of Bar Council is conferred the powers of Civil Court under Code of Civil Procedure, 1908 by:
a) Section 36 of Advocates Act 1961
b) Section 42 of Advocates Act 1961
c) Section 42A of Advocates Act 1961
d) Section 28 of Advocates Act 1961 [AIBE-XIII]

Q.26 The designation 'Senior Advocates' is provided under:
a) Section 16; Advocates Act 1961
b) Section 26; Advocates Act 1961
c) Section 6; Advocates Act 1961
d) Section 15; Advocates Act 1961 [AIBE-XIII]

Q.27 Right to pre-audience is provided by:
a) Section 33 of Advocates Act 1961
b) Section 23 of Advocates Act 1961
c) Section 16 of Advocates Act 1961
d) Section 36 of Advocates Act 1961 [AIBE-XIII]

Q.28 The 'Contempt of Court' belongs to:
a) Entry 77 of Union list and entry 14 of State list in the VIIth schedule of Constitution of India
b) Entry 70 of Union list and entry 40 of State list
c) Entry 67 of Union list and entry 13 of State list
d) None of these [AIBE-XIII]

Q.29 Section 24A of Advocates Act 1961 provides the:
a) Appointment of Attorney General
b) Regular attendance at Law College
c) **Admitted for enrolment in Bar or State Roll**
d) Election to State Bar Council
[AIBE-XII]

Q.30 Punishment for Advocates for misconduct is defined in Advocates Act 1961 by:
a) Section 25
b) Section 33
c) Section 35
d) None of the above [AIBE-XII]

Q.31 Which is the body that award punishments to the advocates for misconduct?
a) Ethics Committee
b) Professional Development Committee
c) Disciplinary Committee
d) High Court [AIBE-XII]

Q.32 Which is the correct statement with regard to the professional ethics of a lawyer?
a) Lawyers have no right to go on strike or give a call for boycott.
b) An advocate shall not influence the decision of a court by any illegal or improper means.
c) An advocate abusing the process of the court is guilty and misconduct.
d) All of the above [AIBE-XII]

Q.33 What is the punishment for advocates if the established finding of the Bar Council is misappropriation?
a) Impose a fine
b) Name of the advocate will be struck off from the rolls
c) Suspension from practice
d) All of the above [AIBE-XI]

Q.34 On being aggrieved by the order of State Bar Council, one can appeal to:
a) High Court
b) Supreme Court
c) Bar Council of India
d) Indian Law Commission
[AIBE-XI]

Q.35 Section 24 of Advocates Act deals with:
a) Qualification of advocates who should be enrolled in the Bar
b) Qualification to become the Advocate General
c) Qualification to become the Solicitor General of India
d) (b) and (c) [AIBE-XI]

Q.36 In which case did the Supreme Court hold that

'misconduct envisages breach of discipline'?
a) P D Gupta Vs. Ram Murti
b) Noratanmal Chourasia Vs. M R Murli
c) P J Ratnam Vs. D Kanikaram
d) None of the above [AIBE-X]

Q.37 Vikramaditya Vs. Smt. Jamila Khatoon is an important case relating to professional misconduct due to which factor?
a) Advocate attending the court with fire arms
b) Not appearing before the court deliberately and intentionally
c) Suppression of material facts with intention to harass poor persons
d) Defrauding the client by exploiting the client's illiteracy
[AIBE-X]

Q.38 Which of the following case is leading case in term of deliberate delay in filing of the suit resulting in huge losses to the complainant?
a) Prof. Krishanraj Goswami Vs. Vishwanath D Mukashikar
b) Pratap Narain Vs. Y P Raheja
c) Babulal Jain Vs. Subhash Jain
d) John D'Souza Vs. Edward Ani
[AIBE-X]

Q.39 Any person aggrieved by an order made by the Disciplinary Committee of the Bar Council of India u/s. 36 or 37 of the Advocates Act may prefer an appeal to the:
a) High Court
b) Supreme Court
c) State Government
d) Central Government [AIBE-X]

Q.40 State Bar Council under the provisions of Section 35 of the Advocates 1961 has the authority to:
a) Reprimand the advocate
b) Suspend the advocate from practice for such period of time as it may deem fit
c) Remove the name of the Advocate from the State Roll of Advocates
d) All of these [AIBE-IX]

Q.41 Which of the following is untrue regarding qualification for a person to be admitted on the State Rolls maintained by State Bar Councils?
a) The minimum age of requirement is 21 years
b) He must be an Indian Citizen
c) He must not have been convicted of an offence involving moral turpitude
d) He must not have been convicted of an offence under the provisions of the Untouchability (Offences) Act 1958 [AIBE-IX]

Q.42 The Bar Council of India rule which stipulated that persons aged 45 years and above could not be enrolled as advocates was struck down by the Supreme Court in:
a) E S Reddi Vs. Bar Council of India
b) Indian Council of Legal Aid and Advice Vs. Bar Council of India
c) P Shanmugam Vs. Bar Council of India
d) Legal Committee Vs. Bar Council or India [AIBE-IX]

Q.43 The Supreme Court held in VC Rangadurai Vs. D Gopalan - An advocate who has been disbarred or suspended from practice must prove after expiration of a reasonable length of time that:
a) He appreciates the insignificance of his dereliction
b) He has lived a consistent life or poverty and integrity
c) He possesses the good character necessary to guarantee uprightness and honour in his professional dealings
d) The burden is on the applicant to establish that he is entitled to resume the privilege of practicing law without restrictions [AIBE-IX]

Q.44 In which famous case, this issue had come up - whether the advocate had committed a professional misconduct and is guilty of the offence of the criminal contempt of the Court for having interfered with and obstructed the course of justice by trying to threaten, overawe and overbear the Court by using insulting, disrespectful and threatening language?
a) Vinay Chandra Mishra, In Re:
b) Ex-Capt. Harish Uppal Vs. Union of India
c) Hikmat Ali Khan Vs. Ishwar Prasad Arya and Ors.
d) None of the above [AIBE-VIII]

Q.45 'Misconduct' would cover any activity or conduct which his professional brethren of good repute and competency would reasonably regard as disgraceful or dishonourable. It may be noted that the scope of 'misconduct' is not restricted by technical interpretations of rules of conduct. This was proven conclusively in the case of:
a) Noratanmal Chaurasia Vs. M R Murli
b) Bar Council of Maharashtra Vs. M V Dahbolkar
c) N G Dastane Vs. Shrikant S Shinde
d) B M Verma Vs. Uttarakhand Electricity Regulatory Commission [AIBE-VIII]

Q.46 Retention of money deposited with advocate for the decree holder even after execution proceedings was held as an instance of misconduct in which case?

a) D C Saxena Vs. Hon'ble Chief Justice of India

b) M Veerbhadra Rao Vs. Tek Chand

c) Shambhu Ram Yadav Vs. Hanuman Das Khatry

d) Prahlad Saran Gupta Vs. Bar Council of India [AIBE-VIII]

Q.47 In which case, where the advocate of one of the parties was asking for continuous adjournments to the immense inconvenience of the opposite party, it was held by the Supreme Court that seeking adjournments for postponing the examination of witnesses who were present without making other arrangements for examining such witnesses is a dereliction of the duty that an advocate owed to the Court amounting to misconduct?

a) N G Dastane Vs. Shrikant S Shinde

b) Sambhu Ram Yadav Vs. Hanuman Das Khatry

c) Noratanmal Chaurasia Vs. M R Murli

d) None of the above [AIBE-VIII]

Q.48 General power of the Bar Council of India to make rules is envisaged under which section of the Advocates Act 1961:

a) S.48

b) S.49

c) S.II-2

d) S.IVA [AIBE-VII]

Q.49 *Seven Lamps of Advocacy* is attributable to:

a) Justice Abbot Parry

b) Justice Heward

c) Justice Bhagwati

d) Justice Grey [AIBE-VII]

Q.50 Which section under the Advocates Act, 1961 speaks of disciplinary powers of the Bar Council of India?

a) 35

b) 37

c) 36

d) 39 [AIBE-VII]

Q.51 S..... of Advocates Act 1961 speaks about Constitution of Legal Aid Committees.

a) 9

b) 10

c) 9A

d) 10A [AIBE-VII]

Q.52 Who has the authority to prescribe qualifications and disqualifications for membership of a Bar Council?

a) State Bar Councils

b) Bar Council of India

c) Supreme Court of India
d) Supreme Court Bar Association
[AIBE-VI]

Q.53 Indian Council of Legal Aid and Advice Vs. BCI case deals with the issue of:
a) Prescribing pre-enrolment training for advocates
b) Prescribing minimum qualification for an advocate
c) Prescribing uniform attire for the advocates appearing in the court of law
d) Prescribing age bar on enrollment of advocates
[AIBE-VI]

Q.54 For transfer of roll from one state to another, an application is made to the:
a) Bar Council of India
b) State Bar Council where one is enrolled
c) State Bar Council where one seeks transfer
d) High Court of the state where one is enrolled [AIBE-VI]

Q.55 Which of the following committees cannot be constituted by State Bar Council?
a) Special Committee
b) Disciplinary Committee
c) Legal Aid Committee
d) Legal Education Committee
[AIBE-VI]

Q.56 "The fundamental aim of Legal Ethics is to maintain the honour and dignity of the Law Profession, to secure a spirit of friendly co-operation between the Bench and the Bar in the promotion of highest standards of justice, to establish honourable and fair dealings of the counsel with his client opponent and witnesses; to establish a spirit of brotherhood in the Bar itself; and to secure that lawyers discharge their responsibilities to the community generally." Whose statement is this?
a) Chief Justice Marshall
b) Chief Justice Coke
c) Chief Justice Halsbury
d) Chief Justice Bacon [AIBE-V]

Q.57 The Supreme Court has held that an advocate cannot claim a lien over a litigation file entrusted to him for his fees. No professional can be given the right to withhold the returnable records relating to the work done by him with his clients matter on the strength of any claim for unpaid remuneration. The alternative is the professional concerned can resort to other legal remedies for such unpaid remuneration. Refer to the specific case:
a) R D Saxena Vs. Balram Prasad Sharma

b) V C Rangadurai Vs. D Gopalan
c) Emperor Vs. Dadu Rama
d) G Naranswamy Vs. Challapalli [AIBE-V]

Q.58 Duty of an advocate towards his client is detailed out in which rules of Bar Council of India?
a) 33 to 38
b) 11 to 33
c) 23 to 27
d) 33 to 36 [AIBE-V]

Q.59 Which section under the Advocates Act 1961 deals with disqualification as to enrolment?
a) S.25A
b) S.26A
c) S.27A
d) S.24A [AIBE-V]

Q.60 When was the Advocates Act introduced?
a) 1962
b) 1959
c) 1961
d) 1966 [AIBE-IV]

Q.61 The Bar Council of India consists of following as ex-officio member:
a) Attorney General of India
b) Solicitor General of India
c) Both (a) & (b)
d) None of the above [AIBE-IV]

Q.62 Indian Bar Committee was constituted first time under the chairmanship of Sir Edward Chamier in the year:
a) 1927
b) 1961
c) 1949
d) 1923 [AIBE-IV]

Q.63 Power of Disciplinary Committee under the Advocates Act is provided under:
a) Section 42
b) Section 53
c) Section 40
d) Section 36 [AIBE-IV]

TOPIC 12: PUBLIC INTEREST LITIGATION

(4 questions are, generally, asked from this subject)

Q.1 In which case a prison inmate sent a letter to the Supreme Court, describing physical torture, which became a pioneer in public interest litigation, though the court later abandoned the practice of considering letters ?

(A) Hussainara Khatoon vs. Bihar case

(B) Sunil Batra vs. Delhi Administration

(C) Mukti Morcha vs. Union of India

(D) The Narasimha Rao case

[AIBE-XIX]

Q.2 In the early 1980s, a social activist group discovered severe exploitation of labourers working in stone quarries near Delhi. The workers, including many children, were working in extremely hazardous conditions, living in makeshift shelters, and were effectively trapped in a cycle of debt and forced labour. The conditions revealed systematic violations of fundamental human rights. The Supreme Court was approached to look into the dire circumstances of the working persons there and one of the following views of the Court was sustained in the said case, identify from the following:

(A) The Court established that the right to free legal aid is a mere directive principle and cannot be enforced as a fundamental right.

(B) The judgment primarily focused on providing monetary compensation to the affected labourers without addressing systemic issues of bonded labour.

(C) The Supreme Court recognized the right against forced labour as a fundamental right derived from the right to life and human dignity under Article 21.

(D) The Court ruled that only government agencies, and not social activists, could file petitions concerning labour rights.

[AIBE-XIX]

Q.3 Read the given statements and choose the correct option.

Statement 1: In PIL cases, the Court plays a passive role similar to traditional cases.

Statement 2: PIL is primarily focused on individual disputes.

(A) Both statements are true.

(B) Only Statement 1 is true.

(C) Only Statement 2 is true.

(D) Both statements are false.

[AIBE-XIX]

Q.4 Given below are two statements, one labelled as Assertion (A) and the other labelled as Reason (R).

Assertion (A): The concept of "locus standi" is relaxed in PIL cases.

Reason (R): PIL allows any public-spirited person to approach the court on behalf of those who cannot represent themselves.

In the context of the above two statements, which one of the following is correct ?

(A) Both (A) and (R) are true, and (R) is the correct explanation of (A).

(B) Both (A) and (R) are true, but (R) is not the correct explanation of (A).

(C) (A) is true, but (R) is false.

(D) (A) is false, and (R) is true.

[AIBE-XIX]

Q.5 Which of the following cases may be considered as the first reported case of PIL in India?

a) S.P. Gupta v Union of India

b) Hussainara Khatoon v State of Bihar

c) M.C. Mehta v Union of India

d) Kalyaneshwari v Union of India

[AIBE-XVIII]

Q.6 Which among the following is considered as the father of PIL in India?

a) Justice S.R. Das

b) Justice V.R. Krishna Iyer

c) Justice P.N. Bhagwati

d) Justice HR Khanna

[AIBE-XVIII]

Q.7 Against which of the following a PIL cannot be filed?

a) Against a State Government

b) Against Central Government

c) Against a private party

d) Against Municipal Corporation

[AIBE-XVIII]

Q.8 In the light of the guidelines issued by the Supreme Court of India, on which of the following issues a PIL cannot be entertained by the Court?

a) Bonded labour matters

b) Petition from jail for premature release

c) Matters pertaining to neglected children

d) Petitions against police for refusing to register a case

[AIBE-XVIII]

Q.9 Which of the following categories of cases will not be entertained as Public Interest Litigation (PIL)?

a) Family pension

b) Petitions from riot victims

c) Neglected children

d) **Landlord-Tenant matter**

[AIBE-XVII]

Q.10 Who is known as the Father of Public Interest Litigation in India?
a) Justice A.N. Ray
b) Justice Y.V. Chandrachud
c) Justice R.S. Pathak
d) **Justice P.N. Bhagwati**
[AIBE-XVII]

Q.11 Which of the following is not a real purpose of Public Interest Litigation?
a) Vindication of the rule of law
b) Facilitate effective access to justice
c) Meaningful realization of fundamental rights
d) **Getting famous and making wealth** [AIBE-XVII]

Q.12 In Hussainara Khatoon Vs State of Bihar, _____ emerged as a basic fundamental right.
a) **Right to Speedy Justice**
b) Right to a Clean Environment
c) Right to Free Legal Aid
d) None of these [AIBE-XVII]

Q.13 Misuse of mechanism of PILs means:
a) Filing PILs for protection of private interest
b) Filing PILs for oblique motive
c) Filing PILs only for publicity
d) **All of the above** [AIBE-XVI]

Q.14 The phrase "file a PIL, ostensibly in public interest but, in fact, to serve personal or private interests" means:
a) filing PIL for protection of only public interest
b) filing PIL for protection of both public and private interest
c) filing PIL for protection of only private interest
d) **filing PIL alleging it to be in public interest, but actually seeking protection of private interest** [AIBE-XVI]

Q.15 Filing of frivolous PILs results in:
a) Increasing backlog of cases
b) Wastage of resources
c) Lesser availability of time for hearing other genuine cases
d) **All of the above** [AIBE-XVI]

Q.16 Anuradha Bhasin Vs. Union of India on 10 January, 2020 relates to a challenge under Article 32 of the Constitution seeking issuance of an appropriate writ:
a) For setting aside orders of the Government by which all modes of communication including Internet have been shut down in J&K
b) For setting aside orders of the Government by which private property was sought to be acquired in J&K

c) For setting aside orders of the Government by which J&K was constituted as a UT
d) for setting aside orders of the Government by which Ladakh was separated [AIBE-XV]

Q.17 The utility of Public Interest Litigation:
a) Liberalized *locus standi*
b) The proceedings are non-adversarial
c) Procedural requirements are liberalized
d) All of the above [AIBE-XV]

Q.18 The petitioner, a professor of political science who had done substantial research and deeply interested in ensuring proper implementation of the constitutional provisions, challenged the practice followed by the State of Bihar in re-promulgating a number of ordinances without getting the approval of the legislature. The court held that the petitioner as a member of public has 'sufficient interest' to maintain a petition under Article 32. This relates to the case of:
a) Parmanand Katara Vs. Union of India AIR 1989 SC 2039
b) D C Wadhwa Vs. State of Bihar AIR 1987 SC 579
c) Neeraja Choudhari Vs. State of Madhya Pradesh AIR 1984 SC 1099
d) Chameli Singh Vs. State of U. P. AIR 1996 SC 1051 [AIBE-XV]

Q.19 "Where a legal wrong or a legal injury is caused to a person or to a determinate class of persons by reason of violation of any constitutional or legal right or any burden is imposed in contravention of any constitutional or legal provision or without authority of law or any such legal wrong or legal injury or illegal burden is threatened and such person or determinate class of persons by reasons of poverty, helplessness or disability or socially or economically disadvantaged position unable to approach the court for relief, any member of public can maintain an application for an appropriate direction, order or writ in the High Court under Article 226 and in case any breach of fundamental rights of such persons or determinate class of persons, in this court under Article 32 seeking judicial redress for the legal wrong or legal injury caused to such person or determinate class of persons." - Justice Bhagwati in the case of:
a) Peoples Union for Democratic Rights Vs. Union of India
b) Ashok Kumar Pandey Vs. State of West Bengal
c) S P Gupta Vs. Union of India

d) Janata Dal Vs. H S Chowdhary [AIBE-XV]

Q.20 Public Interest Litigation is relaxation of which of the following requirements?
a) Jurisdiction
b) Locus Standi
c) Both (a) & (b)
d) None of the above [AIBE-XIV]

Q.21 Which of the following is not a case of Public Interest Litigation?
a) Kesavananda Bharati Vs. State of Kerala AIR 1973 SC 1461
b) Vineet Narain Vs. Union of India AIR 1998 SC 889
c) Union of India Vs. Association for Democratic Reforms AIR 2002 SC 2112
d) Vincent Panikurlangara Vs. Union of India AIR 1987 SC 990 [AIBE-XIV]

Q.22 The purpose of writ of 'Quo Warranto' is?
a) To compel public authority to perform duty
b) To restrain public authority to do illegal act
c) To oust illegal occupant of a public post
d) All of the above [AIBE-XIV]

Q.23 Writ of 'Certiorari' can be issued against:
a) Judicial and Quasi-Judicial bodies
b) Quasi-Judicial and Administrative bodies
c) Administrative bodies only
d) None of the above [AIBE-XIV]

Q.24 Who was the Chief Justice of India when the Concept of PIL was introduced to Indian judicial system?
a) M Hidayataullah
b) A M Ahmadi
c) A S Anand
d) P N Bhagwati [AIBE-XIII]

Q.25 In which country was the concept of PIL originated?
a) United Kingdom
b) United State of America
c) India
d) Australia [AIBE-XIII]

Q.26 'Mandamus' may be issued by:
a) Supreme Court
b) High Court
c) District Court
d) Both (a) & (b) [AIBE-XIII]

Q.27 Which of the following writs means to produce the body of a person?
a) Certiorari
b) Quo Warranto
c) Prohibition
d) Habeas Corpus [AIBE-XIII]

Q.28 A landmark Habeas Corpus

petition was filed during emergency, that is
a) Kesavananda Bharati Vs. State of Kerala
b) Golaknath Vs. State of Punjab
c) M C Mehta Vs. Union of India
d) ADM Jabalpur Vs. Shivkant Shukla [AIBE-XII]

Q.29 Who can move PIL in High Court and Supreme Court?
a) Any public-spirited person
b) NGO or association with public spirit
c) Group of public-spirited persons who have no personal interest
d) All of the above [AIBE-XII]

Q.30 Delhi Domestic Working Women's Forum Vs. Union of India (1995) 1 SC 14 - In this PIL which issue was exposed before the court?
a) The plight of some domestic maids who were sexually assaulted by army men
b) Abolition of child labour
c) Unemployment of domestic servants in Delhi
d) Poor salary of maid servants [AIBE-XII]

Q.31 Which one is a case of public interest?
a) Vishakha Vs. State of Rajasthan
b) Minerva Mills Ltd. Vs. Union of India AIR 1980
c) Municipal Council, Ratlam Vs. Vardhichand AIR 1980
d) All of the above [AIBE-XII]

Q.32 "Custodial death is perhaps one of the worst crimes in a civilized society governed by the Rule of Law" - In which case Supreme Court made this remark?
a) A K Gopalan Vs. State of Madras
b) M C Mehta Vs. Union of India
c) D K Basu Vs. State of Bengal
d) Vishakha Vs. State of Rajasthan [AIBE-XII]

Q.33 Due to the outcome of this case, slum dwellers were benefitted:
a) N K Chanda Vs. State of Haryana
b) Olga Tellis Vs. Bombay Municipal Corporation
c) PV Narasimha Rao Vs. Union of India
d) Ratlam Municipal Council Vs. Vardhichand [AIBE-XI]

Q.34 A Public Interest Litigation can be filed under:
a) Article 226 of Constitution and Article 32 of the Constitution
b) U/s. 133 of Criminal Procedure Code
c) (a) and (b)
d) None of the above [AIBE-XI]

Q.35 Supreme Court, in a PIL known as Kamal Nath case,

evolved:

a) Basic Future and Basic Structure doctrine

b) Public Trust doctrine

c) Separation of Power doctrine

d) Public Interest doctrine

[AIBE-XI]

Q.36 Vishakha Vs. State of Rajasthan case is related to:

a) Sexual Harassment at Workplace

b) Protection of Civil Rights

c) Uniform Civil Code

d) None of the above [AIBE-XI]

Q.37 PIL is criticized on the ground of:

a) Private motive

b) Political ends

c) Tremendous increase in the litigation

d) All of the above [AIBE-X]

Q.38 When can the Supreme Court refuse to grant remedy under Article 32?

a) Delay

b) Malicious petition

c) Infructuous petition

d) All of the above [AIBE-X]

Q.39 Filing with the court to object own or another's imprisonment is called:

a) Writ of Quo Warranto

b) Habeas Corpus

c) Writ of Prohibition

d) None of the above [AIBE-X]

Q.40 Which writ is issued by the Court to quash the wrongful order of a lower court?

a) Mandamus

b) Quo Warranto

c) Prohibition

d) Certiorari [AIBE-X]

TOPIC 13: ALTERNATE DISPUTE REDRESSAL INCLUDING ARBITRATION ACT

(4 questions are, generally, asked from this subject)

Q.1 Which of the following is a characteristic of mediation ?

(A) The mediator imposes a binding decision.

(B) It involves a neutral third party who facilitates negotiation between the parties.

(C) The mediator acts as a judge and renders a verdict.

(D) It is always court-ordered.

[AIBE-XIX]

Q.2 A dispute arises between ABC Ltd and XYZ Pvt Ltd regarding a contract that both parties had entered into. The agreement includes an arbitration clause, which states that any disputes shall be referred to arbitration. However, the parties fail to agree on the appointment of an arbitrator. Which of the following provisions of the Arbitration and Conciliation Act, 1996 would be applicable to resolve the issue of the appointment of an arbitrator ?

(A) The court will appoint an arbitrator under Section 11 if the parties fail to agree on one.

(B) The parties must mutually select an arbitrator, and if they fail, the arbitration will not take place.

(C) The arbitrator must be appointed by the Indian Council of Arbitration (ICA) in all cases.

(D) The parties can resolve the appointment issue by opting for conciliation instead of arbitration.

[AIBE-XIX]

Q.3 Which of the following is not an advantage of using ADR ?

(A) It is generally faster than litigation.

(B) It offers more confidentiality than traditional court cases.

(C) It always results in a binding decision.

(D) It is often less expensive than court proceedings. [AIBE-XIX]

Q.4 Kiran and Meera are involved in an arbitration, where Kiran was awarded Rs. 10 lakhs as compensation. Meera refuses to pay the amount, arguing that the award was not enforceable because of certain procedural irregularities in the arbitration process. Kiran decides to approach the court to enforce the arbitral award. Which of the following provisions of the Arbitration and Conciliation Act, 1996 governs the enforcement of an arbitral award ?

(A) Section 34 of the Act deals with

the enforcement of an arbitral award.

(B) Section 36 of the Act allows for the automatic enforcement of an arbitral award unless set-aside by the court.

(C) Section 9 of the Act governs the enforcement of arbitral awards.

(D) Section 11 of the Act deals with the enforcement of arbitral awards, not the appeal. [AIBE-XIX]

Q.5 Which of the following is not a recognized alternate dispute resolution mechanism under the Code of Civil Procedure, 1908?

a) Arbitration

b) Conciliation

c) Lok Adalat

d) Negotiation [AIBE-XVIII]

Q.6 Which of the following is an incorrect statement with respect to Lok Adalat?

a) No court fee is required in Lok Adalat.

b) Lok Adalat can deal with all civil and criminal matters.

c) Award of Lok Adalat is a deemed decree.

d) No appeal against the award of Lok Adalat is allowed.

[AIBE-XVIII]

Q.7 Which of the following is incorrect with respect to arbitration agreement as per the Arbitration and Conciliation Act, 1996?

a) Arbitration agreement may be written as well as oral.

b) Arbitration agreement may be in the form of a separate agreement.

c) Arbitration agreement may be in the form of an arbitration clause in a contract.

d) Arbitration agreement may be for all or certain disputes which may arise between the parties.

[AIBE-XVIII]

Q.8 In which of the following circumstances an arbitrator may not be challenged as per the Arbitration and Conciliation Act, 1996?

a) When a justifiable doubt as to his independence arises

b) When a justifiable doubt as to his impartiality arises

c) When he possesses the qualifications agreed by the parties

d) When he becomes ineligible as per the seventh schedule of the Act

[AIBE-XVIII]

Q.9 The arbitral tribunal shall not be bound by _____ in the determination of Rules of Procedure.

a) The Code of Civil Procedure, 1908

b) The Indian Evidence Act, 1872

c) The Code of Criminal Procedure, 1973

d) **Both the Code of Civil Procedure, 1908 and the Indian Evidence Act, 1872** [AIBE-XVII]

Q.10 Which of the following sections deals with "Arbitration Agreement" in Arbitration and Conciliation Act, 1996?
a) Section 6
b) **Section 7**
c) Section 8
d) Section 9 [AIBE-XVII]

Q.11 Under what circumstances the arbitral proceedings can be terminated?
1. Final arbitral award
2. Interim award
3. Where the arbitral tribunal issues an order for the termination
a) **1 and 3**
b) 1 and 2
c) 2 and 3
d) 1, 2 and 3 [AIBE-XVII]

Q.12 Under Section 29 of the Arbitration and Conciliation Act 1996, in arbitral proceedings with more than one arbitrator, any decision of the arbitral tribunal ______.
a) shall be made by all members
b) shall be made by 2/3 majority of its members
c) shall be made by the chief arbitrator
d) **shall be made by the majority of its members** [AIBE-XVII]

Q.13 An arbitration proceeding is a:
a) Judicial proceeding
b) **Quasi-judicial proceeding**
c) Administrative proceeding
d) None of the above [AIBE-XVI]

Q.14 What is ad hoc arbitration?
a) It is a proceeding administered by the parties themselves with rules created solely for that specific case.
b) Parties make their own arrangements with respect to all aspects of the arbitration, including the laws and rules.
c) The seal of arbitration, the language and the scope and issues to be resolved by means of arbitration.
d) **(a), (b) and (c)** [AIBE-XVI]

Q.15 Reference to the Arbitration is provided in which section of the Arbitration and Conciliation Act, 1996:
a) Section 7
b) **Section 8**
c) Section 9
d) Section 10 [AIBE-XVI]

Q.16 The Section of the Arbitration and Conciliation Act dealing with the time of commencement of arbitral proceeding is:
a) Section 20
b) **Section 21**

c) Section 22
d) None of the above [AIBE-XVI]

Q.17 "The UNCITRAL Model Law and Rules do not become part of the Arbitration Act so as to become an aid to construe the provisions of the Act." - held in the case of:
a) Union of India Vs. East Coast Boat Builders and Engineers Ltd.
b) Union of India Vs. M C Mehta
c) Tata Press Ltd. Vs. Union of India
d) Union of India Vs. Indian Charge Chrome Ltd. [AIBE-XV]

Q.18 According to Section 7(4) of the Arbitration and Conciliation Act, an arbitration agreement is in writing if it is contained in:
a) A document signed by the parties
b) An exchange of letters, telex, telegrams or other means of telecommunication which provide a record of the agreement
c) An exchange of statements of claim and defence in which the existence of the agreement is alleged by one party and not denied by the other
d) All of the above [AIBE-XV]

Q.19 Waiver of right to object deviance from arbitration agreement is mentioned under ………… of the Arbitration and Conciliation Act.
a) Section 7
b) Section 4
c) Section 20
d) Section 22 [AIBE-XV]

Q.20 The Arbitration Act 1996 repeals:
a) The Arbitration Act 1940
b) The Arbitration (Protocol and Convention) Act 1937
c) The Foreign Awards (Recognition and Enforcement) Act 1961
d) All of the above [AIBE-XV]

Q.21 BATNA stands for:
a) Bilateral Agreement to Negotiation and Arbitration
b) Best Alternative to a Negotiated Agreement
c) Bilateral Trade Negotiated Agreement
d) None of the above [AIBE-XIV]

Q.22 Section 9 of the Arbitration and Conciliation Act 1996 deals with:
a) Interim measures by the court
b) Discretionary powers of the court
c) Both (a) & (b)
d) None of the above [AIBE-XIV]

Q.23 In which of the following cases, the Supreme Court held that an International Commercial

Arbitration is one which has its juridical or legal seat of arbitration outside India?

a) Bhatia International Vs. Bulk Trading S.A. (2002) 4 SCC 105

b) Bharat Aluminum Company Vs. Kaiser Aluminum Technical Services Inc. (2012) 9 SCC 552

c) Booz Allen and Hamilton Inc. Vs. SBI Home Finance Limited (2011) 5 SCC 532

d) Vimal Kishor Shah Vs. Jayesh Dinesh Shah (2016) 8 SCC 788 [AIBE-XIV]

Q.24 Which one is a Foreign Award?

a) An award in an arbitration where at least one party in non-Indian

b) An award passed in a foreign seated arbitration

c) An award passed in arbitration where both the parties are non-Indian

d) None of the above [AIBE-XIV]

Q.25 What is the maximum duration within which fast track arbitration must be completed?

a) 6 months

b) 12 months

c) 18 months

d) 24 months [AIBE-XIII]

Q.26 Which among the following is not an ADR method under Section 89 of CPC 1908?

a) Mini Trial

b) Judicial settlement through Lok Adalat

c) Conciliation

d) None of the above [AIBE-XIII]

Q.27 What is the maximum number of Conciliators allowed in conciliation proceeding:

a) 1

b) 2

c) 5

d) None of the above

[AIBE-XIII]

Q.28 What is the status of a settlement agreement in conciliation proceeding?

a) Non-binding

b) Same as a settlement award

c) Unlike a settlement award

d) None of the above [AIBE-XIII]

Q.29 The Indian legal system has evolved a new technique of alternate dispute resolution which is popularly known as Lok Adalat. It owes its origin to the statutory recognition by passing of:

a) Legal Service Corporation Act 1974

b) Legal Aid and Advice Act 1949

c) Legal Services Authorities Act 1987

d) None [AIBE-XII]

Q.30 Which of the following is an innovative form of Alternative Dispute Resolution mechanism?
a) Bar Council of India
b) Election Commission
c) Comptroller and Auditor General
d) Lok Adalat [AIBE-XII]

Q.31 Part III of Arbitration and Conciliation Act 1996 formalizes:
a) Process of Conciliation
b) Process of Arbitration
c) Enforcement of Foreign awards under New York and Geneva Conventions
d) All of the above [AIBE-XII]

Q.32 Section 22B of Legal Services Authority Act empowers the central and state authorities to:
a) Abolish Lok Adalat
b) Works of Lok Adalat
c) Powers of Lok Adalat or permanent Lok Adalat
d) None of the above [AIBE-XII]

Q.33 The language which is to be used in the arbitral proceedings is decided by:
a) The Tribunal
b) Parties to decide by mutual understanding
c) The petitioner
d) The defendant [AIBE-XI]

Q.34 The Arbitral proceeding shall stand terminated:
a) On making of the final award
b) By an order of the arbitral tribunal
c) When the parties to the dispute agree to terminate proceedings
d) All of the above [AIBE-XI]

Q.35 Every Award of a Lok Adalat is deemed to be:
a) Order of District Collector
b) Order of Income Tax Commissioner
c) Decree of a Civil Court
d) (a) and (b) [AIBE-XI]

Q.36 The Arbitration and Conciliation Act 1996, Section 18-27 states:
a) The Conduct of Arbitral Proceedings
b) Receipt and Written Communications
c) Extent of judicial intervention
d) Awarding final decision [AIBE-XI]

Q.37 The objective of the EU directive on mediation is:
a) Reducing backlogs of cases at the courts in the member states
b) Dividing the cases between all dispute resolution methods
c) Economical reasons in times of crisis, thus ensuring that mediators will have a proper income
d) Ensuring better access to alternate dispute resolution in cross border commercial

conflicts [AIBE-X]

Q.38 In most EU member countries, which of the following is the most visible form of ADR?
a) Mediation
b) Arbitration
c) Litigation
d) Conciliation [AIBE-X]

Q.39 Part III of Arbitration and Conciliation Act 1996 formalizes:
a) Process of Conciliation
b) Process of Arbitration
c) Enforcement of Foreign Awards under New York and Geneva conventions
d) All of the above [AIBE-X]

Q.40 The conciliation proceedings:
a) Can be used as evidence in any judicial proceedings
b) Can be used as evidence only in Arbitral proceedings
c) Can be used as evidence only on the discretion of the Judge or arbitrator
d) Cannot be used as evidence in any judicial or arbitral proceedings [AIBE-IX]

Q.41 Which is an incorrect statement?
a) An Arbitral award is a contract.
b) An Arbitral award must be in writing and signed.
c) An Arbitral award included an interim award.
d) None of the above [AIBE-IX]

Q.42 The present Arbitration and Conciliation Act of 1996 is based on:
a) Constitution of India
b) Supreme Court of India guidelines
c) European Commercial Arbitration Procedure
d) UNCITRAL [AIBE-IX]

Q.43 The provisions of the Arbitration and Conciliation Act of 1996 have to be interpreted being uninfluenced by the principles underlying the 1940 Act. This observation was laid down in:
a) MMTC Ltd. Vs. Sterlite Industries (India) Ltd.
b) Sundaram Finance Ltd. Vs. NEPC Ltd.
c) Olympus Superstructures Pvt. Ltd. Vs. Meena Vijay
d) Orma Impex Pvt. Ltd. Vs. Nissai Asb Pte. Ltd. [AIBE-IX]

Q.44 The judgement in _____ skews the delicate balance, carefully crafted by the Model Law (and enshrined in s 34), between finality of arbitral awards on one hand and permissible judicial review on the other.
a) Renu Sagar Power Co. Ltd. Vs.

General Electric Co.
b) ONGC Vs. Saw Pipes Ltd.
c) Sundaram Finance Ltd. Vs. NEPC
d) Olympus Superstructures Pvt. Ltd. Vs. Meena Vijay Khetan
[AIBE-VIII]

Q.45 The Supreme Court in .... held that irrespective of where the 'central management and control is exercised' by a company, companies incorporated in India, cannot choose foreign law as the governing law of their arbitration.
a) TDM Infrastructure (P) Ltd. Vs. UE Development India (P) Ltd.
b) Comed Chemicals Ltd. Vs. C N Ramchand
c) Shreejee Traco (I) Pvt. Ltd. Vs. Paperline International Inc.
d) Bhatia International Vs. Bulk Trading [AIBE-VIII]

Q.46 Which Section of the 1996 Arbitration Act permits the parties to engage in conciliation process even while the arbitral proceedings are on?
a) Sec.30
b) Sec.10
c) Sec.40
d) Sec.20 [AIBE-VIII]

Q.47 Amendments made in the year .... through the insertion of Sec..... to the Civil Procedure Code introduced provisions to enable the courts to refer pending cases to arbitration, conciliation and mediation to facilitate early and amicable resolution of disputes.
a) 1989, 98
b) 1990, 88
c) 1999, 89
d) 2001, 88 [AIBE-VIII]

Q.48 S.89 of the Civil Procedure Code was incorporated through the Civil Procedure Code Amendment Act of .... which is the prominent provision that discusses about the jurisdiction of Civil Courts in applying Alternate Dispute Resolution mechanisms.
a) 1989
b) 1999
c) 1988
d) 2009 [AIBE-VII]

Q.49 In which case the Supreme Court held that Part I of the Arbitration and Conciliation Act would equally apply to International Commercial Arbitration held outside India, unless any or all provisions have been excluded by agreement between the parties?
a) Bhatia International Vs. Bulk Trading S A
b) United India Ins. Co. Ltd. Vs. Associated Transport Corpn. Ltd.

c) Hakam Singh Vs. Gammon (India) Ltd.
d) Ajmera Brothers Vs. Suraj Mal Naresh Kumar Jain [AIBE-VII]

Q.50 Establishment of Permanent Lok Adalats is envisaged under S..... of the Legal Services Authority Act of 1987.
a) 22B
b) 22A
c) 22(1)
d) 22 [AIBE-VII]

Q.51 In which year by an amendment of the Code of Civil Procedure Sec.89 has been included in the Code, which gives importance to mediation, conciliation and arbitration?
a) 2002
b) 2004
c) 2013
d) 2012 [AIBE-VI]

Q.52 Under The Arbitration and Conciliation Act, an arbitration agreement may be in the form of:
a) an arbitration clause in a contract only
b) in the form of a separate agreement only
c) an arbitration clause in a contract or in the form of a separate agreement
d) commercial custom [AIBE-VI]

Q.53 A decision by the arbitral tribunal that the contract is null and void shall:
a) Entail ipso jure the invalidity of the arbitration clause
b) Not entail ipso jure the invalidity of the arbitration clause
c) Entail de facto invalidity of the arbitration clause
d) None of the above [AIBE-VI]

Q.54 The arbitral tribunal shall not be bound by the:
a) Code of Civil Procedure, 1908 or the Indian Evidence Act 1872
b) The Indian Evidence Act 1872
c) Code of Civil Procedure, 1908
d) None of the above [AIBE-VI]

Q.55 .... is the process whereby interested parties resolve disputes, agree upon courses of action, bargain for individual or collective advantage, and/or attempt to craft outcomes which serve their mutual interests.
a) Expert determination
b) Arbitration
c) Conciliation
d) Negotiation [AIBE-V]

Q.56 The commencement of arbitral proceedings is not dependent on interim relief being allowed or denied under S.9 of the Arbitration and Conciliation Act

1996. Supreme Court, in which case, held so?

a) Firm Ashok Traders & Anr. Vs. Gurumukh Das Saluja & Ors.

b) MMTC Ltd. Vs. Sterlite Industries (India) Ltd.

c) National Thermal Power Corporation Vs. Flowmore (P) Ltd.

d) Magma Leasing Ltd. Vs. NEPC Micon Ltd. [AIBE-V]

.

Q.57 Which provision of Hindu Marriage Act 1955 deals with conciliation?

a) S.23

b) S.23(2)

c) S.23(3)

d) S.22 [AIBE-V]

Q.58 Which section under the Civil Procedure Code, 1908 deals with the settlement of disputes outside the court:

a) S.98

b) S.99

c) S.89

d) S.88 [AIBE-V]

Q.59 The Indian Council of Arbitration was established in:

a) 1956

b) 1976

c) 1965

d) 1996 [AIBE-IV]

Q.60 '*Lex Arbitri*' means:

a) Arbitral tribunal sitting in India can apply the law of Singapore

b) Just Law

c) Arbitrary Law

d) None of these [AIBE-IV]

Q.61 In India, the Arbitration & Conciliation Act was enacted in:

a) 1992

b) 1993

c) 1994

d) 1996 [AIBE-IV]

Q.62 Section 10(i) of the Arbitration & Conciliation Act talks about:

a) Power of Arbitration

b) Numbers of Arbitrators

c) Capacity of Arbitrations

d) None of the above [AIBE-IV]

TOPIC 14: ADMINISTRATIVE LAW

(3 questions are, generally, asked from this subject)

Q.1 Which of the following best defines delegated legislation ?

(A) Legislation passed by local governments.

(B) Laws enacted by Parliament or the Legislature.

(C) Laws made by an administrative authority under powers given to them by Parliament.

(D) A judicial decision made by an administrative tribunal. [AIBE-XIX]

Q.2 In 2020, at Dhorodo village the Panchayat elections could not happen due to Covid pandemic while the tenure of the Panchayat was getting over that year itself. Mr. Haribansh represented the people that year at the Panchayat post dissolution of the Panchayat tenure and made a law exercising the delegated power vide the Panchayati Raj Act of the state to restrict their economic activities per day to ₹100 only. In which of the following case this is allowed or restricted ?

(A) MCD vs. Birla Cotton Mills

(B) Patna University vs. Amita Tiwari

(C) Jalan Trading vs. Union of India

(D) None of these [AIBE-XIX]

Q.3 Which of the following is/are not ground/s for judicial review of administrative action ?

(1) Illegality (2) Irrationality (3) Proportionality (4) Public opinion

(A) Only (2)

(B) (2) and (4)

(C) (1), (2) and (3)

(D) Only (4 [AIBE-XIX]

Q.4 In which of the following landmark cases, it was held that principles of natural justice were applicable not only to judicial and quasi-judicial functions, but also to administrative functions?

a) A.K. Kraipak v Union of India

b) Ram Jawaya Kapoor v State of Punjab

c) Sonic Industries Rajkot v Municipal Corporation, Rajkot

d) Maneka Gandhi v Union of India [AIBE-XVIII]

Q.5 In which of the following judgment the Supreme Court had comprehensively reconsidered S.P. Sampath Kumar v Union of India case?

a) J.B. Chopra v Union of India

b) L. Chandra Kumar v Union of India

c) R.K. Jain v Union of India

d) S.K. Sarkar v Vinay Chandra

Mishra [AIBE-XVIII]

Q.6 Who among the following defined administrative law as 'the law relating to the control of government power'?
a) Ivor Jennings
b) Wade
c) K.C. Davis
d) Garner [AIBE-XVIII]

Q.7 Which of the following writ can be issued against a usurpation of public office?
a) Writ of Mandamus
b) Writ of Certiorari
c) **Writ of Quo Warranto**
d) Writ of Prohibition [AIBE-XVII]

Q.8 Ridge Vs Baldwin's case deals with:
a) Corporation
b) **Natural Justice**
c) State Liability
d) Delegated Legislation [AIBE-XVII]

Q.9 Meaning of "Audi alteram partem" is:
a) **A person cannot be condemned without being heard**
b) An adjudicating authority must give a speaking order
c) No man can be a judge in his own case
d) No one should fear the courts [AIBE-XVII]

Q.10 What is meant by procedural *ultra vires*?
a) It is the non-observance of the procedural norms by the rule making authority
b) It may make the rule ultra vires due to non-observance of the rule making authority and hence become void
c) It means the lacuna in the procedure of law
d) **(a) and (b)** [AIBE-XVI]

Q.11 The ground of "error of law apparent on the face of the record" is connected with which of the writ?
a) Quo-warranto
b) Mandamus
c) Habeas corpus
d) **Certiorari** [AIBE-XVI]

Q.12 Parliament may by law establish Administrative Tribunals under .... of the Constitution.
a) Article 323B
b) Article 323A
c) Article 233
d) Article 323 [AIBE-XV]

Q.13 A. K. Kraipak Vs. Union of India relates to:
a) Likelihood of bias
b) Delegated legislation
c) Administrative discretion
d) Notice [AIBE-XV]

Q.14 Judicial control of Delegated Legislation may be exercised on the ground of:
a) Doctrine of ultra vires
b) Malafides
c) Exclusion of judicial review
d) All of the above [AIBE-XV]

Q.15 The Supreme Court of India has issued the direction to make the CBI independent agency so that it can function more effectively and investigate crimes and corruptions at high places in public life in the case of:
a) Union of India Vs. Association for Democratic Reforms AIR 2002 SC
2112
b) Bangalore Medical Trust Vs. B S Muddappa (1991) 45 Sc 54
c) Vincent Panikurlangara Vs. Union of India (1987) 2 SC 165
d) Vineet Narayan Vs. Union of India AIR 1998 SC 889
[AIBE-XIV]

Q.16 Which of the following Courts / Tribunals cannot entertain a Public Interest Litigation?
a) Supreme Court
b) High Court
c) Central Administrative Tribunal
d) None of the above [AIBE-XIV]

Q.17 Delegated legislation was declared constitutional in:
a) Berubari case
b) Re Delhi Laws Act case
c) Kesavananda Bharati case
d) Maneka Gandhi case
[AIBE-XIII]

Q.18 The provision for Administration Tribunals added by:
a) 42nd Amendment
b) 44th Amendment
c) 24th Amendment
d) 43rd Amendment [AIBE-XIII]

Q.19 'Droit Administration' is a system of administration:
a) French system
b) British system
c) American System
d) Irish System [AIBE-XII]

Q.20 The word 'Ombudsman' is derived from:
a) French Administration
b) British Administration
c) Swedish Administration
d) German Administration
[AIBE-XI]

Q.21 Under Section 3 of the Commission of Inquiry Act 1952, an Inquiry Commission is appointed by:
a) Central Government or State Government
b) Union Public Service

Commission
c) State Public Commission
d) Supreme Court of India
[AIBE-XI]

Q.22 It refers to an authority derived from official character merely, not expressly conferred upon the individual character, but rather annexed to official position:
a) Designation
b) Ex-Officio
c) Appointment
d) Ad interim [AIBE-X]

Q.23 The term sabbatical is connected with:
a) Paid leave for study
b) Paternity leave
c) Maternity leave
d) Quarantine leave [AIBE-X]

Q.24 In cases in which a specific act confers a discretionary power on an authority:
a) The Court can direct the manner in which the power is exercised
b) The Court can direct that the power be exercised in accordance with law
c) Both (a) and (b)
d) Neither (a) nor (b) [AIBE-IX]

Q.25 Which of the following statements hold true for adjudicatory bodies?
a) Doctrine of *Stare Decisis* applies to them
b) Doctrine of *res judicata* does not apply to them
c) Inherent lack of jurisdiction in a tribunal cannot be cured or created by the act of the parties
d) None of the above [AIBE-IX]

Q.26 The requirement to give reasons in administrative decisions which affect rights and liabilities has been held to be mandatory by the Supreme Court in:
a) S N Mukherjee Vs. Union of India
b) State of Orissa Vs. Dr. Binapani Dei
c) State of Maharashtra Vs. Jalgaon Municipal Council
d) Motilal Padampat Sugar Mills Co. Ltd. Vs. State of U. P. [AIBE-VIII]

Q.27 In State of Karnataka Vs. Union of India AIR 1978 SC 68, appointment of a Commission by the Union Government under S.3(1) of the Commission of Inquiry Act (60 of 1952) to look into the charges of corruption etc. against the Chief Minister and other ministers of a State was challenged. It was held:
a) Arbitrary under Art.14
b) Violates federal principle
c) Jurisdiction of the Court is ousted and hence violates the Basic Structure of the Constitution

d) Federal Structure is not jeopardized [AIBE-VIII]

Q.28 The Constitution of India has recognized the concept of tribunals as instruments of quasi-judicial administrative adjudication:
a) Art.39(a) and 39(b)
b) Art.323A and 323B
c) Art.368
d) Art.202A and 202B [AIBE-VII]

Q.29 *'Nemo judex in causa sua'* meaning "No man shall be a judge in his own cause" was first stated by ………. in Dr. Bonham s Case.
a) Lord Grey
b) Lord Heward
c) Lord Coke
d) Lord Moulton [AIBE-VII]

Q.30 Writ of *Certiorari* is issued against:
a) Lower courts or quasi-judicial bodies
b) Public Officials
c) Wrongful confinement
d) Usurpation of public office [AIBE-VI]

Q.31 '*Audi Alteram Partem*' means:
a) Bias
b) Hear the other side
c) No one can be a judge in his own case
d) None of the above [AIBE-VI]

Q.32 The Second Administrative Reforms Commission is constituted:
a) 31st August 2004
b) 31st August 2006
c) 31st August 2005
d) 31st August 2007 [AIBE-VI]

Q.33 If a Quasi-judicial authority violates the principles of natural justice, the appropriate writ would be:
a) Mandamus
b) Habeas Corpus
c) Quo Warranto
d) Certiorari [AIBE-V]

Q.34 Maxim '*delegatus non potest delegare*' means:
a) A delegate can further delegate
b) A delegate cannot further delegate
c) A delegate must protest delegation objectively
d) None of the above [AIBE-IV]

TOPIC 15: COMPANY LAW

(2 questions are, generally, asked from this subject)

Q.1 As per Section 2(84) Share means share in the share capital of a Company and includes ....
(1) Debentures (2) Preference Shares (3) Stocks (4) Bonds

(A) (1) and (2)
(B) (1), (2) and (3)
(C) Only (3)
(D) (1), (2), (3) and (4) [AIBE-XIX]

Q.2 Section 43 of the Companies Act, 2013 provides for ....
(A) Issue of Shares at Premium
(B) Kinds of Shares Capital
(C) Buy Back of Shares
(D) Reduction in Share Capital
[AIBE-XIX]

Q.3 In which of the following situations a One Person Company (OPC) will mandatorily get converted into either private or public company?
a) In case the paid-up share capital of an OPC exceeds twenty-five lakh rupees
b) In case the paid-up share capital of an OPC exceeds fifty lakh rupees.
c) In case the paid-up share capital of an OPC exceeds seventy-five lakh rupees.
d) In case the paid-up share capital of an OPC exceeds one crore rupees. [AIBE-XVIII]

Q.4 What is the minimum number of directors required for a public company as per the Companies Act, 2013?
a) 2
b) 3
c) 5
d) 7 [AIBE-XVIII]

Q.5 ABC Private Limited Company chose to convert itself into a public company. It can do so by altering its Memorandum of Association and Articles of Association and by passing _____.
a) Ordinary Resolution
b) **Special Resolution**
c) Board Resolution
d) None of these [AIBE-XVII]

Q.6 Doctrine of "lifting of or piercing the corporate veil" is associated with:
a) Labour Law
b) **Company Law**
c) Banking Law
d) Service Law [AIBE-XVII]

Q.7 Section 8 of the Companies Act, 2013 contains provision relating to:

a) Incorporation of Company
b) **Formation of companies with charitable objects, etc.**
c) Effect of Registration
d) Effect of Memorandum and Articles [AIBE-XVI]

Q.8 The verification of the Registered Office shall be furnished to the Registrar within a period of incorporation:
a) **30 days**
b) 60 days
c) 90 days
d) 120 days [AIBE-XVI]

Q.9 Minimum number of directors in a Public Company:
a) 3
b) 10
c) 12
d) 5 [AIBE-XV]

Q.10 An associate company, in relation to another company, means:
a) A company in which that other company has a significant influence, but which is a subsidiary company of the company having such influence and includes a joint venture company
b) A company in which that other company has a significant influence, but which is not a subsidiary company of the company having such influence and includes a joint venture company
c) A company in which that other company has a significant influence, but which is not a subsidiary company of the company having such influence and does not include a joint venture company
d) A company in which that other company has full shares, and is a subsidiary company of the company having such influence and includes a joint venture company
[AIBE-XV]

Q.11 Which Court or Authority has the power to punish any person for contempt of the National Company Law Tribunal?
a) Supreme Court
b) High Court
c) National Company Law Appellate Tribunal
d) National Company Law Tribunal [AIBE-XIV]

Q.12 It deals with the Internal Management and Affairs of company:
a) Prospectus
b) Article of Association
c) Memorandum of Association.
d) Debenture [AIBE-XIV]

Q.13 A prospectus which does not include complete particulars of the quantum or price of the securities

included therein in known as:
a) Shelf Prospectus
b) Memorandum
c) Red Herring Prospectus
d) Issuing house [AIBE-XIII]

Q.14 When there is no profit in one year or the profit of a company is not enough to pay the fixed dividend on preference shares, the arrears of dividend are to be carried forward and paid before a dividend is paid on the ordinary shares. This is called:
a) Participating preference shares
b) Cumulative preference shares
c) Non-cumulative preference shares
d) Non-participating preference shares [AIBE-XIII]

Q.15 Articles of a company can be altered by:
a) The directors of the company
b) The officials of the company
c) Shareholders by passing an ordinary resolution
d) Shareholders by passing a special resolution [AIBE-XII]

Q.16 Under the Companies Act, every person subscribing to the Memorandum of a company must take at least:
a) 100 shares
b) 20 shares
c) 10 shares
d) 1 share [AIBE-XII]

Q.17 The Minimum number of persons required to incorporate a Public Company is:
a) 5
b) 10
c) 7
d) 2 [AIBE-XI]

Q.18 A private company can commence business as soon as it receives:
a) Certification of Incorporation
b) Letter of Intent
c) Occupation Certificate
d) None of the above [AIBE-XI]

Q.19 What is the maximum number of partners in banking business?
a) Eight
b) Ten
c) Twelve
d) Sixteen [AIBE-XI]

Q.20 Minimum number of members required to apply for Incorporation Certificate in a Public Ltd. Company is:
a) 7
b) 3
c) 2
d) 50 [AIBE-X]

Q.21 'A' does not fall under the clause of Memorandum of Association. 'A' here is:

a) Subscription
b) Director
c) Capital
d) Situation [AIBE-X]

Q.22 The Serious Fraud Investigation Office:
a) Takes up cases Suo motu
b) Takes up cases for investigation on the basis of application made by the people concerned
c) Takes up cases for investigations referred to it by Central Government
d) All of the above [AIBE-IX]

Q.23 How is the net worth of a Foreign Company calculated for the purpose of Corporate Social Responsibility?
a) The net worth will be calculated as per Section 198 of Companies Act. 2013.
b) It shall be calculated as per Section 197 of the Companies Act 2013.
c) It shall be calculated as per Section 197 and Section 361 of the Companies Act 2013.
d) It shall be calculated as per Section 198 and Section 381 of Companies Act 2013. [AIBE-IX]

Q.24 Which of the following actions can be taken by a Registrar under Section 4(5) of the Companies Act 2013?
a) He can direct the Company to change its name within a period of 6 months after passing an ordinary resolution
b) Take action for striking off the name of the Company from the Registrar of Companies
c) Order winding up of the Company on his own accord
d) All of these [AIBE-IX]

Q.25 Which of the following companies will have to constitute Corporate Social Responsibility Committee under the Companies Act 2013?
a) A Company having a net profit of 2.5 crores in a financial year, a net worth of 300 crores and a turnover of rupees 800 crore
b) A Company having a net profit of 3 crores in a financial year, a net worth of 300 crores and a turnover of rupees 600 crore
c) A Company having a net profit of 5 crores or more, a net worth of 500 crores and a turnover of rupees 1000 crore or more
d) A Company having a net profit of 5 crores or more, a net worth of 500 crores and a turnover of rupees 5000 crore or more [AIBE-IX]

Q.26 Who among the following is authorized to issue regulations regarding shelf prospectus?
a) SEBI

b) Central Government
c) Company Law Board
d) National Company Law Tribunal [AIBE-IX]

Q.27 Which of the following services cannot be provided to the Company by an Auditor appointed under the provisions of the Companies Act 2013?
a) Internal Audit
b) Actuarial services
c) Managerial services
d) All of these [AIBE-IX]

Q.28 Provisions regarding Corporate Social Responsibility are incorporated in the Companies Act 2013 under:
a) Section 101
b) Section 111
c) Section 135
d) Section 235 [AIBE-VIII]

Q.29 What is Corporate Social Responsibility among the following?
a) Employee benefits
b) Project based protection of national heritage
c) Programs undertaken outside India
d) Mere donations [AIBE-VIII]

Q.30 The Companies Act of 1956 accords recognition only to accounting standards whereas under Section 2(7) of the Companies Act of 2013, the recognition is accorded to both accounting and .... standards.
a) Financing
b) Auditing
c) Business
d) Responsibility [AIBE-VIII]

Q.31 Companies Act 2013 allows the formation of:
a) Two persons company only
b) Seven persons company only
c) Two or more persons company only
d) One person company also [AIBE-VIII]

Q.32 .... of the Companies Act 2013 requires disclosure in the prospectus of names and addresses of CFO about sources of promoters' contribution among other things.
a) Section 36
b) Section 37
c) Section 26
d) Section 38 [AIBE-VIII]

Q.33 Sec.253 of the Companies Act 2013 deals with:
a) Determination of Sickness
b) Liability of Directors
c) Promoters
d) Memorandum [AIBE-VIII]

Q.34 Under the Companies Act 2013, any company having a net worth of rupees 500 crore or more or a turnover of rupees 1,000 crore or more or a net profit of rupees 5 crore or more should mandatorily spend ……. of their net profits per fiscal on Corporate Social Responsibility activities.

a) 3%

b) 5%

c) 10%

d) 2% [AIBE-VII]

Q.35 The ………. Guidelines constitute one of the most comprehensive CSR tools available to companies.

a) OECD

b) OACF

c) OECG

d) ASEAN [AIBE-VII]

Q.36 The 2013 Companies Act has increased the limit of the number of members in Private Company from 50 to:

a) 100

b) 200

c) 300

d) 150 [AIBE-VII]

Q.37 The Standards on Auditing have been accorded legal sanctity in the 2013 Act and would be subject to notification by the:

a) NFRA

b) NFRA

c) NARF

d) SEBI [AIBE-VII]

Q.38 SFIO stands for:

a) Serious Fraud Investigation Office

b) Serious Force Institution Office

c) Serious Form Investigation Office

d) Serious File Investigation Office [AIBE-VII]

Q.39 Which provision of the Companies Act 2013 discusses about the issue of bonus shares out of its free reserves or the securities premium account or the capital redemption reserve account, subject to the compliance with certain conditions such as authorization by the articles, approval in the general meeting?

a) S.36

b) S.43

c) S.63

d) S.33 [AIBE-VII]

Q.40 Which of following is a ground recognized under the Companies Act for automatic adjournment of the General Meeting?

a) Absence of Chairman of the meeting

b) Quorum of the meeting is not present

c) Meeting is held at a place different from what was prescribed

in the notice
d) Death of any of the directors prior to the meeting immovable property is situated [AIBE-VI]

Q.41 Which of the following meetings can be called by members?
a) Extra-ordinary General Meeting
b) Annual General Meeting
c) Statutory meeting
d) Special meeting [AIBE-VI]

Q.42 Which of the following powers can be exercised by the Board of Directors without holding a meeting?
a) Power to issue debentures
b) Power to invest funds of the company
c) Power to make loans
d) Power to appoint additional director [AIBE-VI]

Q.43 Which of following is not a ground for compulsory winding up of a company?
a) Oppression of minority
b) Loss of substratum
c) Non-holding of annual general meeting
d) Losses to the company
[AIBE-VI]

Q.44 Trading activities of a company were stopped temporarily in view of the trade depression with an intention to continue the same when the conditions improve. A petition was preferred into the tribunal for winding up of the company. The petition:
a) Is liable to be dismissed
b) Will succeed
c) Will be kept pending till the conditions improve
d) Will not be admitted [AIBE-V]

Q.45 Amalgamation of companies in national interest is dealt under:
a) Section 388 of the Companies Act
b) Section 378 of the Companies Act
c) Section 396 of the Companies Act
d) Section 390 of the Companies Act [AIBE-V]

Q.46 Under Section 171 of the Companies Act, a general meeting of a company may be called by giving a notice in writing for not less than:
a) 21 days
b) 30 days
c) 40 days
d) 14 days [AIBE-V]

Q.47 A private limited company limits the number of members to:
a) 30
b) 40
c) 50

d) 150 [AIBE-V]

Q.48 Upon failure to hold Statutory Meeting, the penalty for the defaulting Company shall be:
a) Rs.500 per day of default
b) Wound up
c) Rs.1000 per day of default
d) None of these [AIBE-IV]

Q.49 Free transferability of shares is mandatory in a:
a) Listed Company
b) Company Ltd. by shares
c) Public Ltd. Company
d) Foreign Company [AIBE-IV]

Q.50 The *Memorandum of Association* of a listed company shall be as per:
a) Table A
b) Table B
c) Table C
d) Table D [AIBE-IV]

Q.51 Which of the following clauses from Memorandum of Association cannot be amended?
a) Objects Clause
b) Liability Clause
c) Association Clause
d) Registered office Clause
[AIBE-IV]

TOPIC 16: ENVIRONMENTAL LAW

(2 questions are, generally, asked from this subject)

Q.1 A manufacturing company in the city of Surat named as "X" has been discharging untreated industrial waste into a nearby river, violating the provisions of the Environment Protection Act, 1986 and the Water (Prevention and Control of Pollution) Act, 1974. This has resulted in severe pollution, making the river water unsafe for drinking and harming aquatic life. Local farmers and residents, who rely on the river for irrigation and daily needs, have started facing health issues and crop failures due to the contaminated water. Despite multiple complaints to the local pollution control board, no action has been taken against the company.

Based on the above problem, select the correct answer:

(A) It is the violation of Section 24 of the Water (Prevention and Control of Pollution) Act, 1974.

(B) It is the violation of Section 40 of the Water (Prevention and Control of Pollution) Act, 1974.

(C) It is not the violation of the provisions of the laws stated in the problem.

(D) It is the violation of Section 23 of the Water (Prevention and Control of Pollution) Act, 1974.

[AIBE-XIX]

Q.2 Which of the following Acts is popularly known as Umbrella Legislation ?

(A) The Water (Prevention and Control of Pollution) Act, 1974

(B) The Air (Prevention and Control of Pollution) Act, 1981

(C) The Factories Act, 1948

(D) The Environment (Protection) Act, 1986

[AIBE-XIX]

Q.3 In which of the following cases, the Supreme Court of India had explained the Precautionary Principle in detail?

a) Vellore Citizens' Welfare Forum v Union of India

b) A.P. Pollution Control Board v M.V. Nayudu

c) Indian Council for Enviro-Legal Action v Union of India

d) M.C. Mehta versus Kamal Nath

[AIBE-XVIII]

Q.4 Which of the following is a landmark case on the public trust doctrine in Environmental Law?

a) Vellore Citizens' Welfare Forum v Union of India

b) Olga Tellis v Bombay Municipal Corporation

c) Indian Council for Enviro-Legal Action v Union of India
d) M.C. Mehta versus Kamal Nath [AIBE-XVIII]

Q.5 Under which section of the Environment (Protection) Act, 1986 an appeal to the National Green Tribunal lies?
a) Section 4A
b) **Section 5A**
c) Section 6A
d) Section 7A [AIBE-XVII]

Q.6 Which one of the following fundamental duties relates to Environmental Protection?
a) Article 51A(b)
b) **Article 51A(g)**
c) Article 51A(j)
d) Article 51A(k) [AIBE-XVII]

Q.7 Basel Convention is associated with one of the following:
a) International trade in endangered species of wild fauna and flora
b) Climate change
c) Protection of ozone layer
d) **The control of transboundary movement of hazardous waste and their disposal** [AIBE-XVI]

Q.8 In which of the following case, the Supreme Court, first of all, made an attempt to look into the question regarding the extension of the right of life to the right to health and other hygienic conditions-
a) **The Rural Litigation and Entitlement Kendra Vs State of Uttar Pradesh**
b) M. C. Mehta Vs Union of India
c) V. Lakshmipathy Vs State of Karnataka
d) F. K. Hussain Vs Union of India [AIBE-XVI]

Q.9 According to Environmental Protection Act 1986 'environmental pollutant' means:
a) Any solid, liquid or gaseous substance present in such concentration as may be, or tend to be, helpful to environment
b) Only gaseous substance present in such concentration as may be, or tend to be, injurious to environment
c) Any solid, liquid or gaseous substance present in such concentration as may be, or tend to be, injurious to environment
d) Any solid, liquid present in such concentration as may be, or tend to be, injurious to environment [AIBE-XV]

Q.10 National Green Tribunal cannot exercise its Jurisdiction with reference to:
a) Wild Life (Protection) Act 1972
b) Scheduled Tribes and Other Traditional Forest Dwellers (Recognition of Forest Rights) Act 2006

c) The Public Liability Insurance Act 1991

d) Both (a) & (b) [AIBE-XV]

Q.11 Public Liability Insurance Act was enacted in:

a) 1991

b) 1993

c) 1995

d) 1997 [AIBE-XIV]

Q.12 Environmental Impact Assessment (EIA) is mandatory under:

a) Indian Forest Act

b) Air Act

c) Wild Life Protection Act

d) Environment Protection Act [AIBE-XIV]

Q.13 Environmental impact assessment (EIA) is mandatory under:

a) Indian Forest Act

b) Air Act

c) Wild Life Protection Act

d) Environment Protection Act [AIBE-XIII]

Q.14 Which of the following appears to contribute to global cooling rather than global warming?

a) Nitrous Oxide

b) Aerosols

c) Methane

d) CFC [AIBE-XIII]

Q.15 The Convention on Climate Change was the outcome of:

a) The Stockholm Conference

b) The Nairobi Conference

c) The Vienna Conference

d) The Rio De Janeiro Conference [AIBE-XII]

Q.16 The Costal Regulation Zone notification was issued by the Central Government in:

a) 1986

b) 1988

c) 1991

d) 1997 [AIBE-XII]

Q.17 The case Krishna Gopal Vs. State of M. P. relates to:

a) Water pollution

b) Air and water pollution

c) Noise and air pollution

d) Water and noise pollution [AIBE-XI]

Q.18 Within the purview of Water Act, the meaning of stream is defined as:

a) Includes a river but not a water course

b) Includes a water course but not a river

c) Includes river and water course, but not subterranean waters

d) Includes a river, a water course and subterranean river [AIBE-XI]

Q.19 Which is the leading case on environment?
a) M C Mehta Vs. Union of India
b) Union of India Vs. H S Dhillon
c) Maneka Gandhi Vs. Union of India
d) None of the above [AIBE-X]

Q.20 The Environment (Protection) Act 1986 came into force on:
a) 18th November 1986
b) 19th November 1986
c) 20th November 1986
d) 21st November 1986 [AIBE-X]

Q.21 Which of the following is a function of Central Pollution Control Board under the provisions of Section 16 of the Air (Prevention and Control of Pollution) Act 1981?
a) To carry out and sponsor investigation and research relating to problems of pollution and prevention, control or abatement of pollution.
b) To improve the quality of air
c) Both (a) and (b)
d) Neither (a) nor (b) [AIBE-IX]

Q.22 The destruction of fish by use of explosive or by poisoning the water is prohibited by:
a) Indian Environment (Protection) Act 1986
b) The Water (Prevention and Control of Pollution) Act 1974
c) Indian Fisheries Act 1897
d) The National Green Tribunal Act 2010 [AIBE-IX]

Q.23 Which of the following is not included in the definition of 'cattle' as given under the Indian Forest Act 1927?
a) Rams
b) Kids
c) Kitten
d) None of these [AIBE-IX]

Q.24 Under the Wild Life (Protection) Act 1972, any person who teases an animal in a zoo may be punished:
a) With fine which may extend to 5000
b) With imprisonment which may extend up to 1 year
c) Both (a) and (b)
d) Neither (a) nor (b) [AIBE-IX]

Q.25 The Water (Prevention and Control of Pollution) Act 1974 regulates:
a) The discharge of hazardous pollutants into the nation's surface water
b) The emission of hazardous air pollutants
c) Waste disposal of sea
d) The transportation of hazardous materials [AIBE-VIII]

Q.26 It was held by the Supreme

Court that noise pollution beyond permissible limits cannot be tolerated, even if such noise was a direct result of and was connected with religious activities - in the case of:

a) Vellore Citizens Welfare Forum Vs. Union of India

b) Church of God (Full Gospel) in India Vs. KKR Majestic Colony Welfare Association

c) Rural Enlightenment Kendra Vs. Union of India

d) Narmada Bachao Andolan Vs. Union of India [AIBE-VIII]

Q.27 According to Environmental (Protection) Act of 1986, "environmental pollutant" means:

a) Any solid, liquid or gaseous substance present in such concentration as may be, or tend to be, injurious to environment

b) Any substance present in such concentration as may be, or tend to be, injurious to environment

c) Any solid, liquid or gaseous substance present in such concentration as may be, or tend to be, injurious to a person

d) Any solid, liquid or gaseous substance present in such concentration as may be, or tend to be, injurious to the society

[AIBE-VIII]

Q.28 National Conservation Strategy and Policy Statement on Environment and Development is a major environmental policy in India and it was passed in the year:

a) 1988

b) 1982

c) 1992

d) 1990 [AIBE-VII]

Q.29 .... of the Environmental Protection Act 1986 defines 'Environment'.

a) Section 2(a)

b) Section 3(a)

c) Section 1(a)

d) Section 11(a) [AIBE-VII]

Q.30 Polluter Pays Principle means:

a) Polluter should bear the cost of pollution as the pollute is responsible for pollution

b) Polluter should not necessarily bear the cost of pollution as the polluter may not be responsible for pollution

c) Polluter may bear the cost of pollution as the polluter may be responsible for pollution

d) None of the above [AIBE-VII]

Q.31 "Pollution is a civil wrong. By its very nature, it is a tort committed against the community as a whole. A person, therefore, who is guilty of causing pollution, has to pay damages (compensation) for restoration of the environment.

He has also to pay damages to those who have suffered loss on account of the act of the offender. Further, the offender can also be held liable to pay exemplary damages so that it may act as a deterrent for others not to cause pollution in any manner. However, the Court cannot impose any pollution fine in absence of any trial and finding of guilty under the relevant statutory provisions." - This observation was made in:
a) M C Mehta Vs. Kamal Nath
b) Calcutta Tanneries Case
c) M C Mehta Vs. UoI
d) A P Pollution Control Board Vs. M V Nayudu [AIBE-VII]

Q.32 India became a party to the International Convention on Biological Diversity in:
a) 1992
b) 1995
c) 1994
d) 2000 [AIBE-VII]

TOPIC 17: CYBER LAW

(2 questions are, generally, asked from this subject)

Q.1 Which of the following is/are included under Section 2(1)(w) of the Information Technology Act, 2000 describing the Intermediary ?

(1) Cyber Cafes
(2) Telecom Regulators
(3) Social Media Platforms
(4) Internet Service Providers

(A) (1), (2) and (3)
(B) (1), (3) and (4)
(C) (1), (2) and (4)
(D) (1), (2), (3) and (4) [AIBE-XIX]

Q.2 Malti, a small business owner, runs an online clothing store. Recently, she noticed that her website had been hacked, and her customers' personal information, including names, addresses, and payment details, was stolen. Shortly after, some of her customers reported unauthorized transactions on their accounts. Malti wishes to file a complaint against the incident. On the basis of the above problem, select the correct option:

(A) It is punishable under Section 66 of the Information Technology Act, 2000.
(B) It is punishable only under the criminal laws.
(C) It is punishable under Section 66 of the Information Technology Act, 2000 and the customers can also claim the compensation under certain circumstances.
(D) The customers do not have any legal remedy under the Information Technology Act, 2000. [AIBE-XIX]

Q.3 In which of the following cases, Section 66A of the Information Technology Act, 2000 was struck down by the Supreme Court?

a) Shreya Singhal v Union of India
b) Kartar Singh v State of Punjab
c) K.A. Abbas v Union of India
d) Maneka Gandhi v Union of India [AIBE-XVIII]

Q.4 In which of the following cases, an electronic record shall not be attributed to the originator as per the Information Technology Act, 2000?

a) Electronic record sent by the originator himself
b) Electronic record sent by an authorised person
c) Electronic record sent by an automated system programmed by him
d) Electronic record sent by an unauthorised person

[AIBE-XVIII]

Q.5 Mr. A, who was aggrieved by an order made by the Controller or an adjudicating officer, made an appeal to Cyber Appellate Tribunal. Later, Mr. A, aggrieved by an order of the Cyber Appellate Tribunal, may prefer an appeal _____.
a) In any District Court
b) In a higher tribunal
c) **Only in the High Court**
d) Only in the Supreme Court [AIBE-XVII]

Q.6 Mr. X, a person who is intended by Mr. Y, an originator, to receive the electronic record is, under the IT Act, known as _____.
a) Intermediary
b) Originators agent
c) **Addressee**
d) Key holder [AIBE-XVII]

Q.7 Cyber-crime is _____ in nature:
a) Tangible
b) **Intangible**
c) Of mental violence
d) None of the above [AIBE-XVI]

Q.8 Cyber law deals with:
a) All activities concerning the Internet
b) IPR
c) E-commerce
d) **All of the above** [AIBE-XVI]

Q.9 Section 66A of Information Technology Act was held unconstitutional in the case of:
a) Justice K S Puttaswamy Vs. Union of India
b) M P Sharma Vs. Satish Chandra
c) Shreya Singhal Vs. Union of India
d) Gagan Harsh Sharma Vs. The State of Maharashtra [AIBE-XV]

Q.10 An attempt to acquire sensitive information such as usernames, passwords, and credit card details (and sometimes, indirectly, money) by masquerading as a trustworthy entity in an electronic communication - is known as:
a) Pharming
b) Smishing
c) Phishing
d) Didling [AIBE-XV]

Q.11 The authentication to be affected by the use of asymmetric crypto system and hash function is known as:
a) Public Key
b) Private Key
c) Digital Signature
d) Electronic Governance [AIBE-XIV]

Q.12 Cyber Terrorism under Section 66F shall be punishable:
a) With imprisonment which may

extend to three years, or with fine not exceeding two lakh rupees or with both
b) With imprisonment for a term which may extend to seven years and shall also be liable to fine
c) With imprisonment which may extend to imprisonment for life
d) With imprisonment of either description for a term which may extend to ten years and shall also be liable to fine [AIBE-XIV]

Q.13 Section 66A was invalidated by the Supreme Court of India in:
a) Anvar P V Vs. P K Basheer (2014)10 SCC 473
b) Shreya Singhal Vs. Union of India AIR 2015 SC 1523
c) Dr. Prafulla Desai Vs. State of Maharashtra AIR 2003 SC 2053
d) State (NCT of Delhi) Vs. Navjot Sandhu (2005) 11 SCC 600
[AIBE-XIII]

Q.14 Which section of the Information Technology (Amendment) Act 2008 deals with the validity of contracts formed through electronic means?
a) Section 12
b) Section 10A
c) Section 11
d) Section 13 [AIBE-XIII]

Q.15 Which chapter of Cyber Law provides the legal recognition to Digital Signature?
a) Chapter III
b) Chapter IV
c) Chapter IX
d) Chapters IX and X [AIBE-XII]

Q.16 Which Act is covering the Cyber-crimes?
a) Indian Telecommunication Act
b) Indian Penal Code
c) Indian Evidence Act
d) Information Technology Act

[AIBE-XII]

Q.17 Information Technology Act was enacted in:
a) 1988
b) 1996
c) 2000
d) 2004 [AIBE-XI]

Q.18 Government of India passed Information Technology Act in 2000 with objective:
a) To provide legal sanction to all transaction for e-commerce
b) To facilitate electronic filing of all documents to the government
c) To amend Indian Penal Code, Indian Evidence Act, to punish the cyber crimes
d) All of the above [AIBE-XI]

Q.19 The Chairperson of Cyber Appellate Tribunal is appointed by the:

a) Central Government in consultation with the Chief Justice of India

b) State Government in consultation with the Chief Justice of the High Court

c) Central Government

d) Central Government in consultation with Controller of Certifying Authority [AIBE-X]

Q.20 The Controller of Certifying Authorities in India must maintain a database of the disclosure records of:

1. Certifying Authority 2. Cross Certifying Authority

3. Foreign Certifying Authority

a) 1 and 2

b) 2 and 3

c) 3 and 1

d) 1, 2 and 3 [AIBE-IX]

Q.21 Under Section 37 of the IT Act 2000, the Certifying Authority can suspend the Digital Signature Certificate if:

1. The subscriber is found guilty of malpractice

2. The subscriber is involved in cyber terrorism

3. The subscriber requests for the same

4. in public interest

a) 1 and 2

b) 2 and 3

c) 3 and 4

d) 4 and 1 [AIBE-IX]

Q.22 In the cases before Cyber Appellate Tribunal, the appellant:

a) Cannot appear in person without a legal practitioner

b) Cannot authorize a legal practitioner to appear on his behalf

c) Cannot authorize his officer to appear on his behalf

d) Cannot authorize his relative who is neither his officer nor a legal practitioner to appear on his behalf [AIBE-IX]

Q.23 In India, which of the following authorities has the power to block websites?

a) CERT-In

b) NCIIPC

c) C-DAC

d) Ministry of IT [AIBE-IX]

Q.24 Which among the following is authorized under the Information Technology Act 2000 to prescribe the security procedures and practices for the purpose of sections 14 and 15 of the Act?

a) Central Government

b) State Government

c) Certifying authority

d) Issuing authority [AIBE-IX]

Q.25 With reference to Cyber Crimes, worm attack:
a) Needs the virus to attach
b) Does not need the virus to attach
c) Needs the host to attach
d) Does not need the host to attach [AIBE-VIII]

Q.26 An attempt to acquire sensitive information such as usernames, passwords, and credit card details (and sometimes, indirectly, money) by masquerading as a trustworthy entity in an electronic communication - is known as:
a) Salami attacks
b) Phishing
c) Data diddling
d) Forgery [AIBE-VIII]

Q.27 The Act to provide legal recognition for the transactions carried out by means of electronic data interchange and other means of electronic communication, commonly referred to as 'Electronic Commerce' is dealt under:
a) Information Technology Act
b) Information and Communication Technology Act
c) Information Communication Act
d) Information and Cyber Space Act [AIBE-VIII]

Q.28 'Asymmetric Crypto System' under Information Technology Act means a system of a secure key pair consisting of a private key for creating a digital signature and:
a) An individual key to verify the digital signature
b) A lock to verify the digital signature
c) A public key to verify the digital signature
d) A Government key to verify the digital signature [AIBE-VIII]

Q.29 Sec 43A of the Information Technology Act deals with:
a) Compensation for failure to protect data
b) Punishment for sending offensive messages
c) Identity theft
d) Impersonation [AIBE-VIII]

Q.30 Section 3 of Information Technology Act 2000 which was originally 'Digital Signature' was renamed as _____ in ITAA 2008:
a) 'Digital Signature and Electronic Signature'
b) 'Digital Signature and E-Signature'
c) 'Digital and Electronic Signature'
d) None of the above [AIBE-VII]

Q.31 Which among the following are the Digital Signature certifying authorities in India?
a) M/s. SafeScrypt
b) M/s. NCERT

c) M/s. MTL
d) All of the above [AIBE-VII]

Q.32 Section 43 of the Information Technology Act deals with:
a) Criminal liability
b) Civil liability
c) Both the above
d) None of the above [AIBE-VII]

Q.33 "Where a body corporate is negligent in implementing reasonable security practices and thereby causes wrongful loss or gain to any person, such body corporate shall be liable to pay damages by way of compensation to the person so affected." Which section of the Information Technology Amendment Act 2008 envisages so?
a) 43
b) 43A
c) 43B
d) 43C [AIBE-VII]

TOPIC 18: INTELLECTUAL PROPERTY LAWS

(2 questions are, generally, asked from this subject)

Q.1 Soham, an independent software developer, created a mobile app called "FitLife" that provides personalized fitness plans. He registered the app's name and logo under trademark law and copyrighted the app's source code. However, six months after its launch, Soham discovered a competing app called "FitLyfe", with a similar logo and features, being marketed by a large tech company. Soham believes the competing app copied elements of his source code and intentionally used a confusingly similar name and logo to mislead customers.

Under trademark law, can Soham claim infringement for the use of a similar name and logo by the competing app ?

On the basis of the above problem, select the correct option:

(A) Yes, if he can prove that the names are confusingly similar.

(B) No, because the competing app has a different name and logo.

(C) Yes, but only if the competitor is a small business.

(D) No, trademark infringement can only occur if there is identical copying. [AIBE-XIX]

Q.2 What is the duration of copyright protection for literary works in India?

(A) 50 years from the creation of the work

(B) 60 years from the date of publication

(C) Lifetime of the author plus 60 years

(D) 10 years from the date of first sales [AIBE-XIX]

Q.3 Imagine an IPL team sets up a company to sell its own range of clothes. What type of intellectual property can the team use to show that the clothes are made by them?

a) Patents

b) Geographical Indications

c) Trademarks

d) Registered designs [AIBE-XVIII]

Q.4 How long do patents usually last for?

a) 10 years

b) 20 years

c) 25 years

d) 50 years [AIBE-XVIII]

Q.5 Who shall be the Registrar of Trademarks for the Purpose of Trade Marks Act, 1999?

a) **Controller General of Patents, Designs and Trademarks**

b) Controller General of Copyright,

Designs and Trademarks
c) Director General of Patents, designs, and trademarks
d) Director General of Copyright, Designs and Trademarks
[AIBE-XVII]

Q.6 Which one of the following is not a type/s of IPR?
a) Copyright
b) Patents
c) Designs
d) **Historical indications**
[AIBE-XVII]

Q.7 The term 'WIPO' stands for:
a) World Investment Policy Organization
b) **World Intellectual Property Organization**
c) Wildlife Investigation and Policing Organization
d) World Institute for Prevention of Organized Crime [AIBE-XVI]

Q.8 A company wishes to ensure that no one else can use their logo:
a) Copyrights
b) **Trade mark**
c) Patent
d) Industrial designs [AIBE-XVI]

Q.9 Under the Patents Act, which of the following are not patentable?
a) A method of agriculture or horticulture
b) A presentation of information
c) Topography of integrated circuits
d) All of the above [AIBE-XV]

Q.10 World Intellectual Property Organization (WIPO) has replaced pre-existing:
a) GATT
b) BIRPI
c) TPRM
d) PCT [AIBE-XV]

Q.11 Which of the following is an infringement of a Registered Trade mark?
a) Use of a mark identical to the Trade mark in relation to goods without authorization
b) Advertising of that Trade mark such that the advertisement is against the reputation of the Trade Mark
c) Use of that Trade mark as a business name without authorization
d) All of the above [AIBE-XIV]

Q.12 Which of the following is wrong in respect of the law of Copyright?
a) Copyright protects only the expression and not idea.
b) There is no copyright in respect of a fact.
c) There is no copyright in a government work.
d) Copyright does not require registration. [AIBE-XIV]

Q.13 Intellectual Property Appellate Board is established under which Act?
a) The Copyright Act 1957
b) The Patents Act 1970
c) The Trade Marks Act 1999
d) The Designs Act 2000
[AIBE-XIII]

Q.14 Which is the subject matter of neighboring rights pretention?
a) Performance
b) Dramatic work
c) Geographical Indication
d) New varieties and plant
[AIBE-XIII]

Q.15 A trade mark is a visual symbol applied to articles of commerce with a view to distinguish the articles from other. It is in the form of:
a) A word
b) A device
c) A label
d) All of the above [AIBE-XII]

Q.16 Criminal proceedings against the infringer are enabled in the Copyright Act by invoking the provisions:
a) Sections 13-16
b) Sections 17-27
c) Sections 63-70
d) None of the above [AIBE-XII]

Q.17 The Patents Act became a law in:
a) 1970
b) 1975
c) 1996
d) 1966 [AIBE-XI]

Q.18 Section 2(1)(zb) of the Trade Marks Act 1999 defines the meaning of:
a) License
b) Trade Mark
c) Registration
d) Cancellation [AIBE-XI]

Q.19 Which is not included within the meaning of artistic work under Copyright Act?
a) Drawing
b) Work of architecture
c) Work of craftsmanship
d) Work of carpenter [AIBE-X]

Q.20 Which condition is not required to be satisfied by an invention to be patentable subject matter under Patents Act?
a) Novelty
b) Inventive steps
c) Distinctiveness
d) Usefulness [AIBE-X]

TOPIC 19: LAND ACQUISITION ACT

(2 questions are, generally, asked from this subject)

Q.1 According to the Land Acquisition Act (Land Acquisition, Rehabilitation and Resettlement), 2013, governments can acquire land for:

(i) Strategic purpose (ii) Projects for Families Affected by Projects

(iii) For public-private partnership projects, where government ownership of land will remain with the government

(A) (i) & (ii)

(B) (ii) & (iii)

(C) (i) & (iii)

(D) (i), (ii) & (iii) [AIBE-XIX]

Q.2 Land Acquisition Act, 2013 in India has replaced which earlier legislation ?

(A) Land Acquisition Act, 1956

(B) Land Acquisition Act, 1862

(C) Land Acquisition Act, 1894

(D) Land Acquisition Act, 1874

[AIBE-XIX]

Q.3 Within what period from the date of publication of the declaration, if no award is made, the entire proceedings for the acquisition of land shall lapse as per the Right to Fair Compensation and Transparency in Land Acquisition Rehabilitation and Resettlement Act, 2013?

a) 6 months

b) 12 months

c) 18 months

d) 24 months [AIBE-XVIII]

Q.4 What is the minimum percentage of affected families that need to give their prior consent for acquiring land for private companies as per the Right to Fair Compensation and Transparency in Land Acquisition Rehabilitation and Resettlement Act, 2013?

a) 75%

b) 80%

c) 90%

d) 100% [AIBE-XVIII]

Q.5 According to the Right to Fair Compensation and Transparency in Land Acquisition, Rehabilitation and Resettlement Act, 2013, the appropriate government can acquire the land for which of the following purposes?

1. for strategic purposes relating to naval, military, Air Force and armed forces of the Union

2. project for water harvesting and water conservation structures, sanitation

3. project for project affected families

4. project for sports, healthcare,

tourism, transportation or space programme
a) 1, 2 and 3
b) 2, 3 and 4
c) 1, 2 and 4
d) **1, 2, 3 and 4** [AIBE-XVII]

Q.6 'Specified person' under Right to Fair Compensation and Transparency in Land Acquisition, Rehabilitation and Resettlement Act, 2013 means any person other than _____.
a) Appropriate government
b) Government company
c) Association of persons or trust or society, wholly or partially aided by the appropriate government or controlled by the appropriate government
d) **All of these** [AIBE-XVII]

Q.7 Who appoints the Commissioner for rehabilitation and resettlement under the LARR Act?
a) LARR authority
b) Minister of Environment and Forests
c) Central Government
d) **State Government** [AIBE-XVI]

Q.8 In case of land acquisition by the Central Government for public-private partnership projects, consent of how many affected families is mandated by the LARR Act?
a) 60%
b) **70%**
c) 80%
d) 90% [AIBE-XVI]

Q.9 Under the Land Acquisition Act, the expression 'land' includes:
a) Benefits to arise out of land
b) Things attached to the earth
c) Things permanently fastened to anything attached to the earth
d) All of the above [AIBE-XV]

Q.10 Temporary occupation of waste or arable land, procedure when difference as to compensation exists, is provided under:
a) Section 32 of Land Acquisition Act
b) Section 30 of Land Acquisition Act
c) Section 35 of Land Acquisition Act
d) Section 31 of Land Acquisition Act [AIBE-XV]

Q.11 The Land Acquisition Act 1894 came into force on:
a) First day of January, 1894
b) First day of February, 1894
c) First day of March, 1894
d) First day of April, 1894
[AIBE-XIV]

Q.12 The objectives of Land Acquisition Act 1894 are:

a) An Act to amend the law for the acquisition of land for public purposes and for industry
b) An Act to amend the law for the purchase of land for public purpose and for business
c) An Act to amend the law for the possessions of land for public purpose and for manufacturing
d) An Act to amend the law for the Acquisition of land for public purposes and for Companies
[AIBE-XIV]

Q.13 Under Land Acquisition Act 1894, an industrial concern, ordinarily employing not less than .... workmen owned by an individual or by an association of individuals and not being a Company, desiring to acquire land for the erection of dwelling houses for workmen employed by the concern or for the provision of amenities directly connected therewith shall, so far as concerns the Acquisition of such land, be deemed to be a company for the purpose of this part, and the references to company in [sections 4, 5A, 6, 7 and 50] shall be interpreted as references also to such concern. Fill in the blank:
a) One Hundred
b) Two Hundred
c) Three Hundred
d) Four Hundred [AIBE-XIII]

Q.14 Under Land Acquisition Act 1894 the expression 'Company' means:
a) A company as defined in Section 3 of the Companies Act 1956 other than a Government company referred to in clause (cc)
b) A company as defined in Section 2 of the Companies Act 1956 other than a Government company referred to in clause (c)
c) A company as defined in Section 1 of the Companies Act 1956(1 of 1956) other than a Government referred to in clause (cc)
d) A company as defined in Section 6 of the Companies Act 1956(1 of 1956) other than a Government company referred to in clause (c)
[AIBE-XIII]

Q.15 Under Section 18 of the Land Acquisition Act 1894, which of the following officers is empowered to refer the matter to the court?
a) The Tahsildar
b) The Sub Collector
c) The Deputy Collector
d) The Collector [AIBE-XII]

Q.16 The Collector shall, under the Land Acquisition Act 1894, give immediate .... of any correction made in the award to all the persons included.

a) Approval
b) Stay
c) Announcement
d) Notice [AIBE-XII]

Q.17 The Land Acquisition Act came into force from:
a) 1st March 1955
b) 1st March 1986
c) 1st March 1994
d) 1st March 1894 [AIBE-XI]

Q.18 Under the Land Acquisition Act, the arable land means:
a) Useful for residential purpose
b) Useful for commercial purpose
c) Useful for cultivation
d) Useful for industrial purpose
[AIBE-XI]

Q.19 Fulfilling the constitutional obligation under Article 300A, the Land Acquisition Act is the law providing for:
a) Acquisition of land and taking over possession of land
b) Assessment of compensation
c) Payment of compensation
d) All of the above [AIBE-X]

Q.20 Under Section 25 of the Land Acquisition Act, the amount of compensation awarded by the court:
a) Shall not be less than the amount awarded by the Collector under Section 11
b) Shall not be equal to the amount awarded by the Collector under Section 11
c) Shall not be more than the amount awarded by the Collector under Section 11
d) All of the above [AIBE-X]

www.ingramcontent.com/pod-product-compliance
Lightning Source LLC
Chambersburg PA
CBHW040107180526
45172CB00009B/1256

* 9 7 8 1 6 3 9 7 4 1 5 7 1 *